John W. Carroll undertakes a careful philosophical examination of laws of nature, causation, and other related topics. He argues that laws of nature are not susceptible to the sort of philosophical treatment preferred by empiricists. Indeed, he shows that empirically pure matters of fact need not even determine what the laws are. Similar, and even stronger, conclusions are drawn about causation. Replacing the traditional view of laws and causation as requiring some kind of foundational legitimacy, the author argues that these phenomena are inextricably intertwined with everything else.

This distinctively clear and detailed discussion of what it is to be a law will be valuable to a broad swathe of philosophers in metaphysics, epistemology, the philosophy of mind, and the philosophy of science.

CAMBRIDGE STUDIES IN PHILOSOPHY

Laws of nature

CAMBRIDGE STUDIES IN PHILOSOPHY

General editor ERNEST SOSA

Advisory editors J. E. J. ALTHMAN, SIMON BLACKBURN,
GILBERT HARMAN, MARTIN HOLLIS, FRANK JACKSON,
WILLIAM G. LYCAN, JOHN PERRY,
SYDNEY SHOEMAKER, BARRY STROUD

RECENT TITLES

Laws of nature

John W. Carroll

Department of Philosophy
Rhode Island College

CAMBRIDGE
UNIVERSITY PRESS

Published by the Press Syndicate of the University of Cambridge
The Pitt Building, Trumpington Street, Cambridge CB2 1RP
40 West 20th Street, New York, NY 10011-4211, USA
10 Stamford Road, Oakleigh, Melbourne 3166, Australia

First published 1994
Reprinted 1995

Printed in the United States of America

Library of Congress Cataloging-in-Publication Data is available

A catalogue record for this book is available from the British Library

ISBN 0-521-43334-7 hardback

Contents

Acknowledgments

This book's first three chapters and its first appendix derive from two journal articles: "Ontology and the Laws of Nature" *Australasian Journal of Philosophy* (Carroll 1987), and "The Humean Tradition" *Philosophical Review* (Carroll 1990). By now, there is little precise overlap between the book and the articles, but where there is I thank the publishers of these journals for their permission to reuse the material. Portions of the book were read at Rutgers University, Southern Methodist University, and the 1990 Midwest and Pacific Meetings of the American Philosophical Association. I did important work on the book in the fall of 1988 thanks to a Mellon Presidential Fellowship awarded by New York University.

Janean Miller and Gina Zavota read early drafts of the entire manuscript; their suggestions improved the presentation immensely. By providing some desperately needed advice, and by doing a few (what were for her) simple drawings, Lori Loebelsohn turned my own preliminary sketches into effective illustrations. Many of my students over the last seven years have caught minor glitches in the text, but what's more important, they have kept me honest. Various former teachers stand out as being extremely influential in many ways. Deserving of special note are Stephen Schiffer, John Pollock, David Sipfle, Jules Coleman, Holly Smith, Alvin Goldman, Phil Ehrlich, Myles Brand, and William Galvin (a truly tremendous high school math teacher). Other friends whose impact was less direct but whose support was even more important include the two Leighs, the Mortons, the Browns, the other Village House professors, the Modal Operators, and assorted Carls (especially Gilbert, Brian, and Tom). The support was even greater from my parents, siblings, and in-laws. And, the book would not have been finished when it was if Barbara Celius had not so quickly shown herself to be the world's greatest baby-sitter.

It would be remiss of me not to thank the many trees whose lives were lost because of this book. It has been written and rewritten countless times. Indeed, I fear that a small forest may have been lost for the sake of Section 4.3 alone. Partial responsibility for this arboreal genocide belongs to numerous friends and colleagues. Lila Luce, Alan Nelson, Francis Sheehan, Paul Teller, and especially John Pollock had many useful criticisms when this book was still just a dissertation. Barry Loewer, Arnold Koslow, Paul Boghossian, David Albert, Jonathan Adler, John Richardson, Ed Stein, J. D. Trout, and Julia Driver have had a more recent impact. David Armstrong sent comments on an early draft of Chapter 5 that proved very helpful. Doug Ehring and Ran Lahav, with help from the other members of the Southern Methodist University philosophy department, later forced me to rework this chapter even more drastically. During its many years of creation, on its way to finding a home with Cambridge University Press, the book improved as the result of detailed reviews by Ellery Eells, Daniel Bonevac, Evan Fales, and Lawrence Sklar, along with those of two other anonymous referees. Special thanks to Roy Sorensen for his patience, diligence, and support; I sometimes wonder if he has read more drafts of this book than I. Keith DeRose is by far the most responsible for the slaughter associated with Section 4.3 and for suggesting this ecological acknowledgment.

If I noted every spot Peter Unger or Stephen Schiffer had some influence, the book would be covered with their names. Unger's unorthodox and sharply critical mind has a way of cutting to the heart of most philosophical problems. His most important contribution to this book was his insistence on the present emphasis on centrality. He also promoted the epistemological themes in Chapter 2, reworked the presentation of many of my most basic arguments (especially those for which centrality is key), and suggested organizational changes too numerous to remember. The book would not have been nearly as interesting without his help. Schiffer's early instruction shaped the structure of my dissertation and eventually this book. Indeed, this all began in his metaphysics course at the University of Arizona in the fall of 1984. From the day he showed me the foolishness of some analysis of lawhood I was trying valiantly to defend, to the next semester when he started me thinking about supervenience, to the correct formulation of the central problem with Armstrong's position, to his support during some academically trying times, his influence has been substantial and steadfast.

In Chapter 6, I say that it is contingent that I am married. While that may be true, there is some sort of stupendously real and equally wonderful necessary connection between my wife Ann and myself. With all due respect to Hume, it is Ann, our daughter Erin, and our son Aidan who are the cement of my universe. I owe them the greatest thanks for their love, not to mention their willingness to tolerate my desire to plop myself in front of a computer for hours on end. To them and the rest of my family, I dedicate this book.

1

Centrality

The goal of this book is to provide a better understanding of the concept of a law of nature, to show what lawhood is like, to say how it relates to the rest of our conceptual equipment. Other attempts have been impeded by two factors that in combination present a formidable obstacle. The first is an ensconced way of going about things; in essence, one that sees worthwhile understanding of lawhood as dispensed only by a suitably antiseptic description of the essential differences between laws and nonlaws. The second is a curious feature of laws: Laws have a *modal character* in that not every true proposition, not even every true universal generalization, is a law. For example, suppose that I bought a brand new pair of pants earlier today. After putting on the pants, I placed two nickels in my pocket. Because those pants will be destroyed in a fire tonight, those are the only coins that will ever be in that pocket. Then, there is the true universal generalization that all the coins in my pocket are nickels. Though perfectly true, this proposition is not a law. It fails to be a law because its truth is an "accident"; it is *accidentally true*. In contrast, consider Newton's first law of motion, the generalization that if no force acts on a body, its acceleration is zero. Assuming for the moment that it really is a law, this Newtonian generalization is *not* accidentally true.

The history of science provides many instances of laws or, at least, of propositions that were once thought to be laws. We have already noted Newton's first. Another is Kepler's first law of planetary motion, the principle that all planets have elliptical orbits about the sun. A third case is the generalization that radium atoms have a fifty percent chance of remaining stable for 1600 years. This generalization is interestingly different from the others, because it involves an explicit probabilistic element. To round matters out,

1

there are three more examples that are utilized frequently in the chapters ahead. First, there is the Galilean principle that on earth, all free-falling bodies accelerate at a rate of 9.81 meters per second squared. Second, there is a central tenet from the theory of special relativity, the proposition that no signals travel at speeds greater than the speed of light. Finally, occasionally I invoke Newton's gravitational principle. It states that the gravitational force between two bodies of masses m and m' separated by a distance r is gmm'/r^2 (where g is the gravitational constant).

To those unfamiliar with the problem of laws, it may appear easy to describe the difference between laws and mere accidents.[1] One feature of the accidentally true generalization about the nickels stands out. The generalization that all coins in my pocket are nickels refers to a specific thing in the world: that pocket in the short-lived pair of pants. It is easy to think that, unlike laws, accidentally true propositions include reference to specific things. But the essential difference between laws and accidents must lie elsewhere. This is true for at least two reasons. First, there are many accidentally true generalizations that include no suspicious reference. For example, consider the generalization that all gold spheres are less than ten meters in diameter. It is true, and it includes no suspect singular terms. Yet, intuitively, this generalization is not a law. Rather, it is accidentally true. Even though there are none, in an important sense there *could* have been gold spheres greater than or equal to ten meters in diameter. Second, there appear to be laws or, at least, propositions that could be laws that *do* include reference to particular things. Kepler's first law refers to the sun. Galileo's law refers to the earth. Evidently, the essential difference between laws and accidents cannot be that laws include no reference to specific things. (These examples are discussed again, much more carefully, in Chapter 2.)

The perplexing nature of the problem of laws emerges upon realizing there are laws and accidents that appear to be very similar indeed. Suppose that the fastest that any raven has ever traveled, or will ever travel, is exactly thirty meters per second. Then, consider these generalizations:

---

1 As should be obvious, I am using the word 'accident' for accidentally true propositions, for the true nonlaws, not in its more colloquial use as a term for unintended or unexplained events.

(1) All ravens have speeds less than 31 meters per second.
(2) All signals have speeds less than 300,000,001 meters per second.[2]

Generalization (1) is true, but not a law. What about (2)? Supposing that this aspect of special relativity is correct, it is a law that no signals travel faster than light, and the speed of light is slightly less than 300,000,001 meters per second. So, it is plausible to think that (2) is both true and a law. Now, it is extremely difficult to describe precisely the *significant* differences between (1) and (2). There are differences: The first quantifies over ravens instead of signals, and also cites a different speed. But it would be surprising if these differences account for why (2) may be a law and why (1) is not. So, we are left with a challenging question: What is the difference between laws and accidents?

In the first section of this chapter, I describe both the established framework for understanding lawhood and some of the reasons our investigation is important. Primary among these reasons is this: Lawhood is conceptually intertwined with many other blatantly modal concepts that all have a massive role to play in our habitual ways of thinking and speaking. Besides being part of familiar commonsense practices themselves, these other concepts infiltrate nearly all our ordinary notions; so much so, that there is strong reason to believe that *if there were no laws, there would be little else.* In Section 1.2, I anticipate some of the conclusions that follow from the fact that these lawful notions are so central. Then, in the final two portions of the chapter, I pour the foundations for my investigation, specifying some of the perspectives and convictions that have shaped my metaphysics. To be more specific, in Section 1.3, I describe my methodology. Of particular interest there is some preliminary support for a key tenet, principle (SC), describing one way in which lawhood is tied up with other concepts. In Section 1.4, I discuss where I stand on the issues of the truth, contingency, and universality of laws.

1.1 REDUCTION AND THE WHOLESOME BASE

Many philosophical problems quite obviously arise from everyday thought and talk. For example, epistemologists investigate knowl-

---

2 Similar pairs are commonly discussed in the literature. For one example, see van Fraassen (1989 p. 27).

edge, in part, because of the frequency with which we ascribe knowledge. The ethicist inquires into the nature of moral wrong, in part, because we frequently judge actions as wrong. Yet, any commonsense practice employing lawhood must be more subdued; judgments as to what propositions are laws are not a conspicuous part of our daily routine. So, why should we undertake a philosophical investigation of what it is to be a law of nature?

The traditional answer is twofold. First, despite lawhood's limited role in everyday discourse, it does have a central role in scientific practice. Since science is of such great importance, one of its principal concepts deserves attention. Second, most have correctly recognized that lawhood is conceptually entwined at least with *some* very familiar and extremely interesting concepts. With regard to both past philosophical interest and my own, the most important example of such a concept is the counterfactual conditional. Indeed, it is the account of counterfactuals championed by Roderick Chisholm (1946, 1955) and Nelson Goodman (1947) that, I think, provoked much of the recent philosophical interest in laws of nature.[3] Philosophers have found it hard to imagine what it could be that makes certain counterfactuals true, and so also have wondered what it is that distinguishes laws from accidents.

Given the mood set by logical positivism, many philosophers from the middle part of this century onward have viewed laws and counterfactuals with a certain amount of suspicion. There are several notoriously slippery issues that sustain their doubts. The most significant is a thoroughly epistemological concern. Hume's argument against the idea of necessary connection, though largely of a semantic nature involving – it is now safe to say – suspect semantic assumptions, contained an important and still plausible epistemo-

---

3 As is well known, there are similar accounts of explanation and causation. There is the deductive-nomological (D-N) model of explanation advanced by Hempel and Oppenheim (1948). Hempel and Oppenheim were aware of the importance the D-N model placed on the distinction between laws and accidents. Their paper includes (pp. 152–159) an extended attempt to provide an account of that distinction. They cite discussions of laws by Langford (1941), C. I. Lewis (1946), and Reichenbach (1947) as well as Goodman (1947) and Chisholm (1946). There are also *subsumption* analyses of causation, one of which is discussed in Chapter 5. Elements of the analysis date back to Hume. Braithwaite (1927, p. 470) adopted something like this position (together with an idiosyncratic analysis of lawhood). Also see Pap (1962, p. 255). For still others who have held similar positions about causation, see footnote 11 in Chapter 5.

logical premise. This premise points out our lack of "direct perceptual access" to causal connections:

All events seem entirely loose and separate. One event follows another, but we never can observe any tie between them. They seem *conjoined*, but never *connected* (1955 [f.p. 1748], p. 85).

The skeptical fear that flows from this premise is that our analogous lack of direct perceptual access to lawhood and the counterfactual conditional would prevent us from having knowledge we ordinarily presume ourselves to have. Another part of the story behind the positivist-inspired suspicions is in some very broad sense ontological. To take laws seriously, philosophers dread that they would have to recognize necessary connections or other similarly mysterious entities as really existing in nature. More vaguely, there is also simply the gut feeling that modal stuff is somehow less fundamental than nonmodal stuff. Philosophers feel that, in some way, the secondary nature of the modal stuff needs to be reflected in their philosophy.

Whatever drives the suspicions, the preferred method of squelching them is clear. Convinced that there is a significant class of more basic concepts, philosophers seek a definition of 'law of nature'. They seek an analytic completion of

(S1) P is a law of nature if an only if. . . .

Of course, not just any analytic completion of (S1) suffices. Consider:

P is a law of nature if and only if, for all Q, P would be the case if Q were the case.

Even if this completion were analytic, which it is not, it just wouldn't do. First, many (including Goodman and Chisholm) want to analyze the subjunctive conditional in terms of lawhood. So, an analysis of lawhood in terms of this conditional would generate a disappointing circle. Second, and more to the point, an analysis of lawhood that used the subjunctive conditional would do little to bring lawhood back down to earth. What is desired is a definition showing that lawhood's modal character is harmless, that the appearance of anything otherworldly or occult is only the result of

5

lawhood being a molecular concept, one composed of much more basic, entirely wholesome, notions. Certainly there is to be no reference to any abstract entities – possible worlds, universals, or anything else of that ilk.[4] All told, metaphysicians and philosophers of science desire a definition of lawhood employing no modal concepts and making no reference to modality-supplying entities.

We have already excluded the counterfactual conditional from the class of concepts pure enough to serve in a definition that would stifle Humean suspicions. Besides it, there are several other concepts that clearly have as rich a modal character as lawhood. Causation is one. For one event to cause another, the first must *bring about* or *produce* or – in some sense – *necessitate* the second. Other modally stained concepts include: chance, physical necessity, (causal) explanation, and dispositions. It is sometimes difficult to describe any profound connections between lawhood and these other concepts. In fact, as we'll discover, because lawhood has an almost covert role in everyday thought and talk, some may be tempted to deny that these connections exist at all. Still, so long as our concern is not with uncovering any very interesting ties, it is easy to delineate some relationships that reinforce the desire to avoid causation, chance, et al., in a definition of lawhood. For example, being extremely conservative, there is this much of a link between causation and lawhood: If there is any causation at all, then there is at least one law of nature. Staying as conservative: If there are any instantiated dispositions, then there is at least one law. In much the same spirit, most would agree that if there were no laws, there would be no true (nontrivial) counterfactual conditionals, no true explanations, and so on. What underlies these relationships is that *generality* and some sort of *necessity* are built into all these other concepts. For example, *c* can't cause *e* unless *any* event exactly like *c* in precisely similar circumstances *would* have some chance of causing an event similar to *e*. How could the required generality and necessity obtain without there also being at

4 In claiming that philosophers eschew reference to modality-supplying entities, it appears that I have inexcusably overlooked an important group. It includes Armstrong (1983), Tooley (1987), Dretske (1977), Pargetter (1984), and many others. These authors feel that an appeal to universals or to possible worlds is of tremendous benefit to the study of laws of nature. Because their perspective forces consideration of somewhat idiosyncratic matters, I have chosen to discuss their positions in Appendix A.

least one suitably nonaccidental generalization; that is, without there also being at least one law?

Most of this has been appreciated for as long as there has been a problem of laws. Because these concepts have almost universally been recognized as having a modal character and as inappropriate for use in a definition intended to tame the modality of lawhood, I give them a special name. I call them the *nomic concepts*. Be aware that the counterfactual conditional, lawhood, causation, etc., do not quite exhaust all the nomic concepts. Made-up notions explicitly defined in terms of the concepts just cited are also nomic. For example, in Chapter 5, I introduce the nomic notion of *lawful sufficiency*: *P* is lawfully sufficient for *Q* if and only if *P* physically necessitates *Q*. There are also some ordinary nomic concepts that I have left off my list, ones that are very close cousins of the key nomic concepts; for example, *production* (a close cousin of causation) and *nonaccidentality* (a close cousin of lawhood). Be warned that I introduce the nomic/nonnomic distinction with tremendous reluctance. There are two reasons for my diffidence. First, as it is being used here, the word 'nomic' is very vague; it is not always clear what counts as "a close cousin" of the key nomic concepts or what counts as a disposition. Second, and this is the more important reason for my reluctance, I am afraid that someone will think that the nomic/nonnomic distinction marks something of great metaphysical import. On the contrary, as will become clear, there is no deep metaphysical division here.

In a way, it is a bit arbitrary that I have chosen to focus on the concept of a law of nature. The modal character of laws is no more and no less suspicious than is the modality associated with, say, causation. My focus is likely to appear especially arbitrary because there is also a common presumption that the nomic concepts are interdefinable. Though I have serious doubts about this interdefinability thesis, I do appreciate that the problem of laws has many relatives. At the very least, we should expect lessons about lawhood to carry over to the other nomic concepts. With this in mind, and in part to minimize the appearance of arbitrariness, I discuss chance at some length in Chapter 3, arguing that my most important conclusions about lawhood also apply to chance. Moreover, in that same chapter, scattered about, I briefly use my results about chance and lawhood to draw parallel conclusions about causation, explanation, the counterfactual conditional, and a sample disposition. I also discuss causation at great length in Chapter 5, but by that time our discussion takes on a different slant. By the time the fifth chapter rolls around, our concern is not with the possibility of illuminating nomic modality.

Returning to the question of what concepts can be used in the definition of 'law of nature', let us consider another concept: perception. Though it is not usually thrown in with causation and the other nomic concepts, most philosophers recognize that it too has a nonaccidental character. These thinkers have drawn the same conclusions about some other notions like action, reference, and even such a basic metaphysical notion as persistence (identity over time). The modal character of these concepts is commonly recognized because, as many so-called causal theorists have convincingly argued, there are some easily specified and extremely plausible connections between these assorted concepts and causation. For example, with regard to perception, it is clear that nothing perceives anything else unless there is a causal connection between the perceiver and the entity perceived. Regarding persistence, no single material entity exists at two distinct times if there is no causation linking an entity that exists at one of those two times with an entity that exists at the other time. Following tradition, I do not count perception, persistence, or any of these other concepts as a nomic concept. Introducing some new terminology, we might say that though they are not nomic concepts they do have *nomic commitments*. It is the distinction between the concepts with nomic commitments and those without, not our earlier nomic/nonnomic distinction, that is metaphysically significant. Only a definition of lawhood that uses just terms free of nomic commitment could explain away the otherwordly character of laws.

What is not often recognized, nor its importance always appreciated, is the range of concepts with nomic commitments. It may be that this is often missed because the connections between many of our ordinary concepts and the nomic concepts are not always as apparent as is the connection, say, between perception and causation. Consider, for example, the mundane and ordinary concept of being a table. At first glance, one might think that there is a simple connection with causation. One might think that nothing is a table unless it *supports* other things. But, this proposed connection is obviously incorrect; there are tables that were built, and then destroyed, before they ever supported a single thing. A better, though probably not perfect, suggestion is that nothing is a table unless it is *capable* of supporting other things. It is not crucial, nor is it even very important, that we give a precise and interesting statement of the ties between tablehood and any of the nomic concepts. I suspect that the relationship between being a table and the nomic concepts is much like the relationship between causation and lawhood: Any very interesting connection is difficult to specify. Still, as is the case with these two nomic concepts, it is easy to state a fairly uninteresting and weak connection. It is absolutely clear that nothing is a table unless it exhibits at least one dispositional property. Since no dispositional properties are exemplified unless there is also at least one law of nature, nothing could be a table unless there is at least one law.

Tablehood is not at all exceptional in this regard. Some have thought that colors are some sort of disposition to produce specific visual appearances. Others have thought that part of being of value is to be disposed to be desired. These principles are much too crude to be anywhere close to being true. They do suggest, however, that we can confidently accept that color concepts and the concept of value are also concepts with nomic commitments. If there were no laws of nature, our world would be monochromatic and our lives meaningless. What's more, that would really be the least of our problems. Consider matter itself, or really, the concept of materiality (cf., Armstrong 1961, pp. 184–190; Robinson 1982, pp. 108–112). The atoms making up my desk are material objects – the empty spaces between them are not. But, what is it to be a material object? It is natural to think that something like this is right: The atoms making up my desk are material objects by virtue of being solid. The spaces between the atoms lack solidity. What is solidity? Solidity, it is plausible to think, is something like the property of being *impenetrable* by a sufficiently wide range of other objects. Reasoning as we have before, it is extremely clear that solidity could not be instantiated unless at least one disposition was also instantiated. So, if there were no laws, not only would there be no colored things and nothing of value; in an important sense, there wouldn't be any *things*.

Are there any suitably wholesome concepts, any that can be used in an attempt to legitimize lawhood? Are there any concepts free of nomic commitment? Yes, there are. The truth-functional concepts, standard mathematical concepts (e.g., being prime), and necessity and possibility are pretty clear examples.[5] Less clearly, it may be that spatial and temporal relations lack nomic commitment. This is more controversial because many are tempted to analyze these relations, especially the temporal relations of earlier and later than, in causal terms. Also, though I strongly suspect that this is a mistake, some even hold that certain epistemological concepts like confirmation lack nomic commitment. In any case, what is important to notice is that, even if we are extremely generous, even if we were to place spatiotemporal relations and certain epistemological concepts in the class of concepts lacking nomic commitment, this class still would be very barren. Thus, these considerations greatly support *the centrality of the nomic*. It has become clear that if there were no laws of nature, then there would be very little else. If there were no laws, then there would be no causation, there would be no dispositions, there would be no true (nontrivial) counterfactual conditionals. By the same token, if there were no laws of nature, there would be no perception, no actions, no persistence. There wouldn't be any tables, no red things, no things of value, not even any physical objects.

This focality makes it clear why the topic of laws of nature is so important. It isn't just that *some* concepts are conceptually intertwined with lawhood. Nearly all our ordinary concepts are so plaited. In coming to better understand lawhood, we indirectly gain a better understanding of all these notions. Yet, this is only the first important lesson to be learned from the centrality of the nomic. The second is a lesson about the prospects for definitional success. Even before considering a single attempt to analyze lawhood, it is clear that providing one is at least an extremely arduous

5 I adopt what I take to be standard terminology regarding necessity (and possibility). When I use the word 'necessity' (without qualifiers), I use it in roughly the same way that David Lewis does throughout his work. The way I use this word may be even closer to the way Alvin Plantinga does in *The Nature of Necessity* (1974). Necessity is the notion that is sometimes referred to, probably misleadingly, as *metaphysical necessity* or *broadly logical necessity*. It contrasts with the narrower notion of *(narrowly) logical necessity*, and with the more encompassing notion of *physical necessity*. Plausible examples of necessary propositions include that two plus two is four, that all bachelors are unmarried, and so on. I also adopt the complementary possible worlds lingo, assuming that a proposition is necessary if and only if it is true in all possible worlds. I make similar assumptions about certain cognate terms: Something has a property *essentially* if and only if it has that property in all possible worlds; a proposition is *contingent* if and only if it is true in at least one possible world and false in at least one other.

task. In general, restricting the available vocabulary decreases the likelihood of giving a successful definition. But here, where we seem forced to restrict the vocabulary for the analysis to terms free of nomic commitment, it looks as if the likelihood of success is minuscule. The class of concepts without nomic commitments is just much too barren. Robert Stalnaker has made basically the same point. The definitional part of the reductive program requires

the assumption that the unproblematic factual basis is autonomous – that we can make sense of the world, and of the unproblematic statements describing the world, without relying, explicitly or implicitly, on the propositions whose status is in question (1984, p. 153).

In a minor way, Stalnaker may be wrong insofar as he is skeptical about there *being* an autonomous base; at the very least there are the truth-functional concepts. Still, his point is essentially correct. The class of concepts that is truly autonomous, even if it is nonempty, isn't nearly rich enough to permit the desired analysis.

As the history of our topic has unfurled, many definitions have been proposed and quickly counterexampled. So philosophers have naturally been inclined to weaken the constraints; they have been less stringent about what it would take to show that nomic modality is unproblematic. Among the more interesting ways of weakening the restrictions is by being less demanding about the connection required to obtain between the legitimizing nonmodal base and lawhood. For example, philosophers generally have not been so concerned that their completion of (S1) succeed as a *definition* of 'law of nature'. They would be perfectly satisfied if it were to state a necessary truth, a proposition true in all possible worlds. Respecting this trend, so long as a completion of (S1) is necessarily true, I take it to be an *analysis* of lawhood. So, with my terminology, every definition is an analysis, but not every analysis is a definition. More radically, some may even feel that the constraints can be weakened further, feeling that so long as it can successfully be maintained that lawhood *supervenes* on the wholesome base then the suspicions about lawhood have been addressed. Of course, these natural ways of weakening the constraints do not mesh very well with the overall empiricist approach – they do concede to our nomic language a certain independence. But, given the history of definitional failure, one can understand why they are endorsed.

Though it is already suggested by the preliminary discussion of this chapter, I show in Chapters 2 and 3 that the concepts free of nomic commitment can't by themselves explain the modal character of laws. In fact, in a novel way, I hope to show that nothing even remotely in the spirit of the reductive program is feasible. Setting my sights high, I argue that lawhood does not *supervene* on even the entire class of *nonnomic* concepts. (Remember: The class of nonnomic concepts is much more inclusive than is the class of concepts free of nomic commitment. The former includes enormously many nonnomic concepts that do have nomic commitments.) So, even if we were to weaken the restrictions, by either expanding the base or weakening the required connection, there is no hope of explaining away the otherworldly character of laws. By arguing in this way, it may appear that I attribute some sort of significance to the nomic/nonnomic distinction. This appearance is badly misleading. I rely on that thoroughly vague and metaphysically insignificant distinction only to show how wrong philosophers have been. The big advantage of setting my sights high in this manner is that I can bypass the equally vague matter of what concepts are free of nomic commitment. Even if we forbid appeals only to such concepts as quite clearly have very direct nomic commitments, no definition, no analysis, and no sufficiently strong supervenience thesis can succeed.

1.2 SKIRTING EMPIRICIST INFLUENCES

Among other more crucial claims, Section 1.1 briefly makes the innocuous point that enduring suspicions about lawhood and the other nomic concepts derive from metaphysical and epistemological postulates encouraged by the empiricists. In the middle part of this century, Goodman voiced his misgivings thus:

All this is by way of preface to declaring that some of the things that seem to me inacceptable without explanation are powers or dispositions, counterfactual assertions, entities or experiences that are possible but not actual, neutrinos, angels, devils, and classes (1983 [f.p. 1954] p. 33).

As did the doubts of many others, Goodman's suspicions grew directly out of the logical positivists' general concerns about metaphysics. *P*'s being a law, as much as that God exists, stood in need of some suitable association with the observable. Without such an association, the received doctrine was that we should accept some form of *antirealism* about laws, denying that our law-talk is descriptive of any external reality.

12

Analogous positivist-inspired doctrines underlie other philosophical issues. As with lawhood, it is hard to see what it could be that makes ethical concepts apply. And, of course, numerous tries have been made to interpret ethical sentences in other less puzzling terms. If any of these attempts were successful,

The moral vocabulary would then turn out to be just a different way of putting ordinary, natural, or psychological truths. In that case it would import no particular problems of its own – such as ones of what kind of thing moral facts can be, of how we can know about them, or how they relate to underlying natural facts, and so on (Blackburn 1984, pp. 151–152).

If, however, the desired definitions can't be given, then these particular problems about the ethical arise again with a vengeance, and force the acceptance of some sort of ethical antirealism. In a similar vein, Jerry Fodor, commenting on the problem of intentionality, says with his usual flair that "If aboutness is real, it must be really something else" (1987, p. 97). Ironically, while intended as a challenge to empiricism, Quine's (1980 [f.p. 1951], pp. 20–46) attack on analyticity has the same structure as many empiricist attacks on other concepts. After arguing very convincingly that there is no definition of analyticity in suitably wholesome terms – terms that did not invoke similar semantic concepts like synonymy – Quine denies that there are any analytic truths.

The influence of empiricism on the problem of laws manifests itself in the prevailing demand for a suitably reductive definition of lawhood. Yet, this demand, when conjoined with some of my conclusions, has some grave and apparently unavoidable consequences. In Section 1.1, I argued that what a suitably reductive definition of lawhood amounts to is a definition of lawhood solely in terms free of nomic commitment. But, in that section, we also saw that the centrality of the nomic makes it very unlikely that there could be such a definition. In fact, as I said at the end of Section 1.1, I will argue in Chapters 2 and 3 not only that there is no definition of lawhood in terms free of nomic commitments, but also that lawhood doesn't even supervene on the nonnomic concepts. Viewing matters from anything like a positivist perspective, this nonsupervenience conclusion apparently forces us to adopt some form of antirealism about the nomic.

The seeming inevitability of some sort of nomic antirealism marks the fall of the long-standing empiricist framework. As may already be clear, and as is spelled out a little more carefully in Chapter 4, in addition to undermining all attempts to give a reductive definition of lawhood, the centrality of the nomic provides a certain particularly serious threat to all forms of nomic antirealism. In this regard, it is well worth noting that lawhood and the other nomic concepts – especially dispositions – quickly surfaced as a potential embarrassment for the positivists (cf., Hempel 1971 [f.p. 1950], pp. 428–429). It was plain right away that these concepts strongly resisted the desired association with the observable. Yet the positivists' scientism made the move to some corresponding antirealism unattractive. Disposition terms litter the pages of science. To hold that certain religious sentences do not describe reality was one thing; to hold that many statements of physics do not was quite another. As I see it, the positivists were perfectly correct about at least this: The thought that some of our most secure and familiar scientific terms could not succeed in describing the world is disturbing. But, as has not been adequately appreciated, this threat to science is really only the very tip of the iceberg. The great range of concepts with nomic commitments suggests that accepting some sort of antirealism about the nomic would force us to accept an all-encompassing antirealism. It isn't just the dispositions that are in jeopardy. It isn't just the laws that are at stake. Virtually none of our discourse could be accepted as truly describing the world. We would be stuck holding that all our talk that is apparently about perception, persistence, tables, and other material objects does not characterize mind-independent reality.

The preferred method of squelching the empiricist suspicions is founded on the doctrine that the nomic concepts are secondary, that there is a significant class of concepts that are more basic. But, that doctrine is *hopelessly* false. The distinction between the nomic and nonnomic concepts is unmotivated and tenuous. It's tenuous because the line between the nomic concepts and the nonnomic concepts is a vague one. It is unmotivated because the nomic concepts and the interesting nonnomic concepts are really on a par; they all have nomic commitments. The only difference is this trivial one: With the nomic concepts themselves, the commitment is perfectly obvious; with the others, it's less than perfectly obvious. The distinction between concepts with nomic commitments and those without is better motivated. Some sort of definition, analysis, or suitably strong supervenience relation connecting lawhood and the nomically uncommitted concepts *might* do something to ground the modal character of laws. This distinction is, however, just as vague, it being unclear, for example, whether spatiotemporal and certain epistemological properties and relations have nomic commitments. Furthermore, despite being better motivated, this distinction is still of limited significance. About anything of even slight metaphysical importance, there is just one big network of concepts on a plane in logical space.

The picture emerging from my discussion is one that portrays lawhood and the other nomic concepts very differently than it depicts, say, the ethical concepts. The group of concepts that lack ethical commitments is far richer than the class of concepts lacking nomic commitments. It is very clear that ethical commitments do not extend all the way to standard scientific concepts like temperature and mass. They certainly don't extend all the way to the concept of being a physical object. Indeed, while most of the *nomically* committed concepts *lack ethical* commitments, most of, or even all of, the *ethically committed* concepts *have nomic* commitments. Even more clearly, my discussion suggests that lawhood is very different from analyticity or intentionality. Compared with all the nomically committed concepts, concepts like intentionality and analyticity lead a very isolated existence. For something to be a physical object, there need not be any interesting analytic sentences. Even for there to be middle-sized ordinary things, there need not be any language or thought at all.

If the position I have been advancing is on the right track, a weighty question quickly arises: Is there any work left for the philosopher who is interested in lawhood or in one of the other nomic concepts? Once we recognize (i) that the nomic concepts and the other concepts with nomic commitments form a vast interlocking network, (ii) that this network cannot be explained using only concepts lacking nomic commitments, and (iii) that its resistance to philosophical explanation does nothing to impugn the network, then the natural next step is to better understand the network itself. So, then, we should do what could appropriately be called *conceptual geography*.

There are various ways to do this. Not straying very far from traditional approaches one might seek an analysis of lawhood (or one of the other nomic concepts) in *nomic* terms. But I go at the network in a different way, one that is in the spirit of my earlier

15

remarks. In the past, many have sought an analysis of causation using *only* lawhood, chance, the subjunctive conditional, and assorted nonnomic concepts. Just as ever so many philosophers have not appreciated the centrality of the nomic to our entire conceptual scheme, so these would-be analyzers of causation have not appreciated the centrality of causation to the network of concepts with nomic commitments. As I argue in Chapter 5, there cannot be a successful analysis of causation using in addition to nonnomic concepts, only lawhood, chance, and the subjunctive conditional. Thus, rather than trying to establish connections within the network, I'll show how certain aspects of the network are independent of certain other aspects of the network.

As Chapter 5 starts to suggest, there are very few full-fledged analyses that are even pretty interesting. Once we have set aside pedestrian examples like *x* is a vixen if and only if *x* is a female fox or *x* is a bachelor if and only if *x* is an unmarried male, successful analyses are rare. This is not to disparage the search for analyses. Attempts to analyze knowledge, personal identity, and even lawhood and causation have been extremely useful. Though as far as I can tell these attempts never result in complete and successful analyses, they often do provide us with a better understanding of the concepts. Sometimes they do so merely by revealing a facet of the concept not previously recognized. Sometimes we find some one-way connection between concepts, a notable necessary condition or a notable sufficient condition. In fact, I think this is one attainable and still very worthy goal for the contemporary metaphysician: to discover the analytic connections linking the various parts of conceptual space. Of course, there may be lots of nice fall out from the flipside of this endeavor: We may discover places where there are no such links. Thus, regarding philosophy, my recommendation is that we should not shun the search for analyses, but only that we should at long last come to *expect* philosophically interesting concepts to resist analysis. We should also recognize that their resistance is no threat to realism.

1.3 METHODOLOGY

This book incorporates a methodological precept that is suggested by my constructive conclusions. In evaluating the many analyses of causation and lawhood, it is no surprise that I often rely on the well-known method of counterexample. Thus, I frequently describe some actual or counterfactual situation, reveal what the analysis in question says about that situation, and attempt a philosophically untutored judgment of the plausibility of what is said. In addition to the method of counterexample, however, I employ an especially useful methodology that trades on an interesting conceptual connection that holds between lawhood and the subjunctive conditional, one that falls short of suggesting a full analysis of either concept. Support for this principle comes from a familiar picture of reality which embodies especially vividly the concept of lawhood employed in common sense.

Many have suggested that our devotion to there being some kind of necessity attaching to laws is born of a picture that portrays laws as the decrees of a supreme being.[6] A. J. Ayer puts the point this way:

I think that our present use of the expression 'laws of nature' carries traces of the conception of Nature as subject to command. Whether these commands are conceived to be those of a personal deity or, as by the Greeks, of an impersonal fate, makes no difference here. The point, in either case, is that the sovereign is thought to be so powerful that its dictates are bound to be obeyed. . . . [T]he commands which are issued to Nature are delivered with such authority that it is impossible that she should disobey them (1963 [f.p. 1956], p. 211).

Not being even an armchair etymologist, I do not hazard any guesses about the history of our use of the phrase 'laws of nature'. Nevertheless, the view of laws as the edicts of a lawgiver does provide a useful metaphor. I rely on this metaphor insofar as it underlies a more secular and more detailed picture: *the Laplacean picture*.[7] This worldview includes a portrayal of our universe as completely determined by its temporally local history at any one time together with a statement of what propositions are laws. According to the Laplacean picture, it is *as if* God created the world by designating the initial conditions and the laws. Given God's designations, the

6 Van Fraassen (1989, pp. 1–14) begins his book by reminding us of this view.
7 The obvious reference is to Pierre Simon Laplace and his classic discussion of determinism (1951 [f.p. 1814], p. 4). Prior to Laplace, Jean Le Rond d'Alembert appears to have held a full-blown theistic version of this worldview. See Hahn (1967, pp. 14–15; 1986, pp. 267–270), and Numbers (1977) for historical discussions of these cosmological outlooks and others important to this scientific period.

entire history of our universe, every fact, was completely determined. This picture also has an epistemological vision closely associated with it: that all phenomena can, with enough effort by generations of scientists, be embraced by a collection of laws that are both general and absolutely true (Hahn 1967, p. 6).

Suppose God did create the universe in part by specifying the laws of nature. Since he is an omnipotent sovereign, his laws *cannot* be disobeyed. No matter how attending circumstances might differ, the laws would still govern the course of history. In this way, the Laplacean picture suggests that, for any propositions P and Q, if Q follows from P given the lawful nature of the world, then Q would be the case if P were the case. In slightly more technical terms, the picture suggests:

(LP) If $\Box_{\mathscr{P}}(P \supset Q)$, then $P > Q$.

'$\Box_{\mathscr{P}}P$' abbreviates 'P is physically necessary', and '$P > Q$' abbreviates 'if P were the case, then Q would be the case'.[8] As illustration, suppose that it's a law that all copper expands when heated. Then consider any bit of copper b that, in fact, is not heated. Even if particular circumstances had been different, even if b were heated, the laws governing our world surely would be unchanged. Thus, we naturally accept the counterfactual that if b were (still) copper and heated, then b would expand. That is just what is suggested by (LP). Since it is a law that copper expands when heated,

8 I reluctantly employ standard language about physical necessity: A proposition is physically necessary if and only if it is true in all possible worlds with exactly the same laws as the actual world. Here, the phrase 'the actual world' is not a rigid designator; it does not refer to the same thing in all possible worlds. So, in a Newtonian world, it is physically necessary that massive bodies exert gravitational forces proportional to the inverse square of their distance, because in all possible worlds with exactly the same laws as *that Newtonian world*, massive bodies do exert gravitational forces proportional to the inverse square of their distance. (A proposition is physically possible if and only if its negation is not physically necessary.) In one respect, 'physical necessity' is a misleading name. It incorrectly suggests that the concept has some connection to *physics* or *physicalism*. On the contrary, even if it turns out that *dualism* is true, then, so long as there are laws linking mental properties, it could be the case that some *nonphysical* proposition physically necessitates some other *nonphysical* proposition. A better tag would be 'lawful necessity'. Since it is strongly rooted in the literature, however, I have chosen to stick with the unfortunate phrase.

it is physically necessary that the conjunction of b's being copper and b's being heated implies that b expands.

Though (LP) is suggested by the Laplacean picture, it has some suspicious implications involving *counterlegals*, subjunctive conditionals whose antecedent is physically impossible. For example, suppose c is an X-particle. Also suppose that L_0 is a law, where L_0 is the generalization that all X-particles have spin up. Then, consider the following (false) proposition:

(3) c is an X-particle and c has spin down.

Since L_0 is a law, it is physically necessary that (3) implies that c has spin up. Thus, (LP) endorses the extremely counterintuitive and apparently false conditional:

(4) If c were an X-particle and c had spin down, then c would have spin up.

Some propositions, like (3), are physically impossible because they contradict a law. Others are physically impossible for a different reason. Again suppose that L_0 is a law. Then, rather than focusing on (3), consider the following (false) proposition:

(5) c is an X-particle and c has a .1% chance of having spin up.

In contrast to (3), this conjunction does not contradict L_0; (5) and L_0 both could be true if c were an X-particle, c had a one-tenth percent chance of having spin up, and, despite the odds, c still did have spin up. Even so, (5) is not physically possible. Though there is a possible world in which L_0 and (5) are both true, there is no possible world in which L_0 is a *law* and (5) is also true. Because (5) is physically impossible, it sets up another apparent problem for (LP). Notice that the conjunction of (5) and L_0 entails that c has spin up. Thus, (LP) implies:

(6) If c were an X-particle and c had a .1% chance of having spin up, then c would have spin up.

Yet, very probably, this counterfactual is false. It is not true that if c were an X-particle and had a one-tenth percent chance of having

19

spin up, then c would have spin up; very likely, c *would not* have spin up.[9]

The problem with (LP) is that laws of nature are not so immutable that we can assume that they would still govern were either their truth or their lawhood to be contradicted. We shouldn't have expected the laws to hold no matter how different the attending circumstances might be. We need to weaken (LP). Letting '$\Diamond_{\wp}P$' abbreviate 'P is physically possible', I suggest:

(SC) If $\Diamond_{\wp}P$ and $\Box_{\wp}(P \supset Q)$, then $P > Q$.

This principle is not subject to the same counterexamples as (LP) because (3) and (5) are not physically possible (given that L_0 is a law). (SC) is a prime example of an analytic connection between two concepts that, despite a failure to suggest a complete analysis of either concept, is both highly defensible and philosophically interesting.[10]

---

9 Bennett (1984, pp. 83–84) quickly suggests treating counterfactuals with physically impossible antecedents as philosophers standardly treat counterfactuals with impossible antecedents, as trivially true unless relativized in a certain way. Someone with these sympathies might not accept my counterexamples to (LP), accepting (4) and (6) as true. While I disagree, it is worth noting that none of my later arguments turn on this point. It seems to me that if all unrelativized counterlegals are trivially true, then (LP) is perfectly acceptable. (LP) is significantly *stronger* than the principle that I employ. With it at my disposal, many of my arguments could be simplified.

10 (SC) is a consequence of Pollock's principle of legal conservatism (1984, pp. 116–118). Further support for (SC) comes indirectly from the Chisholm/Goodman account of the subjunctive conditional. For conditionals in which the antecedent is consistent with the laws, their account maintains that $P > Q$ if and only if there is a valid argument of the form:

$$L_1, \ldots, L_r$$
$$\underline{P, I_1, \ldots, I_k}$$
$$Q$$

where $L_1 - L_r$ are laws, and $I_1 - I_k$ are nonlaws *cotenable* with P. Since 'cotenable' is a technical term, this account needs to be supplemented with come characterization of cotenability. Even so, one implication of their account is clear:

(CG) If P is consistent with the laws and Q follows validly from P and the laws, then $P > Q$.

(SC) and (CG) are quite similar. Indeed, assuming that P's being a law entails that it is a law that P is a law, (CG) is *equivalent* to (SC).

How can (SC) be put to good use? In Chapter 2, it is primarily used to test a proposed characterization of the difference between laws and accidents. I ask what would follow from (SC) if that account were correct. When false conditionals are found among the implications, the account is rejected. Completely unobjectionable, this is one useful way of ensuring that a purported solution to the problem of laws preserves lawhood's relationship with the subjunctive conditional. Hence, this approach helps to ensure that a purported solution does not undermine lawhood's subtle role in everyday thought and talk. While most have not been as careful about the connection between lawhood and the subjunctive conditional, this use of the connection is not entirely novel; it has often been used as a constraint on purported solutions to the problem of laws. In Chapter 3, (SC) again is used in a manner that is wholly unobjectionable. But, as well, it is implemented in a fashion that, very far from being time-worn, is quite novel. There, (SC) assists in showing that both lawhood and chance do not supervene on the nonnomic concepts.[11]

Its overt determinism makes the Laplacean picture suspect when viewed as a description of the actual world. Recent science suggests that indeterminism rules. Still, the picture need not be accurate to be valuable. As I see it, this picture contains both some very revealing features and some very misleading features. Both sorts help to frame my discussion. On the revealing side, and as is suggested by the discussion of this present section, the picture embodies the concept of lawhood employed in common sense, the concept we see as naturally intertwined with the subjunctive conditional and with nearly all our ordinary concepts. On the misleading side, and as we will see in Chapter 5, it can easily be taken to suggest an overly strong connection between laws, attending conditions, and causation.

1.4 THREE FEATURES OF LAWS

Although the ties between lawhood and the counterfactual conditional are more crucial, my discussion is shaped to a lesser degree by three fundamental convictions. The first is that all laws are true. The second is that all laws are in some sense general or universal.

---

11 Because (SC) has such an important role in the book, I defend it against possible objections in Appendix B.

The third is that all laws are contingent. Though these doctrines are not always given a careful formulation, they are adopted in some form by most philosophers. Indeed, they are usually taken to be necessary truths. In this portion of the chapter, I formulate and offer some brief considerations in support of the foregoing convictions. I am afraid that these considerations may not sway the minority of philosophers who defend conflicting positions. Because these doctrines are so fundamental, it is difficult to find any common ground on which to engage dissenters. If my fears are justified, it is probably best to view these convictions as three assumptions of my investigation.

a. Truth

In our daily inquiries, we take ourselves to be seeking, and sometimes finding, *truth*. It would be surprising if scientists – our most revered investigators – sought less. So, to the extent that laws are one object of scientific discovery, it is natural to think that laws must be true. We also take many of our counterfactual, dispositional, and causal judgments to be true and suppose that our everyday and scientific explanations do not succeed unless they are true. If our counterfactual, causal, dispositional, and explanatory judgments are sometimes true, then the principles capable of supporting those judgments must also be true. The commonsense practice employing lawhood strongly suggests that there are no false laws of nature.

The assumption that all laws are true can lead to some confusion. Strictly speaking, many propositions that are called 'laws', like Newton's law of gravitation, are not really laws. The scientific theories that recognized them as laws are no longer very strongly confirmed. The true science, very likely, will imply that these generalizations are false, and hence that they are not genuine laws of nature. Confusion is possible because they are still called 'laws' (though not as frequently 'laws of nature') even after they are no longer believed. This sometimes results either because the propositions are given *names* including the word 'law' when they were believed to be laws, or because of a tendency to use the word 'law' to describe any general proposition or any proposition at one time taken to be a law of nature by scientists. One should be wary of this confusion, because, for expository reasons, I frequently rely on

22

simple and familiar generalizations from the history of science (or on even simpler, wholly fictitious examples) that are no longer (or perhaps never were) believed to be true. The points to be made usually require only the possibility of the proposition being a law – not that it actually be a law. (I shall continue to use the word 'law' and the phrase 'law of nature' interchangeably.)

Wittgensteinian instrumentalists (see Musgrave 1981) like S. E. Toulmin (1953) and N. R. Hanson (1969) recognize a distinction between laws and other empirical generalizations and yet maintain that all laws are neither true nor false. More recently, Nancy Cartwright (1983) at least appears to challenge the claim that all laws are true.[12] These positions are motivated by various abstract considerations and are not directly motivated by the commonsense practice employing lawhood or the underlying Laplacean picture. Speaking from the perspective of common sense, the principle that P's being a law entails P is as plausible as the principle that S's knowing P entails P. To my mind, these two principles are clear examples of analytic truths and are as secure as any hypotheses ever advanced in philosophy. I'd sooner believe there are no laws of nature, and all that this would imply, than give up the conviction that all laws are true.

b. Contingency

Since Hume, philosophers have generally admitted that there are at least some contingently true propositions that could be laws of nature. (Whether all laws are contingent is discussed in a moment.) For example, consider Newton's first law of motion. There are possible worlds in which it is true and a law, and there are also possible worlds in which it is false. Any Newtonian world, any world that as a matter of law obeys the general principles of Newtonian

12 It may be that Cartwright is using the word 'law' differently than I do here. By 'law', she may mean either a general proposition or a proposition at one time taken to be a law by scientists. Scriven (1961), who also appears to argue that at least some laws are false, clearly is using the word 'law' in one of these other ways. See Swartz (1985, pp. 3–4) for further discussion. More recently, Woodward claims to have several examples such that "In none of these cases does the holding of a law entail that the corresponding generalization is exactly and exceptionlessly true" (1992, p. 192). While it is clear that Woodward is using the word 'law' to mean "the generalizations and relationships which are taken to be laws within scientific practice" (p. 193), he also seems to think that this is the only proper notion of law for examination.

physics, is a world in which Newton's first is true (and also a law). A world containing decelerating bodies not subject to any force, perhaps a world lawfully obeying the general principles of Aristotelian physics, is a world in which Newton's first is false.

There are two traditional reasons for believing that a contingent proposition could be a law. The first is that it is easy to *imagine* the laws of one possible world being false in another. The second stems from the nature of scientific discovery. There seem to be some generalizations, especially certain quantitative ones, that could be laws and that are also clearly a posteriori. If all laws of nature are necessary truths, then it is not clear why scientists must sometimes conduct their business in the drastically empirical way that they do. Naturally, these two traditional reasons are often challenged. *Necessitarians* maintain that all laws are necessary.[13] They argue that imagination is not a suitable guide to possibility. They also frequently call attention to Saul Kripke's (1972) apparent discovery of a posteriori necessary truths, suggesting that the a posteriori nature of some laws does not prevent them from being necessary. I am not sure what to make of these replies to the traditional considerations. While it is easy enough to show that imagination or conceivability is not an infallible guide to possibility, necessitarians have not shown that imagination, conceivability, or something similar does not set up some presumption for judgments of possibility. And, over twenty years later, Kripke's so-called discovery is still sufficiently controversial to make me reluctant to dismiss the epistemological worry.

Even setting the traditional reasons aside, I see little to recommend the necessitarian position. Theirs is the much stronger claim, maintaining as they do that all laws are necessary, even taking this thesis itself to be a necessary truth. To undermine their position, we need only discover one contingent proposition that could be a law. Consider Newton's gravitational principle. For a long time, it was thought to be a law of nature by many of the most astute people in the history of science. Then more recent science taught us that it was only approximately true. So, it is false and not actually a law. Yet it surely is not necessarily false. Hence, the gravitational principle is contingent. But just as surely, if bodies did attract one another in exactly the way the gravitational principle describes, then

13 See Blanshard (1962), Shoemaker (1980), Swoyer (1982), and Fales (1990).

this principle would be a law of nature. Therefore, there is a contingent proposition that could be a law. I suppose that necessitarians will stubbornly deny that the gravitational principle would be a law if it were true. But that is not an easy position to maintain. Given the way our world is, this principle has pretty much all the makings of a law. Scientists certainly thought it was sufficiently nonaccidental when they believed it to be true.[14]

Is it true, perhaps even necessarily true, that *all* laws are contingent? This is neither a terribly important, nor a terribly interesting, issue. The point that isolates the necessitarians is whether a contingent proposition could be a law. I have briefly argued that one could. That this is so is one thing that makes the problem of laws especially interesting. It is contingent laws that have an especially interesting modal character, involving a contingent modality not identifiable with anything like logical necessity or necessity (simpliciter). There are some minor considerations weighing against the position that all laws are contingent. Necessary truths certainly cannot be disqualified for being too accidental. It is also natural to think that all deductive consequences of laws are themselves laws though the deductive consequences of any proposition include all logical truths. Furthermore, scientists sometimes take certain definitions and pure mathematical statements to be laws. For convenience, I do adopt the position that all laws are contingent. Even if it is not quite correct, assuming that all laws are contingent has the virtue of focusing our discussion on the most interesting group of laws.

c. Universality

Especially when keeping the Laplacean picture in mind, the thesis that laws of nature are in some sense general or universal is very compelling. As evidence, note that we have a natural reluctance to

14 Perhaps the most interesting support for the necessitarian position is that it has an explanation of why laws of nature are counterfactual-supporting: They support counterfactuals in the same way and for the same reasons that the truths of logic and mathematics do. (See Swoyer 1982, p. 209; or Fales 1990, pp. 85–87). This advantage of the necessitarian position is largely illusory. As may already be apparent, I think that the connection between lawhood and the subjunctive conditional is analytic. It really needs no explanation, at least no more so than, say that S's knowing P implies P. As I see it, supporting counterfactuals is just part of what it is to be a law.

accept anything but universally quantified propositions as laws. For example, it is at least strange to think that some particular fact (e.g., that the earth has mass 5.98×10^{24} kilograms) could be a law of nature, no matter how interesting or scientifically important that fact might be. Given this reluctance, it is tempting to maintain simply that all laws are universally quantified. Unfortunately, matters are not that simple. Requiring that laws be universally quantified has the suspicious consequence that two propositions may be logically equivalent though only one of the two is a law. For this and no doubt other reasons, it is difficult to state a universality thesis very precisely. So I leave this conviction in its vague, but immensely plausible, original formulation as the thought that all laws are in some sense general or universal. [15]

Some have advocated a second, and somewhat less plausible, universality thesis: that no laws are spatially or temporally restricted; i.e., that laws do not quantify over limited spatial or temporal regions or refer to any specific spaces or times. This second thesis is troubled by the relatively minor problems of precise formulation that plague the first universality thesis: Consider the generalization that all inertial bodies have no acceleration; more explicitly, the proposition that, for all times t and all x, if x is an inertial body at t, then x has no acceleration at t. Since it quantifies over all times, it is not temporally restricted. It may also be a law. But it entails many temporally restricted generalizations that it would also be natural to count as laws. For example, it entails that, for all x, if x is an inertial body at noon today, then x has no acceleration at noon today. Aside from such problems of formulation, however, I also have some much more interesting doubts about this second universality thesis. I am tempted to think that there could be some fundamental spatially or temporally restricted laws, ones that were not the consequence of any more basic unrestricted law. Certain elementary particles might exhibit some lawful behavior in one section of space, exhibiting some other lawful behavior in a different section of space, though no more general law accounted for this difference in behavior. (A similar point could be made about different epics of time.)

15 Certain attempts to answer to the problem of laws to be discussed in Chapter 2 do hold that all laws are universally quantified. I do not, however, criticize these attempts for this slight failing. The problems concerning the formulation of a universality condition are minor in comparison to the criticisms that are raised.

I suspect that some philosophers are reluctant to admit the possibility of spatially or temporally restricted laws, because there are obviously many spatially or temporally restricted accidents, e.g., that anyone who was the United States president in 1990 was named 'George'. So, admitting the possibility of these laws makes their job of distinguishing laws and accidents that much more difficult. Some have been reluctant to admit that another sort of restricted generalization could a law for similar reasons. These universal generalizations are restricted by virtue of referring to some specific physical object or event. As I said in the introduction to this chapter, the proposition that all the coins in my pocket are nickels is an example by virtue of its reference to my pocket. But Galileo's law and Kepler's first law are also examples by virtue of their respective allusions to the earth and the sun. As I also said above, whether a generalization that refers to a specific physical object or event can be a law of nature is discussed much more carefully in Chapter 2.

d. The role of these convictions

That all laws are true, contingent, and in some sense general inspires some of the simplest attempts to solve the traditional problem of laws. These *naive regularity accounts,* to be discussed in the next chapter, more or less assume that these three necessary conditions together constitute a sufficient condition for being a law. The convictions just discussed play a different role in my book, never being treated as more than individually necessary. In fact, the only aspects of these convictions that I ever place any great weight upon are the thesis that lawhood entails truth and the thesis that a contingent proposition could be a law.

2

Humean analyses

Epistemological questions are often influential in calling our attention to *metaphysical* issues. For example, we are moved to ask what makes an action morally wrong by questions about how we know of an action that it is morally wrong. (I realize that according to the traditional way of classifying philosophical issues, the question of what makes an action morally wrong is a question of ethics, not of metaphysics. But it is, in the relevant sense, a metaphysical issue in ethics.) In much the same way, we are pushed to ask about the nature of mentality and consciousness by questions about how we know facts about other minds. The problem of laws encounters similar epistemological influences. Many are led to investigate what makes a proposition a law by questioning how we know of a proposition that it is a law. Sometimes the epistemological motivation is slightly less direct, coming from questions regarding our knowledge of causation, the counterfactual conditional, or one of the other nomic concepts.

This interplay between epistemological and metaphysical questions encourages *epistemologically oriented* metaphysical viewpoints. Berkeley's idealism is a well-known example. Faced with Descartes's epistemological questions, Berkeley advanced a metaphysical position giving us easy access to the external world. Our perceptions, apparently, constitute the basis of our knowledge of the external world; Berkeley's metaphysics has it that our perceptions (along with God's) are what make it the case that facts about the external world obtain.

As I use this term, *Humean* analyses are analyses of lawhood that avoid any essential reference to mysterious entities, and that are otherwise beyond empiricist reproach;[1] in particular, their analyz-

---

1 By calling these accounts *Humean*, I do not mean to imply that Hume offered one. I take these to be Humean analyses only because of Hume's influence on their

ing vocabulary must not include any expressions with nomic commitments. The very simplest Humean analyses are appropriately known as *naive regularity analyses*. The many straightforward objections to these analyses motivate more plausible Humean accounts. These more plausible accounts are epistemologically oriented in much the same way as Berkeley's idealism. Some of these accounts focus on induction as the source of our knowledge of *laws* and maintain that laws are confirmable by a certain sort of induction, while accidents are not. Other of the more plausible Humean analyses focus on a rather complex concept that arguably is epistemologically relevant to *lawhood;* namely, membership in all true theoretical systems with a best balance of simplicity and strength.

I argue that all Humean analyses fail, demonstrating that the epistemology of laws and lawhood is a poor guide to answering metaphysical questions about lawhood. Readers intrigued by the interplay of epistemology and metaphysics should be patient. Before discussing the analyses suffering the most serious epistemological influences in Sections 2.2 and 2.3, I present in Section 2.1 some criticisms of naive regularity analyses. I hope that the reader's patience is rewarded.

2.1 NAIVE REGULARITY ANALYSES

Although I find it misleading, many philosophers adopt a framework that takes lawhood to be the conjunction of truth and *lawlikeness*. That is, many philosophers accept:

P is a law if and only if P is true and P is lawlike.

'Lawlike' is a made-up term. It simply stands for that property other than truth that a proposition must satisfy in order to be a law. Within this framework, what is needed to give an analysis of lawhood is an analysis of lawlikeness. The only test of an analysis of lawlikeness is the adequacy of the resulting analysis of lawhood.

defenders. Hume, himself, was not much concerned – at least not directly – with lawhood. Regarding his position about the nomic more generally, there is a great deal of controversy. Here's just a sampling of some recent participants in that dispute: Blackburn (1990), Broughton (1987), Costa (1989), Strawson (1989), and Winkler (1991).

By definition, naive regularity analyses are analyses that take lawlikeness to be an essential feature of a proposition. They differ from one another only in how they attempt to analyze lawlikeness. One of their motivations appears to have been the usual motivation attached to "conjunctive analyses" (cf., Unger 1986, pp. 125–126). Having identified some necessary conditions of lawhood, like truth and like contingency and universality (which are usually taken to be necessary conditions of lawlikeness), philosophers conjoined those necessary conditions with the hope that together they would constitute a necessary *and* sufficient condition for lawhood. There is also an epistemological motivation for naive regularity analyses. Not too long ago, it was popular to think that the only empirical evidence needed to confirm that P is a law is the evidence confirming P. By making lawlikeness an essential feature of propositions, and hence a property that arguably can be discovered a priori, naive regularity analyses apparently ensure that the only empirical evidence needed to confirm P's lawhood is the empirical evidence of P's truth.

The naive regularity analysis I discuss is typical. It analyzes lawlikeness thus:

P is lawlike if and only if P is contingent, universally quantified, and unrestricted.[2]

Our naive regularity analysis relies on some standard terminology:

P is unrestricted if and only if P includes only nonlocal, empirical concepts apart from logical connectives and quantifiers.

Local concepts are defined with reference to individual times, places, or objects; the following are examples: being medieval, being American, and being terrestrial. It is difficult to characterize empirical concepts. I suppose, however, that the following would

---

2 This analysis is frequently criticized. None of the problems I raise are completely novel, but I do think that they are raised in an original way. Similar problems are discussed by Armstrong (1983), Nagel (1961, pp. 47–110), Molnar (1974, [f.p. 1969]), Ayer (1963), Goodman (1983, pp. 17–25), Hempel (1966, pp. 54–58), Earman (1984), Mellor (1980), and others.

be examples of nonempirical ones: being a nonphysical spirit, being a Platonic form, and so on.[3] Our naive regularity analysis rules out the initial example of an accidentally true proposition from Chapter 1: the generalization that all coins in my pocket are nickels. While this proposition is true, contingent, and universally quantified, it is not unrestricted.

a. Too weak

Directing us to count as laws propositions that are not, our naive regularity analysis, and others like it, are too weak. Here are three different classes of propositions, each of which shows that our naive regularity analysis fails to put strong enough restrictions on candidates for lawhood.

1. Vacuous generalizations. Let us say that any panda whose fur exemplifies a plaid pattern is a *plaid panda*. (So, as I am using the phrase 'plaid panda', even a panda that has been painted plaid qualifies as a plaid panda.) Then, let us suppose, plausibly enough, that there are no plaid pandas. Because none exist, all plaid pandas weigh five kilograms.[4] This true universal generalization is contingent: There are possible worlds in which there are plaid pandas weighing more than five kilograms. The generalization is also unrestricted because it includes only nonlocal, empirical concepts apart from logical connectives and quantifiers. More generally, if there are no Fs and the universal generalization that all Fs are Gs is contingent and unrestricted, then, according to our naive regularity analysis, that generalization is a law. Hence, not only is it a law that all plaid pandas weigh five kilograms, it is also a law that all plaid pandas weigh 5000 kilograms. So, the analysis

---

3 Sometimes it is assumed that empirical concepts must be *projectible*. I am not making that assumption. Projectibility raises many important issues. Some of these matters are discussed in Section 2.2.

4 Although it *may* be a slight oversimplification, throughout the book, I assume that indicative conditional sentences are accurately represented using the material conditional of predicate logic. (A material conditional sentence '$P \supset Q$' is true if and only if 'P' is false or 'Q' is true.) Very little turns on this assumption. For arguments that it is not an oversimplification, see Jackson (1987) and Lewis (1986, pp. 152–156).

makes science absurdly easy – all we need do to discover laws of nature is conjure up generalizations that are vacuous, contingent, and unrestricted.[5]

Admitting all contingent, unrestricted, vacuous generalizations as laws also leads to problems deriving from certain plausible judgments of physical possibility and principle (SC), our principle relating lawhood and the subjunctive conditional. (See Chapter 1.) Because many of my arguments in this chapter are of a similar form, in presenting this representative argument, I reveal the problems in a rather deliberate manner. To begin, consider Ling-Ling, a panda who visited the Bronx Zoo in 1987.[6] For Ling-Ling to be a plaid panda, some deviant would only need to sneak into her pen, tranquilize her, and dye her fur plaid. So, Ling-Ling's being a plaid panda certainly would have no implications about what propositions are laws of nature. There are possible worlds in which Ling-Ling is a plaid panda and in which the laws are exactly the laws of the actual world. Invoking the standard definition of physical possibility, it follows that it is *physically possible* for Ling-Ling to be a plaid panda. This judgment of physical possibility is the first key to my argument. The second key is a consequence of our naive regularity analysis. According to that analysis, one law of the actual world is that all plaid pandas weigh five kilograms. So, according to our analysis, in every possible world with exactly the same laws as the actual world, the proposition that Ling-Ling is a plaid panda implies that she weighs five kilograms. Therefore, Ling-Ling's being a plaid panda *physically necessitates* her weighing five kilograms. (Here I am relying on the standard definition of physical necessity.) Together with principle (SC), this consequence and the judgment of physical possibility undermine our naive regularity analysis. Principle (SC) says that for all P and Q, if P is physically possible and physically necessitates Q, then Q would be the case if P were the case. So, it should be true that Ling-Ling would weigh five kilograms if she were a plaid panda. But that counterfactual is false. Ling-Ling weighs much more than five kilograms, and her weight

5 W. E. Johnson (1964 [f.p. 1924], pp. 11–12) presents the earliest discussion that I have come across of the problem of vacuous generalizations.
6 The panda I have in mind is not the more famous and – I'm sorry to say – recently deceased Ling-Ling who was housed at the National Zoo for twenty years. The less famous Ling-Ling was quite young when she made her trip from China to the Bronx. I assume that she is still alive, well, and not in the least bit plaid.

would still be much more than five kilograms if she were a plaid panda, if – for example – her fur were dyed plaid.

Along a line already indicated, we can turn this serious problem into an even more serious problem. I have just argued that, because our naive regularity analysis says that it is a law that all plaid pandas weigh five kilograms, it also implies:

(1) If Ling-Ling were a plaid panda, than Ling-Ling would weigh 5 kilograms.

Our analysis also says that it is a law that all plaid pandas weigh 5000 kilograms. So, reasoning as we did before, it follows that:

(2) If Ling-Ling were a plaid panda, then Ling-Ling would weigh 5000 kilograms.

But (1) and (2) cannot both be true. Together with the plausible judgments of physical possibility and our principle (SC), our naive regularity analysis thus not only has *false* counterfactual implications, it has *inconsistent* counterfactual implications.

2. Troublesome concepts. Suppose it is true that all ravens have feathers. (Whether this generalization is also a law is incidental.) And, call anything that is either a raven or a plaid panda a *plaven*. Since there are no plaid pandas and all ravens have feathers, it is true that all plavens have feathers. Moreover, this generalization is contingent and unrestricted. So, according to our naive regularity analysis, it is a law that all plavens have feathers. But, in reality, this is not a law. It is hardly the sort of generalization one would expect to find as part of a serious scientific theory. If additional reasons are desired for denying this generalization the status of law, here a couple. First, since the generalization entails the contingent generalization that all plaid pandas have feathers, that generalization ought also to be a law. It is not. Second, we again encounter problems with counterfactuals. As I said above, it is plausible to think that Ling-Ling's being a plaid panda is physically possible. If the generalization that all plavens have feathers is a law, then that Ling-Ling is a plaid panda physically necessitates that Ling-Ling has feathers. Thus, invoking (SC), it should be true that if Ling-Ling were a plaid panda, then she would have feathers. Since this is not

33

true, our naive regularity analysis must be mistaken. Notice that, because there are lots and lots of ravens, there are lots and lots of plavens. The generalization that all plavens have feathers is not vacuous. Vacuity is not the source of this second problem for our naive regularity analysis. What seems to be the problem is that the generalization contains a troublesome concept in its antecedent, the disjunctive concept of being a plaven.

3. *A puzzle.* Consider the generalization, discussed briefly in Chapter 1, that all gold spheres are less than ten meters in diameter. It is true, contingent, and unrestricted. So, according to our naive regularity analysis, it is a law that all gold spheres are less than ten meters in diameter. Nevertheless, this generalization is not a law. All that prevents there being a gold sphere that big is the fact that no one has been curious enough and wealthy enough to have such a sphere produced. A closely related, often discussed example is the generalization that all gold spheres are less than a *mile* in diameter. According to our naive regularity analysis, it is also a law of nature. Most take this to be a counterexample. Though I agree, I do not think that it is as obvious a counterexample as, say, the generalization that all gold spheres are less than ten meters in diameter. That all gold spheres are less than a mile in diameter is much less accidental. For all I know, there is not enough gold in the entire universe for there to be a one-mile gold sphere. Still, the generalization that all gold spheres are less than a mile in diameter very clearly is not a law. It is sufficiently accidental even if there is not enough gold in the universe for such a tremendous gold sphere. There would only need to be different initial conditions for this generalization to be false.

Another related counterexample derives from an example proposed by Karl Popper (1959, pp. 427–428; also see Armstrong 1983, p. 18). Moas are an extinct species of New Zealand birds. We can suppose that the longest-lived moa – I'll call her 'Marge' – just missed living fifty years, dying on the day before her fiftieth birthday. There was nothing about the genetic structure of moas that prevented any of them from living longer than fifty years. Their early deaths were quite accidental, the longer-lived ones – including Marge – dying as a result of a virus. Coming from India, this virus was blown into New Zealand by a certain wind. In absence of this wind, the virus would never have gotten there. Then, the generalization that all moas die before age fifty apparently is not a law. Since it is a true, contingent, and unrestricted generalization, our naive regularity analysis has the mistaken consequence that it is. Once again we encounter problems involving implications about counterfactuals. Though Marge did contract the fatal virus, it is surely physically possible that Marge be a moa and not contract the virus. According to our naive regularity analysis, it is a law that all moas die before age fifty. If that is correct, then the complex proposition that Marge is a moa and does not contract the virus physically necessitates that Marge die before age fifty. So, according to principle (SC), it should be true that if Marge were a moa and had not contracted the virus, then Marge would have died before age fifty. But that counterfactual is false. If Marge were a moa and had not contracted the virus, then she probably would have lived at least one more day.

The two generalizations about the gold spheres and the generalization about the moas all present a problem for our naive regularity analysis that is quite distinct from the counterexamples presented earlier. These generalizations are not vacuous and involve no obviously troublesome concepts. Furthermore, unlike the earlier counterexamples, for which we could at least point to an apparent source of the problem (i.e., vacuity or troublesome concepts), it is not at all clear what gives rise to these counterexamples.

The puzzle presented by these generalizations and others like them is a serious one. Such accidentally true generalizations exhibit few obvious differences from many laws. Return to some examples discussed briefly in Chapter 1:

(3) All ravens have speeds less than 31 meters per second.
(4) All signals have speeds less than 300,000,001 meters per second.

Like the generalizations about the gold spheres and the one about the moas, (3) is an accident. But (3) exhibits few obvious differences from (4), and (4) may well be a law. Somehow, while keeping lawlikeness an essential feature of propositions, a successful naive regularity analysis must rule that (4) is, and (3) is not, lawlike.

We can turn this sort of puzzle into a conclusive objection against *all* naive regularity accounts. Consider again the generalization that all gold spheres are less than a mile in diameter. That generalization, though it is not a law, could be a law. For example, "if gold

35

were unstable in such a way that there was no chance whatever that a large amount of gold could last long enough to be formed into a one-mile sphere" (Lewis 1986, p. 123), then it might well be a law that all gold spheres are less than a mile in diameter.[7] In such possible worlds, the generalization is a law, and hence it is also lawlike. But, in the actual world, the generalization is true, and not a law. So, in our world, it is not lawlike. Thus, a single proposition is lawlike in one possible world and not lawlike in another. Any essential feature of a proposition must be exhibited by the proposition in all possible worlds. Hence, lawlikeness must not be an essential property of propositions. Since, by definition, all naive regularity analyses take lawlikeness to be an essential feature of propositions, all such analyses fail (cf., Tooley 1987, p. 52).

b. Too strong

In addition to being rejected for being too weak, naive regularity analyses are sometimes rejected for being too strong. Here I discuss one objection, briefly mentioned in Chapter 1, supposedly showing that our naive regularity analysis is too strong. Hoping to avoid a common error, I begin with a subtly fallacious presentation. (Once this error is identified, I present the objection once again in an effective manner.) Assume that our universe is Newtonian and that it is true that, on earth, free-falling bodies accelerate at a rate of 9.81 meters per second per second. Since this generalization includes reference to the earth, it is not unrestricted and hence, according to our naive regularity analysis, it is not a law. Though I have my doubts, many think that this is a counterexample. Many think that, despite what our analysis says, this free-fall principle would be a law if it were true and our universe were Newtonian.

I find this presentation of the example fallacious, because I do not think that this restricted generalization would be a law even if it were true and our universe were Newtonian. It would just be too easy for the generalization to be false; its truth would be too acci-

---

7 One might be tempted to argue that if anything were unstable in this way, then it would not be gold. If this were so, we would lose the impetus for taking the gold sphere generalization to be a law in the imagined world. Nevertheless, while there is perhaps some plausibility to thinking that some sort of stability is an essential property of gold, it is not plausible to think that stability in these large quantities is essential to gold.

dental. If our universe were Newtonian and this generalization were true, it would be the case, for example, that the generalization would be false if only the earth had a much smaller (or larger) mass. To make these considerations more precise, suppose our universe is Newtonian and that the free-fall principle is true. For the earth to have a much smaller mass, a series of cataclysmic explosions need only cause large portions of the earth to leave its atmosphere. Since that is all it would take, it seems that the earth could have significantly less mass without there being a difference in the laws of nature. If so, then it is also possible that the laws be the same, the earth have significantly less mass, and Ling-Ling (that unfortunate panda) be free-falling. Thus, it is physically possible that the earth have significantly less mass and Ling-Ling be a free-falling body. Invoking (SC), if the restricted generalization really is a law, it should be the case that if the earth did have significantly less mass and Ling-Ling were a free-falling body on earth, then she would accelerate at 9.81 meters per second per second. But this counterfactual is false. If the earth had significantly less mass and Ling-Ling were a free-falling body on earth, then she would accelerate at a slower rate. Thus, the free-fall principle wouldn't be a law even if it were true and our universe were Newtonian.

In a way, I am taking what appears to be a controversial position about this generalization and its status as a law. Scientists certainly called it a law then they thought that our universe was Newtonian. Who am I to maintain that these *scientists* had misjudged what the laws were? Two remarks may help to lessen my burden. First, scientists who called it a law may have been using the word 'law' in a derivative way (e.g., as a term for any general proposition or any proposition once taken to be a law) just as scientists do today when they refer to Newton's principle of gravitation as a law, knowing full well that this generalization is false. Second, it may be that the phrase '. . . is a law' is *context-dependent*. Several authors have convincingly argued that the verb 'to know' is context-dependent, that whether it is true to say, '*S* knows *P*' depends on its context of utterance.[8] Specifically, they have argued that context determines

---

8 For more on context-dependence, see Lewis (1983b, pp. 233–249). DeRose's (1992) paper contains a helpful discussion of the context-dependence of epistemological terms. Also see Unger (1986) and Cohen (1988). Van Fraassen (1980, p. 118) denies that sentences of science are context-dependent. His original argu-

how *nonaccidental* S's believing *P* must be in order for it to be true to say, '*S* knows *P*'. Given the parallels between lawhood and knowledge with respect to their connection to nonaccidentality, it would be surprising if the phrase '. . . is a law' were not similarly context-dependent. Context may determine just how accidental *P* can be and it still be true to say, '*P* is a law'. If this is correct, then a lawhood sentence may be true in one context, and false in another. So, a paragraph back when I uttered sentences denying the free-fall principle the status of law, I may not have been contradicting scientists who thought that our universe was Newtonian and who may have uttered sentences attributing it the status of law. The context could have become more demanding. (Further support for the context-dependence of '. . . is a law' comes from the frequently acknowledged context-dependence of counterfactual conditional sentences and sentences including modal expressions like 'can', 'may', and 'must'.)

There is a nonfallacious way of using Galileo's law to raise a problem for our naive regularity account. Even though this generalization would not be a law if it were true and our universe were Newtonian, it would be a law in a different sort of universe. In one such a universe, it is true that on earth free-falling bodies accelerate at a rate of 9.81 meters per second per second. But, in addition, the acceleration of free-falling bodies is much more immutable. In particular, it is insensitive to changes in the mass of the earth. If the earth had a significantly smaller (or larger) mass and Ling-Ling were a free-falling body, then she would still accelerate at a rate of 9.81 meters per second per second. Other similar examples of restricted laws are occasionally discussed in the literature:

ment went something like this: Science does not imply that context is one way or another; therefore, scientific sentences are not context-dependent. In response to objections raised by Stalnaker (1984, pp. 149–50), van Fraassen (1989, p. 36) has slightly weakened his conclusion, holding that if the truth of a sentence '*P*' is context-independent, then so is the truth of '*P* is a law'. Van Fraassen has apparently missed the point of Stalnaker's criticisms. *Nothing* follows about the context-independence of scientific sentences from the fact that science does not imply that contexts are one way or another. As Stalnaker says, "For scientific statements to be both determinate and context-dependent, all that is required is that scientific practice provide a context for the interpretation of the language it uses to describe the world" (p. 150). I highly recommend Stalnaker's extended discussion of van Fraassen's position.

Suppose, for example, the world were as follows: All the fruit in Smith's garden at any time are apples. When one attempts to take an orange into the garden, it turns into an elephant. Bananas so treated become apples as they cross the boundary, while pears are resisted by a force that cannot be overcome. Cherry trees planted in the garden bear apples, or they bear nothing at all. If all these things were true, there would be a very strong case for its being a law that all the fruit in Smith's garden are apples (Tooley 1987, 120–22).

These sorts of examples, though patently hypothetical, are sufficient to show that our naive regularity analysis is too strong.[9]

One might hope that we only need to fiddle with the definition of lawlikeness, making it a bit weaker, to avoid the problem of restricted laws. But that is not so. The tempting revision is to weaken the characterization of lawlikeness so that some, but not all, restricted generalizations could be laws. That is not a worthwhile enterprise within a naive regularity analysis. My discussion of the free-fall principle includes considerations, much like the earlier argument concerning the generalization that all gold spheres are less than a mile in diameter, undermining all naive regularity analyses. I have in essence argued that the free-fall claim would be true, but not a law, in one universe and that it would be true, and a law, in another universe. It would be true, but not a law, if it were true and our universe were Newtonian. It would be true, and a law, in the universe in which the acceleration of free-falling bodies is uninfluenced by changes in the mass of the earth. So, a single restricted generalization can be a law in one possible world, while being an accident in another possible world. Thus, lawlikeness must be a contingent feature of propositions. Using exactly the same words used at the end of Section 2.1a, we may conclude: Since, by definition, all naive regularity analyses take lawlikeness to be an essential feature of propositions, all such analyses fail.

9 Nearly all the points just made about Galileo's law could also be made about Kepler's first law of planetary motion. Many (e.g., Nagel 1961, p. 57; Bigelow and Pargetter 1990, p. 233) cite the latter as an example of a restricted law, but they appear to be mistaken about what sort of conditions must obtain in order for it to be a law. As I see it, Kepler's first is not actually a law, nor would it be a law even if it were true and our universe were Newtonian (cf., Lyon 1977, p. 118). Like Galileo's law it would be just too accidental in a Newtonian universe. Kepler's first would be a law, however, in a very different sort of possible world, one where the sun and the orbits of the planets are much more immutable than they would be if our universe were Newtonian.

39

c. Reactions

For the most part, Humeans have recognized that there are defeating objections to all naive regularity analyses. (They have been especially impressed by the fact that these analyses are much too weak.) It looks as if there must be a nonessential feature of propositions other than truth that distinguishes laws from accidents. The project for Humeans is specifying what that additional feature is. As I indicated in the opening pages of this chapter, Humeans have looked to epistemological considerations for advice. At last, we are ready to examine those Humean analyses that are most strongly influenced by these considerations.

Regarding any law of nature, there are two pertinent, but distinct, things I can know. I can know *it*, or I can know *that it is a law of nature*. For example, with regard to Newton's first, assuming for the moment that it is a law, I can know *that* all bodies experiencing no force have no acceleration, or I can know *that it is a law* that all bodies experiencing no force have no acceleration. When we investigate our reasons for believing the law of nature itself, we are considering the epistemology of *laws*. When we investigate our reasons for believing that it is a law of nature, we are considering the epistemology of *lawhood*. Some Humeans are influenced by the epistemology of laws, while others are influenced by the epistemology of lawhood. In the next section, I discuss the analyses proposed by Humeans influenced by the epistemology of laws.

2.2 INDUCTION, LAWS, AND LAWHOOD

Recognizing that induction is part of the epistemology of at least many laws, Nelson Goodman proposed that the difference between laws and accidents is that laws, though not accidents, are confirmable by a *less-than-complete* induction. Goodman's proposal is most favorably seen as emerging from the problem troublesome concepts present naive regularity analyses. He noticed that for some concepts F and G, the generalization that all Fs are Gs is not confirmable by a less-than-complete induction. Goodman's classic example involves the concept of being grue. (We'll say x is grue if and only if x is green and examined before the year 2000 or blue otherwise.) The generalization that all emeralds are grue is not confirmable by a less-than-complete induction; if a person who had no prior knowledge of emeralds were to examine a nonempty and nonexhaustive sample of emeralds, the examination would not be reason to conclude that all emeralds are grue. Similarly, the generalization that all plavens have feathers fails to be confirmable by a less-than-complete induction. Since there are no plaid pandas, if someone who had no prior knowledge of plavens (and hence didn't already know that there are no plaid pandas) were to examine a nonempty and nonexhaustive sample of plavens, the sample would include only ravens. So, were this person to examine such a sample, the examination would not be reason to conclude that all plavens have feathers. Introducing a bit of Goodman's terminology, the concept of having feathers is not *projectible* with respect to the concept of being a plaven.

Adopting the framework employed by naive regularity analyses, the framework analyzing lawhood as lawlikeness plus truth, Goodman offers the following analysis of lawlikeness:

P is lawlike if and only if P is contingent, universally quantified, and confirmable by a less-than-complete induction (cf., 1983, p. 22).[10]

Because confirmability by a less-than-complete induction is a disposition, Goodman's analysis of lawlikeness (and hence his analysis of lawhood) appears not to be reductive. But, for Goodman, this appearance is both deceptive and fleeting. The disposition term is to be analyzed away by relying on a certain picture of epistemology. This picture has it that there are significant *principles of confirmation*. Given any set of evidence and given any proposition, the principles of confirmation dictate whether the set of evidence confirms the proposition. So, for example, one deductive principle might dictate that the set of evidence consisting of the proposition that all moas are black and the proposition that Marge is a moa confirms the proposition that Marge is black. Inductive principles might tell us that a set of evidence consisting of propositions attributing grue to several different emeralds does not confirm that all emeralds are grue. Goodman's initial hope is that the principles of confirmation do not use any nomically committed terms. If so,

10 After stating this proposal, Goodman revises it (1983, p. 23). I rely on the unrevised proposal because it is simpler. In any case, the objections I raise apply to both the proposal stated here and his revision.

then his further hope is that confirmability by a less-than-complete induction can be characterized solely in terms free of nomic commitment by appealing to the principles of confirmation.[11]

Whether he could succeed in doing that and whether this picture of epistemology is correct, two things are very worrisome about this approach. First, there is a serious worry about its ability to preserve the *objectivity of lawhood*. Since the principles of confirmation concern the rationality of certain belief-forming processes, it is at least somewhat plausible to think that these principles are in many ways dependent on the psychological characteristics of cognizers (cf., Goldman 1986; Harman 1986). If confirmability by a less-than-complete induction is characterized in terms of the principles of confirmation, then it too may be dependent on people's psychologies. In that case, Goodman's analysis of lawlikeness would make lawhood overly subjective. That would be a mistake. Lawhood is objective in that, at least usually, it is not dependent on the psychological characteristics of cognizers. For example, assuming that it is a law that no signals travel at speeds greater than the speed of light, this would still be a law even if every person's beliefs changed, even if humans had very different psychologies, and even if there were no cognizers. Occasionally, a proposition's status as a law does depend on psychological factors. For example, if we were to have drastically different psychologies, then some actual psychological laws might be false and hence would not be laws. But these are the exceptional cases. In raising this objectivity issue, I am not trying to advance a full-fledged objection to Goodman's position. I am not prepared to argue that his position makes lawhood inappropriately subjective. In part, that is because I do not know how confirmability by a less-than-complete induction is to be characterized using the principles of confirmation. I do not even know

11 Though this is the program Goodman sets out in "The Problem of Counterfactual Conditionals" (1947; see especially pp. 126–127), he deviates from it slightly in later works. His "Prospects for a Theory of Projection" (Goodman 1983 [f.p. 1953], pp. 84–124) suggests that projectibility is used in the principles of confirmation. So, one principle might say something to the effect that:

Given that G is projectible with respect to F, an examination of a samples of Fs all of which are Gs is reason to believe that all Fs are Gs.

Then, projectibility is to be analyzed not in terms of the principles of confirmation, but in terms of *entrenchment*. Objections similar to those presented in the text also arise for Goodman's more recent approach to the problem.

what the principles of confirmation are. My point is just to show that the plausibility of Goodman's position rests on a somewhat questionable assumption.[12]

My second worry about Goodman's position is more serious. I doubt that there is a legitimate understanding of the phrase 'confirmable by a less-than-complete induction' that makes Goodman's analysis of lawhood at all plausible. Consider the third class of counterexamples to our naive regularity analysis, a class of cases designed to show that our naive regularity analysis is too weak. In order for Goodman's analysis of lawlikeness to succeed, each of the generalizations in this class must not be confirmable by a less-than-complete induction. For example, the generalization that all gold spheres are less than ten meters in diameter must not be so confirmable because, though all of Goodman's other conditions for lawhood and lawlikeness are clearly satisfied, it is not a law. There lies the problem. It is hard to believe that there is a legitimate understanding of the phrase 'confirmable by a less-than-complete induction' that gives rise to these consequences. Prima facie, the concepts involved in all the generalizations in the third class of counterexamples are projectible. Goodman apparently asks confirmability by a less-than-complete induction to do too much work.

Let us study another proposal in the spirit of Goodman's position that may appear to be an improvement:

P is a law if and only if P is a contingently true generalization and the principles of confirmation dictate that the *to-be-specified* set of evidence confirms P.

Notice that, without a specification of the to-be-specified set, strictly speaking, this is not an analysis of lawhood. It is only a proposal as to the form the correct analysis will take. I shall discuss some attempts at completing the analysis momentarily.[13] The similarities

12 Some philosophers would be unmoved by this worry: Braithwaite (1927, 1928), Rescher (1969), and Wilson (1986, p. 88) are subjectivists regarding lawhood. I take their positions to be even more extreme, and more at odds with common sense, than those positions discussed in Section 1.4 (Chapter 1) that either deny that all laws are true or deny that some laws are contingent.

13 This proposal, in a way, is a simplified version of an account of lawhood discernible in Skyrms (1980). For my criticisms of a full-blown Skyrmsian account, see Carroll (1990, pp. 207–211). Tooley (1987, pp. 58–63) offers similar criticisms.

with Goodman's position should be apparent. There is the thought that certain sets of evidence confirm some, but not all, generalizations. The ones that are confirmed, it is hoped, are the laws. The defender of such a position, like Goodman, needs to assume that the confirmability of a proposition by a set of evidence is not overly dependent on our psychologies. As I said about Goodman's position, this is a questionable assumption.

One possible completion is to specify the to-be-specified set so that it includes all and only the nonnomic facts. This, however, leads to an incorrect analysis. The principles of confirmation (if there really are any) surely dictate that the set of nonnomic facts, which includes the fact that there are no gold spheres greater than ten meters in diameter, confirms the generalization that all gold spheres are less than ten meters in diameter. But, as I have pointed out before, this generalization is not a law. We need to complete the analysis in some other way. Instead of including only nonnomic *facts*, it is tempting to specify the to-be-specified set so that it includes a few false propositions. Why? Well, suppose we could include the false proposition that there are gold spheres over ten meters in diameter. Then, the principles of confirmation would dictate that the set of evidence does not confirm the generalization that all gold spheres are less than ten meters in diameter. So, the position under discussion would have the intuitive consequence that this generalization is not a law. Unfortunately for the Humean, though it is tempting, and may even be necessary, to include false propositions, it is also impossible to specify reductively the to-be-specified set so that only the appropriate false propositions get in. To see this, suppose we include the false proposition that there is a signal traveling faster than light. Then, the position under consideration has the unintuitive consequence that it is not a law that no signals travel faster than light. It seems that the to-be-specified set must include some false propositions, like the proposition that there is a gold sphere greater than ten meters in diameter. It must exclude other false propositions, like the proposition that there is a signal traveling faster than light. A plausible explanation of why this latter proposition should not be included in the relevant set is that it *is not* physically possible. A plausible explanation of why the proposition that there is a gold sphere greater than ten meters in diameter should be included is that it *is* physically possible. It looks as if the defender of this proposal needs to specify that only physically possible propositions be included in the set of evidence. But such a specification is not available; such a specification would make the position under consideration nonreductive.

2.3 SIMPLICITY, STRENGTH, AND BEST BALANCE

Faced with the failure of naive regularity analyses, it is natural to ask why scientists do not *accept* the counterexamples to our naive regularity analysis as laws. Scientists presumably do have reasons for accepting as laws only the propositions that they do. Whatever those reasons are, they may help Humeans to advance the correct reductive analysis. Letting their metaphysics be shaped by the epistemology of lawhood in this way, many philosophers identify simplicity, strength, and best balance between them as the concepts epistemologically relevant to lawhood. Problems ultimately emerge for analyses of this sort because these concepts, though of the appropriate nature to be part of the epistemology of lawhood, are ill-suited for the analysis of lawhood.

a. Motivation

In response to the problem posed by vacuous generalizations, it is tempting to maintain that no vacuous generalizations are laws. This move fails, however, because there are vacuous laws. Newton's first is a good example. If our universe were Newtonian, it would be a law that if no force is exerted on a body, it has no acceleration, and it would still be the case that there are no such bodies.[14]

14 Is Newton's first vacuous, or would it be vacuous if our universe were Newtonian? I think so, but why depends on exactly what Newton's first law is. For no particular reason, I have opted for the formulation:

(a) If no force is exerted on a body, it has no acceleration.

But some suppose that the correct formulation is

(b) If no *net* force is exerted on a body, it has no acceleration.

If (a) is the correct formulation, then Newton's first law would be vacuous in any Newtonian universe with more than one body because of Newton's law of gravitation. So if our universe were Newtonian, the law would be vacuous. But, if (b) is the correct formulation, then the law might be nonvacuous in a New-

There are other vacuous laws. C. D. Broad (1935) has identified an entire class of them (c.f., Ayer 1963, p. 224; Armstrong 1983, p. 22). These laws are derivable from more general laws relating a quantitatively measurable property to one or more other quantitatively measurable properties. As illustration, consider Newton's law of gravitation. It states that the gravitational force between two bodies is the product of their masses, the gravitational constant g, and the inverse square of their distance. Since there are infinitely many values of mass, there are likely to be many values of mass that are not instantiated by any object in our universe. So, let m_1 and m_2 be two such values. Then, Newton's law of gravitation entails the vacuous generalization that the gravitational force between bodies of mass m_1 and m_2 separated by a distance of r is $(gm_1m_2)/r^2$. It is natural to think that this vacuous generalization is a law. There is a further problem with maintaining that there are no vacuous laws. Consider the vacuous generalization that all unicorns are white. It is logically equivalent to the generalization that all nonwhite things are nonunicorns. Yet the latter is not vacuous – there are nonwhite things. So, even with a necessary condition requiring that laws be nonvacuous, an analysis might imply that it is a law that all nonwhite things are nonunicorns. Presumably, that would be a mistake.

Let's step back as do some Humeans, and ask why scientists would accept, for example, that it is a law that the gravitational force between bodies of mass m_1 and m_2 separated by a distance r is $(gm_1m_2)/r^2$. Obviously, it is not *because* this generalization is vacuous that they accept it as a law. It looks as if scientists would accept this generalization as a law precisely because it is entailed by a non-vacuous generalization already accepted as a law, Newton's law of gravitation. It is tempting to think that this is the case generally. It is tempting to think that every vacuous generalization believed to be a law is believed to be a law because it is entailed by some non-vacuous law. Then, it is a short step from epistemology to meta-

tonian universe, even one with more than one body, because the forces on a body might cancel each other out. Nevertheless, if our universe were Newtonian, it seems highly unlikely given the number and diversity of bodies exerting forces that there would be such a body and, more important, it is clear that the status of Newton's first as a law does not depend on the existence of such a body (cf., Earman 1984, p. 193; Earman and Friedman 1973, p. 341).

46

physics. Perhaps what might *make* vacuous generalizations laws is that they are entailed by nonvacuous laws. As a result, some philosophers (e.g., Smart 1985, p. 276; Nagel 1961, p. 60; Braithwaite 1953, p. 305) have been tempted to invoke the concept of a *basic law*. Basic laws are thought of as the fundamental postulates of the true physical theory. These philosophers have been tempted to suggest that the basic laws are all and only the nonvacuous, contingent, unrestricted generalizations, while allowing that there may be vacuous, nonbasic laws. (According to this approach, any contingent proposition entailed by the basic laws is counted as a nonbasic law.)[15]

This proposal, tempting though it may be, does not solve the problem of vacuous laws. Without some further constraint on basic laws, nearly all the troublesome vacuous generalizations qualify as nonbasic laws, because nearly all such generalizations are entailed by some nonvacuous, contingent, unrestricted generalization. For example, according to this proposal, the generalization that all nonwhite things are nonunicorns qualifies as a basic law, and the generalization that all unicorns are white qualifies as a nonbasic law. Furthermore, the suggestion implies that no basic laws are vacuous, and that consequence does not mesh well with the history of science. Newton's first law, Galileo's law of falling bodies, Boyle's law, and others arguably are vacuous and were once accepted as laws. Yet, at the time they were first accepted as laws, they were not derived from any more fundamental laws – they were accepted as basic laws.

Still, there might be something right in spirit about the proposal. The suggestion ties lawhood to the relationships between propositions in a theoretical *system*. Perhaps all that is needed is

15 A distinction between basic and other sorts of laws was perhaps first invoked to deal with laws referring to specific physical objects (cf., Reichenbach 1947, p. 361; Hempel and Oppenheim 1948, p. 152). But the move is even less successful in this regard. First, as Nagel (1961, p. 56) points out, many restricted propositions that were thought to be laws, like Kepler's first law of planetary motion, are not entailed by the relevant basic laws; they are entailed by basic laws together with some to-be-specified class of particular facts. But it proved to be extremely difficult to specify that class of facts without counting certain accidents as laws. Second, there were confusions concerning restricted laws. As I argued in Section 2.1b, philosophers tended to count too many restricted generalizations as laws, thinking, for example, that Galileo's free-fall principle would be a law if it were true and our universe were Newtonian.

47

different constraints on what it is to be a basic law – maybe non-vacuity is too strong and maybe other constraints are needed instead. In other words, maybe the proposal is correct in invoking systemic considerations and just needs to do so in a more sophisticated way. The approach to laws advocated by John Stuart Mill (1947 [f.p. 1843]), Frank Ramsey (1978 [f.p. 1928]), John Earman (1984), and David Lewis (1973, 1983a, 1986) is a much more sophisticated example of a reductive account of lawhood that ties lawhood to the relationships between propositions in a theoretical system.

b. The systems approach

An especially accessible formulation of the systems approach is Lewis's early formulation:

> [A] contingent generalization is a *law of nature* if and only if it appears as a theorem (or axiom) in each of the true deductive systems that achieves a best combination of simplicity and strength (1973, p. 73).

This is the formulation that I discuss at length below, though, not surprisingly, there are many others. An attractive feature of the systems approach is that it appears to deal with the problem of vacuous laws. There is no explicit exclusion of vacuous generalizations from the realm of laws, and yet only those vacuous generalizations that are theorems or axioms in each of the true deductive systems achieving a best combination of simplicity and strength qualify as laws. That is promising. The analysis at least conforms well with the epistemology behind our acceptance of some vacuous generalizations as laws. For example, we accepted Newton's first law of motion as a law, because it was an axiom in a simple, strong, and at the time thought to be true theoretical system: Newtonian physics. Also, vacuous generalizations entailed by Newton's law of gravitation were accepted as laws because they were theorems of that same system. Another attraction of the systems approach is that it holds the promise of addressing the problem of restricted laws. Some particular facts might appear as axioms in all the true deductive systems achieving a best combination of simplicity and strength, in which case a restricted generalization may well appear as a theorem in that system (cf., Lewis 1986, p. 123; Earman 1978, p. 180).

48

c. Problems

I agree that a proposition's being part of a true theoretical system with a best combination of simplicity and strength is epistemologically relevant to that proposition's being a law. Simplicity, strength, and best balance between them are part of the epistemology of lawhood.[16] That is what is appealing about the systems approach. But, the analysis needs to be rejected. Simplicity, strength, and best balance do not belong in a reductive analysis of lawhood. Let us begin by considering simplicity at some length. The problems involving strength and best balance are similar. So, once my point has been made with respect to simplicity, I can make analogous points with respect to the other two concepts much more briefly. Keep in mind that though the points to be made are similar, they are independent. Any one could be true without the others.

In any use relevant to our present topic, the ordinary sense of the phrase 'simpler than' is (at least) *triadically relational* and also *subjective* (cf., Armstrong 1983, p. 67; van Fraassen 1989, pp. 56–57, 148). This is especially obvious when it is used in the comparison of two tasks. For example, solving systems of linear equations is simpler than composing a sonnet for the typical mathematician, although composing a sonnet is simpler than solving a system of linear equations for the typical poet. This elementary example suggests that simplicity, as applied to tasks, is at least a triadic relation; a sentence of the form '. . . is simpler than _____' is always elliptical for sentences of the form '. . . is simpler than _____ for ★★★'. The example also suggests that simplicity is subjective: Simplicity is apparently dependent on the *psychological abilities* and *background knowledge* of those to whom the simplicity is relative. It is because of the psychological abilities and background knowledge of typical poets that for them, composing sonnets is simpler than solving systems of linear equations. It is also because of psychological factors that solving systems of linear equations is simpler for typical mathematicians. In regard to its relational and subjective nature, simplicity is much like *color appearance*. Notice that the moon appears green to my wife, but not to someone like me with some color deficiencies. So, apparently, color appearance is relational; a sentence

---

16 Their role is, however, probably not as central, or as uniquely tied to lawhood, as my discussion above suggests. See Chapter 4.

49

like 'The moon appears green' is always elliptical for a sentence like 'The moon appears green to my wife'. Color appearance is also subjective, because the moon's appearing green to my wife and not to me depends on our psychologies.

Simplicity continues to exhibit this relational and subjective nature when used to describe scientific hypotheses. This is brought out in the following hypothetical example. Suppose there are two cultures, the Right-Brainers and the Left-Brainers, each of which has data relating two quantities, x and y. Experimental limitations make it such that additional data for new values of x and y will not be forthcoming, nor will more precise measurements be possible. Two hypotheses are being considered by the two cultures. The first hypothesis says that x and y are related by the equation:

$$y = \sin x,$$

and the second says that they are related by the equation:

$$y = x - \frac{x^3}{6} + \frac{x^5}{120}.\text{[17]}$$

To the degree of precision experimentally possible and for the values of x examined, the two hypotheses conform to the data equally well. They are, however, different hypotheses (see Table 2.1). Continuing the example, let us suppose that Right-Brainers are excellent at geometry. They discovered early in their history that for any two right triangles with congruent acute angles, the ratios of the length of their corresponding sides to the length of the hypotenuses are identical. Trigonometry is taught at an early age. These Right-Brainers, however, are not quite so adept at algebra. Polynomials of degree higher than two are perplexing and are thought to be so much esoteric mathematical theory. The reverse is true of the Left-Brainers. They are excellent at algebra and weak in geometry. Trigonometry, though recently formulated, is considered so much esoteric mathematics. The Left-Brainers are, however, whizzes at calculation.

Now, what are the facts about simplicity in this example? Consider the sentence, 'The trigonometric equation is simpler than the polynomial equation'. Is it true or false? Evidently, the sentence is

---

17 For those wondering why there is such close agreement between the two hypotheses, the polynomial equation includes the first three terms of the Maclaurin series for the sine function. See, for example, Swokowski (1975, p. 457).

Table 2.1

Data		Hypotheses	
x	y	$\sin x$	$x - \dfrac{x^3}{6} + \dfrac{x^5}{120}$
.0	.00	.00	.00
.5	.48	.48	.48
1.0	.84	.84	.84
1.5	1.00	1.00	1.00
2.0	.92	.91	.93

incomplete. Considered outside of a richer context, we are left wondering who we are talking about. Given the drastic differences in their abilities and background knowledge, it seems that *for the Right-Brainers,* the trigonometric equation is simpler than the polynomial equation, while it seems that *for the Left-Brainers,* the polynomial equation if simpler than the trigonometric equation. Thus, the ordinary sense of 'simpler than' continues to be at least a triadic relation when used to describe scientific hypotheses. It also continues to be subjective. It is because of the psychological abilities and background knowledge of the Right-Brainers that for them, the trigonometric equation is simpler than the polynomial equation. It is because of those same psychological factors that for the Left-Brainers, the polynomial equation is simpler.[18]

The relational and subjective nature of simplicity really raises two different problems for the systems approach. That simplicity is

18 In the middle part of this century, it was popular to maintain that there was a less relational, objective concept of simplicity. One of the primary projects in the philosophy of science was thought to be the analysis of this concept (cf., Popper 1959, and especially Goodman 1958 and elsewhere). In response to my example, some may claim that on the objective and less relational sense of the word 'simple', at most the *beliefs* about which hypothesis is the more simple would differ for our two communities. While I agree that understanding simplicity better is an important project in the philosophy of science, I deny that there is a less relational and objective concept of simplicity. I think my example succeeds in showing that the ordinary sense of the word is triadically relational and subjective. Those who claim that there is some other sense of 'simple' need to say what it is. The analyses actually advanced are notorious for having failed to provide a concept of simplicity suitable for accounts of scientific confirmation. I doubt that they do any better providing one suitable for the systems approach to lawhood. Hesse's entry in *The Encyclopedia of Philosophy* (1967, pp. 445–448) surveys much of the relevant literature.

at least a triadic relation shows that the systems approach is not a genuine analysis of lawhood; it is incomplete. We are told to consider all the true deductive systems achieving a best combination of simplicity and strength, but we have not been told to whom the simplicity is relative. The subjectivity of simplicity presents a more serious problem. Its subjectivity implies that what systems are simpler than what other systems depends on the psychological abilities and background knowledge of those to whom the simplicity is relative. So, even if we are eventually told to whom the simplicity is relative, the systems approach evidently will have mistaken consequences about lawhood. It will mistakenly imply that the difference between laws and accidents depends on subjective factors.

Basically the same criticisms can be made about the systems approach's appeal to strength. Consider two true theoretical systems including exactly the same unrestricted astronomical generalizations as axioms. The only difference in their axioms is that the first includes a statement of the current mass and position of the sun, while the second contains a statement of the current mass and position of Mount Everest. *For astronomers,* the first is the stronger system. That is a relational judgment, one relatum of which is a group of scientists. Furthermore, the truth of this relational judgment depends on the *interests* of the astronomers. There is no difference in the sheer number of propositions in the systems. The size and location of the sun as opposed to the size and location of Mount Everest alone can hardly account for the difference in strengths. The difference in the strengths has something to do with the fact that the first system includes propositions that astronomers find more interesting. The strengths of the two systems could be different for people with different interests. So, by appealing to strength, the systems approach is open to criticisms identical to those arising from its appeal to simplicity. First, the relational nature of strength suggests that the systems approach, strictly speaking, is not a genuine analysis of lawhood. We have not been told to whom the strength is relative; we have no idea whose interests are pertinent. Second, the subjectivity of strength suggests that even if we were told to whom the judgments of strength were relative, the systems approach would entail that lawhood is inappropriately subjective. Lawhood should not be sensitive to the interests of any group of cognizers.

It may be that basically the same two problems arise with regard to the comparisons of the balance of simplicity and strength. Remember that according to the systems approach, laws are those generalizations that are theorems in all the true deductive systems achieving a *best* combination of simplicity and strength. But, ordinarily we use 'better' as a relation to people or their *purposes*. For example, caffeinic coffee is better than decaffeinated coffee for college students cramming for a final. Decaf is better for most people concerned about their health. So, the failure to give a complete analysis and the threat to the objectivity of lawhood may also arise because of the systems approach's appeal to best balance.

A different problem for the systems approach may also grow out of the relational nature of strength and best balance. Since a single person can at one time have many different interests and purposes, a defender of the systems approach – strictly speaking – cannot complete the analysis just by saying to whom the strength and best balance are relative. The defender must say which of the person's interests and purposes the judgments of strength and best balance are relative to. In doing so, those interests and purposes need to be selected carefully. To make the analysis plausible, it seems that the interests and purposes should be those closely tied to scientific endeavors, especially *scientific explanation*. So, the defender of the systems approach may not be able to pick out the most appropriate interests and purposes without invoking *nomic* concepts. It is unlikely that the systems approach can be completed so that it is truly a *Humean* analysis.

Lewis is not troubled by the relational and subjective natures of simplicity, strength, and best balance. In more recent work (1986, p. 123), he makes it very clear that according to his analysis, for a generalization to be a law it must be part of all the true deductive systems with a best combination of simplicity and strength, given *our actual* and *present* standards of simplicity, strength, and best balance. This addition does appear to complete his analysis. *We* are the persons the judgments of simplicity, strength, and best balance are relative to. Lewis's proposal also avoids having lawhood depend on psychological factors by making the judgments of simplicity, strength, and best balance relative to our actual and present standards. So, in possible worlds where we have different standards of simplicity, strength, or best balance, what propositions are laws is still determined by our *actual* standards. In this way, lawhood usually cannot be instantiated or fail to be instantiated as the result of a change in our psychologies. Though ingenious, the proposal is, as it stands, questionable. First, it is ad hoc: Why suppose that it is the *actual* standards of simplicity, strength, and best balance that are the standards conceptually tied to lawhood? Why not other possible standards of simplicity, strength, and best balance? Why, too, is it *our standards* – the standards of *our* culture *now* – that make propositions laws? Why not the standards of any other culture at any other time? Second, the proposal suggests that if other possible cognizers or cognizers from other cultures or cognizers from our culture at earlier times merely have different standards of simplicity, strength, and balance, then they cannot even *have* our concept of lawhood. Third, psychological abilities, background knowledge, interests, and purposes vary drastically from person to person even within our culture at the present time. Which are we to fix upon for the analysis of lawhood? Finally, on a related note, Lewis has not addressed my final worry, the additional worry stemming from the relational nature of strength and best balance. To really make the analysis plausible he needs to pick out the relevant interests and the relevant purposes carefully. It may well be that they need to be picked out nomically.[19]

d. Conclusions

In sum, the problem for the systems approach is this. Defenders of that approach invoke concepts relevant to our rationally believing propositions to be laws. Those concepts are relational and subjective in important ways. But those concepts cannot be relational and subjective in these ways and be part of what it is to be a law. I am not suggesting that these Humeans are incorrect about the epistemology of lawhood. Given what I have said so far, they may be absolutely right that the correct way to *discover* what propositions are laws of nature is via consideration of simplicity, strength, and

---

19 In Carroll (1990, pp. 198–202), I raise another criticism of Lewis's particular version of the systems approach. I should also mention that, because of issues involving probabilistic laws, Lewis revised his analysis. I briefly discuss his revisions in that same article (see p. 206).

best balance. Prima facie, these factors could be relational and subjective in the ways described and still be epistemologically relevant to lawhood. The analogy with color appearance is again instructive. Green appearance is a relational and subjective concept; yet it is epistemologically relevant to the color green. It is green appearances that typically are associated with our perceptual beliefs about the greenness of objects. The epistemology of lawhood can be heavily flavored with the psychological. The problem for the systems approach is that the metaphysics of lawhood cannot. Again, we have found epistemology to be a poor guide for answering metaphysical questions.

2.4 EPISTEMOLOGY AND METAPHYSICS

At the beginning of the chapter, I pointed out that Descartes's epistemological concerns led Berkeley to put forward his reductions of physical objects. The epistemological importance of perception to our beliefs about the external world led to Berkeley's idealism. Much later, it led *phenomenalists* to seek a reduction of physical object propositions to pure appearance propositions. In a similar fashion, epistemological questions about the mentality of others led many to seek an analysis of mental concepts. The epistemological importance of behavior to our beliefs about other minds led *behaviorists* to seek an analysis of mental concepts in purely behavioral terms. Engrossed by epistemological worries, the search for epistemologically oriented analyses of this sort takes on an aura of legitimacy.

Yet the history of philosophy teaches us that epistemology can be a bad guide to metaphysics. This, fortunately, has been recognized with regard to the problem of the external world and the problem of other minds. Impressed by the failings of phenomenalist and behaviorist analyses, the sensible philosopher rejects phenomenalism and behaviorism. I am in the process of suggesting that we adopt a similar stance with regard to lawhood and all nomic concepts. We have just undertaken a careful survey of the most popular Humean analyses, the reductive analyses of lawhood that have tended to be epistemologically oriented. They are all subject to defeating objections. It may well be that epistemological considerations are as poor a guide to the analysis of lawhood as they are to the analysis of physical object propositions and mental concepts.

55

In order to complete my argument to that conclusion, I offer, in the next chapter, another objection to all Humean analyses. The analogy with phenomenalism may give the reader a hint of what is to come. In addition to rejecting phenomenalism because there are straightforward problems with extant phenomenalist analyses, most philosophers admit that Descartes's evil genius is a genuine possibility, in effect admitting that two possible worlds – ours and the evil genius world – could agree on their pure appearance facts, while disagreeing on their physical object facts. The evil genius world is a world in which we have all the sensory appearances we actually do, but all or most of our physical object beliefs are false. In a way, admitting the possibility of the evil genius is simply to admit that evidence for physical object propositions can *underdetermine* what physical objects there are. Similarly, I raise a further challenge to all Humean analyses by arguing that two possible worlds could agree on a proposition's characteristics free of nomic commitment, while disagreeing on its status as a law. Evidence for laws and lawhood can fail to determine what propositions are laws.

3

Humean supervenience

There is a new panacea in philosophy. Faced with the failure to legitimize certain realist practices by producing a suitable analysis, say, of ethical concepts in terms of purely natural ones or mental concepts in terms of purely physical ones, many have clung to *supervenience*. One particularly famous use of a supervenience notion occurs in G. E. Moore's ethical theory. Of intrinsic value, he says, "It is *impossible* that of two exactly similar things one should possess it and the other not, or that one should possess it in one degree, and the other in a different one" (1958 [f.p. 1922], p. 261). More recently, as Jaegwon Kim points out, many have thought that psychophysical supervenience "acknowledges the primacy of the physical without committing us to the stronger claims of physical reductionism" (1984, pp. 155–156). Though there are many different treatments of supervenience, the concept is almost always spelled out in modally rich terms and is usually taken to describe a deep metaphysical dependency.

Because of the criticisms raised in the previous chapter, from any perspective even scarcely resembling empiricism, the last hope of maintaining a realism about laws is the hope of upholding that lawhood somehow supervenes on a suitably wholesome base. Given the desire to account for lawhood in thoroughly unobjectionable terms, the natural position for Humeans to adopt is that no two possible worlds have propositions that agree on their features *free of nomic commitments* and disagree on their status as laws. The pivotal portion of this chapter, Section 3.1, undermines this neo-Humean claim. In fact, this section argues that even a somewhat weaker thesis is false. As is discussed in Chapter 1, the class of *concepts free of nomic commitments* is a subclass of the class of *nonnomic concepts*. The former includes the truth-functional concepts, necessity and possibility, mathematical concepts, and more controversially spatiotemporal concepts. The latter includes all these concepts, but others as well, even some that have very strong and very obvious nomic commitments. For example, as I have pointed out before, though perception is a nonnomic concept, it has nomic commitments; nothing perceives anything unless there is a *casual* connection between the perceiver and the creature perceived. Because of the overlap, any two possible worlds agreeing on the nonnomic concepts instantiated by a proposition P also agree on the concepts free of nomic commitment instantiated by P. With this in mind, Section 3.1 argues against the thesis that no two possible worlds have propositions that agree on all their *nonnomic* features and also disagree on their status as laws. I take this thesis to be *Humean supervenience about lawhood*.[1] The distinction between the nomic concepts and the concepts with no nomic commitments is really the significant one. It is the distinction that is crucial for empiricist attempts to explain away the otherworldly character of laws. But some tough questions about what concepts are free of nomic commitment are easily avoided by being generous about what can be in the explanatory base. Even admitting the nonnomic concepts does not make any interesting supervenience claim tenable.

If the argument of Section 3.1 is sound, then lawhood and our many other concepts with nomic commitments form a vast interlocking network. What we as philosophers should be doing is trying to understand that network better – we should be doing some *conceptual geography*. Just so, in Section 3.2, I take a short, but serious, look at what my approach to lawhood suggests about (objective) chance. The partial map of conceptual space that emerges shows that chance is nonsupervenient in the same way the lawhood is. Following the discussion of chance, I return to some leftover issues from Section 3.1. In Section 3.3, I discuss two supervenience theses about lawhood that are weaker than Humean supervenience. Though these positions might appeal to some desperate souls, ultimately they are nearly as difficult to defend as their stronger cousin. Furthermore, I go on to show that they are also much too feeble for their assigned work. Thus, whatever its effectiveness

---

1 Humean supervenience about lawhood should not be confused with the thesis Lewis (1986, p. xi) calls 'Humean supervenience'. One important difference is that Lewis takes his thesis to be contingent. Regardless of whether it is true or false, Humean supervenience about lawhood is clearly noncontingent. My terminology here is more in line with Tooley's (1987, p. 29).

may be in other areas of philosophy, I suspect that it will become abundantly clear that supervenience is not a way to deter the threat of nomic antirealism. In the fourth and final section, some comparisons are made between supervenience issues about lawhood and corresponding issues as they arise in ethics and the philosophy of mind.

Before beginning, two preliminary points should be brought to the reader's attention. The first concerns some new business: the role principle (SC) plays in my nonsupervenience arguments. Though they work reasonably well without it, (SC) is very supportive. It states that if a proposition P is physically possible and physically necessitates a proposition Q, then Q would be the case if P were the case. Symbolically, it can be stated:

(SC) If $\Diamond_{\mathscr{P}}P$ and $\Box_{\mathscr{P}}(P \supset Q)$, then $P > Q$.

As a matter of fact, for the added support, we do not need the full power of (SC). Two of its consequences are enough. The first, (SC$\star$), says that if P is physically possible and Q is a law, then Q would (still) be a law if P were the case. The second, (SC$'$), says that if P is physically possible and Q is not a law, then Q would (still) not be a law if P were the case. The derivations of (SC$\star$) and (SC$'$) are straightforward, and so are discussed only briefly in a footnote.[2] The second preliminary point concerns some old business: the consequences of this chapter for Humean analyses of lawhood. For those who were not convinced of Humeanism's dire condition by the arguments of Chapter 2, my nonsupervenience arguments provide a wholly independent criticism. To appreciate this point, remember that the Humean project is to advance a *necessarily* true, nomic-free, completion of:

(S1) P is a law of nature if and only if. . . .

2 To derive (SC$\star$) from (SC), suppose that P is physically possible, and also suppose that Q is a law. Since Q is a law, Q is a law in every possible world with the same laws as the actual world, and so it is physically necessary that Q is a law. Also every proposition physically necessitates a physically necessary one. So, P physically necessitates that Q is a law. Since P physically necessitates that Q is a law and part of our initial supposition is that P is physically possible, it follows from (SC) that if P were the case, then Q would be a law. (The derivation of (SC$'$) is extremely similar and so is left to the reader.)

59

Hence, for it to succeed, the nonnomic features instantiated by P must strictly determine whether P is a law; no two possible worlds could agree on the nonnomic features instantiated by one or more propositions and yet disagree on whether those propositions are laws. Hence, by arguing against Humean supervenience, I am undermining a basic presupposition of Humeanism. Nonsupervenience entails the failure of all Humean accounts.

3.1 THE MIRROR ARGUMENT

Consider a possible world, U_1. In it, there are exactly five X-particles, five Y-fields, and not much else. Since the beginning of time, the X-particles have been traveling in a line at a constant velocity toward a staggered string of Y-fields. (See Figure 3.1.) Particle b, the first X-particle to enter a Y-field, does so, say, at high noon. Then, each hour on the hour, for the next four hours, another X-particle enters another Y-field. When their time comes, the particles all pass through their respective fields quite quickly, without any change in direction, never to enter a Y-field again. While in their Y-fields, all the X-particles have spin up. Unlike any of the other particles, particle b has an interesting mirror right along, though not in, its path to the Y-field. This mirror is on a well-oiled swivel and so can easily be twisted between two positions, positions c and d. It is in fact in position c and so does not interfere with b's flight. If twisted to position d, however, the mirror would deflect b out and away from all the fields. Clearly, the generalization, L_1, that all X-particles subject to a Y-field have spin up could be a law in such a world. So let us make that our final key supposition about U_1.

Possible world U_2 is just a little different. As in U_1, there are exactly five X-particles, exactly five Y-fields, and not much else. The X-particles again travel in a line, and each enters its Y-field at exactly the same time and place that it did in U_1. There is even that same twistable mirror. The only concrete differences in the histories of U_1 and U_2 are confined to the brief time period immediately following b's entrance into its Y-field. Specifically, in U_2, when b enters its field, it does not acquire spin up. Aside from this nonnomic difference, there must be at least one decidedly nomic difference between U_1 and U_2: L_1 is not a law in U_2. Given my

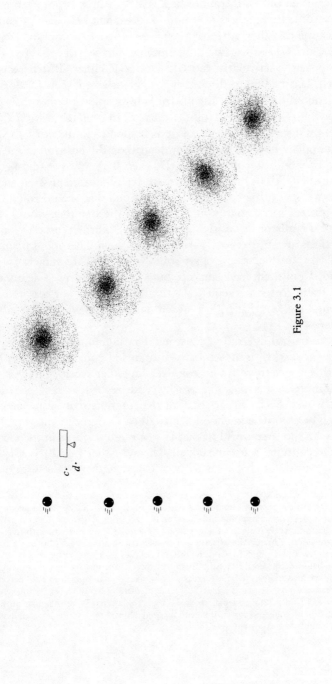

Figure 3.1

description of U_2, L_1 cannot be a law because it is not even true. I do assume that there is *some* nomic agreement between U_1 and U_2. I assume that they agree on their laws of particle motion.[3]

U_1 and U_2 are just two different ways our world could be. There is nothing particularly remarkable about either. But here is the catch. It is natural to think that L_1's status as a law in U_1 does not depend on the fact that the mirror is in position c rather than position d. It is very clear that if the mirror had been in position d, then L_1 would still be a law. It is just as natural to think that L_1's status as a nonlaw in U_2 also does not depend on the position of the mirror. L_1 would not be a law in U_2 even if the mirror had been in position d. All of this suggests there are two more possible worlds that we should be considering: (i) the one that would result were the mirror in position d in U_1, and (ii) the one that would result were the mirror in position d in U_2. In the former, exactly four X-particles are subject to a Y-field, all of them have spin up, and L_1 is a law. In the latter, exactly four X-particles are subject to a Y-field, all of them have spin up, but L_1 is an accident. The question the friends of supervenience must face is how they are going to ground the fact that L_1 is a law in one of these worlds but not the other.

L_1 is true, universally quantified, contingent, and unrestricted in both worlds. L_1 is also equally simple and equally strong in both worlds. Since there are no cognizers in either world, there may be no difference between the worlds with regard to how well L_1 is confirmed. So it appears that all the concepts that Humeans have taken to comprise lawhood must fail to recognize either that L_1 is a law in the first world or that L_1 is a mere accident in the second. These concepts must mistakenly dictate either that L_1 is a law in both worlds or that L_1 is an accident in both worlds. Of course,

3 Usually when hypothetical cases are deployed, it is within the method of cases. Some philosopher is interested in criticizing a specific analysis of some concept, and so describes a hypothetical situation *in other terms*. Then the reader is asked to judge intuitively whether the concept in question applies. If the intuitive judgment doesn't match the dictates of the analysis, then so much the worse for the analysis. But U_1 and U_2 (and the other examples to be described in this chapter) are being deployed differently. In this chapter, I am not interested in criticizing any specific analysis. My interest is whether certain concepts need even determine whether a proposition is a law. So I have *stipulated* what the laws are in each universe. I find nothing suspicious about the stipulations. Were this, say, an investigation of counterfactuals, it would be quite natural to describe a possible world by stipulating all or some of the laws.

with the differences in laws, there are accompanying differences in the counterfactuals: In the first world, if b were subject to a Y-field, then b would have spin up; in the second world, it might not. But counterfactual considerations are nomic, and hence are off limits. As I see it, though these worlds differ on whether L_1 is a law, they agree on the concepts *free of nomic commitments* that are instantiated by L_1. In fact, it seems that L_1 has all the same *nonnomic* features in these two worlds. It is for this reason that I reject Humean supervenience about lawhood. The only factors that distinguish these two worlds are factors that Humeans think cannot account for L_1's lawhood.

This argument can be made more precise by appealing to principles (SC$\star$) and (SC′). It is very plausible to think that it is physically possible in U_1 that the mirror be in position d. After all, all this claim of physical possibility requires is that there be at least one possible world with exactly the same laws as U_1 in which that mirror is so situated. This possible world might have a history that is nothing like U_1's. It could have millions upon millions of X-particles in Y-fields all with spin up. How could we begin to think of laws as nonaccidental and also think that what the laws are depends in this way on whether that mirror is in position d? (Though I do not bother to spell them out, precisely parallel reasons could be given in support of it being physically possible in U_2 that the mirror be in position d.) Keeping all of this in mind, let $U_{1\star}$ be the world that would result if the mirror were in position d in U_1. Then, since it is physically possible in U_1 that the mirror be in position d, and since L_1 is a law in U_1, it follows from (SC$\star$) that in U_1, if the mirror were in that position, then L_1 would be a law. Thus, since $U_{1\star}$ is the possible world that would result if the mirror were in a position d in U_1, L_1 is a law of $U_{1\star}$. Let $U_{2\star}$ be the world that would result if the mirror were in position d in U_2. Since b is not subject to a Y-field in $U_{2\star}$ and all the other X-particles subject to a Y-field in U_2 do have spin up, L_1 is true in $U_{2\star}$. But it must be accidentally true. Invoking (SC′), it follows, from the fact that it is physically possible in U_2 that the mirror is in position d and the fact that L_1 is not a law of U_2, that L_1 is not a law of $U_{2\star}$.

Yet it also appears that $U_{1\star}$ and $U_{2\star}$ agree on their nonnomic facts. What changes need to be made to U_1 and U_2 to accommodate the supposition that the mirror is in position d is determined by such factors as the events leading up to b's passing by the mirror and the laws governing these events. Since U_1 and U_2 agree on their histories up until b enters the Y-field, there is perfect agreement on the events leading up to b's passing the mirror. Since U_1 and U_2 agree on the laws governing particle motion, there is also perfect agreement on the laws governing these events. Thus, $U_{1\star}$ and $U_{2\star}$ must agree on all nonnomic facts. Therefore, $U_{1\star}$ and $U_{2\star}$ are a counterexample to Humean supervenience. They agree on the nonnomic concepts instantiated by L_1. Yet, they disagree on whether L_1 is a law of nature.[4]

What is especially compelling about this argument is that it permits us to set aside *at least some* questions about possibility. Were I simply to have described $U_{1\star}$ and $U_{2\star}$ directly, without having described U_1 and U_2, then my argument would have started (and finished) with a judgment about the possibility of the very worlds constituting the counterexample. Since judgments of possibility are notoriously difficult to defend, this would have made it just too tempting for Humeans to deny the crucial judgments. Rather than starting with such judgments, my argument begins with

---

4 The $U_{1\star}/U_{2\star}$ is just one counterexample to supervenience. We shall encounter another in Section 3.3. I believe there are still more. I hold, for instance, that many *empty* universes exist. As I see it, there is a world devoid of all material objects and events in which the general principles of Newtonian mechanics are laws; there is another empty world in which the general principles of Aristotelian physics are laws. These valiant claims, however, are difficult to establish convincingly. They can be supported using principle (SC) if one is willing to assume that in each of two lawful worlds it is physically possible that no material objects or events exist (ever). This, however, is much more contentious than either of the statements of physical possibility used to set up the $U_{1\star}/U_{2\star}$ counterexample. Still, I do accept that many empty possible worlds exist. To suppose there is an empty Aristotelian world and an empty Newtonian world is easy enough. Prima facie, such a supposition involves no contradiction. In the absence of any counterargument, I embrace these bereft possibilities. Are there worlds nonnomically just like the actual world but with different laws; perhaps a lawless possible world in nonnomic agreement with the actual world (cf., Jackson 1977, p. 5; Bigelow and Pargetter 1990, p. 243)? As far as I know, there *may* be a world with different laws that is nonnomically just like our universe. It is difficult for me to tell, given my limited knowledge of our world's laws and history. It is clear, however, that no lawless possible world nonnomically agrees with the actual world. Remember that many nonnomic concepts have nomic commitments. Perception is just one example. Since the actual fact that I am perceiving my computer is a nonnomic fact, in order for any other world to be in nonnomic agreement with the actual world, in that world I must perceive my computer. But, because of perception's nomic commitments, unlawful perception is impossible. I would not perceive my computer (or anything else) in a world with no laws.

descriptions of worlds that do not themselves challenge Humean supervenience, and that are otherwise unremarkable. Then, the counterexample is constructed in an intuitive way, as occurred in the third paragraph of this section. It can also be derived from (SC) and a few secondary assumptions as happened in paragraphs five and six.

I wish we could set aside *all* questions about possibility, but we cannot. There are some questions that might be raised about the possibility of U_1 and U_2. These questions range from the foolhardy to the insightful. Toward one end of the spectrum, there are questions about what are really rather incidental features of U_1 and U_2. For example, some may be bothered by the fact that there are so few things in each of these universes. Could there really be a possible world that contained only five particles, five fields, and a mirror on a swivel? Or again, the sorts of considerations that make some philosophers (wrongly) suspicious of vacuous laws might lead someone to question the possibility of a law governing only five interactions all that occur within the span of five hours. These questions, and others like them, border on being silly because it is so clear how these features could be cut from the examples. As far as my argument is concerned, U_1 and U_2 could just as easily have included 5,000,000 X-particles, 1,000,000 of which have movable mirrors along their paths, all heading toward 5,000,000 Y-fields. In U_1, the 5,000,000 X-particles would all have spin up while in their Y-fields. In U_2, only 4,000,000 would – the million with the mirrors along their path would not. The particles also need not have entered their fields every hour on the hour; the Y-fields (even if there were 5,000,000 of them) could have been so spread out that an X-particle entered a Y-field once every year instead. And, of course, all of this doesn't have to be going on in worlds with only X-particles, Y-fields, and moveable mirrors. It could all take place in an isolated portion of an ordinary universe, one much like ours, that includes people, tables, and all sorts of things.

More toward the middle of the spectrum is a slightly more interesting question about *the interdependency of the laws*. I require that the laws governing particle motion be the same in U_1 and U_2 to ensure agreement on the laws governing what would happen if the mirror were in position d. Yet not all the same laws govern the behavior of X-particles in Y-fields in these two worlds. After all, L_1

is not a law of U_2, and it is a law of U_1. This somewhat isolated disagreement on what the laws are may bother some. Especially if one has sympathy with the systems approach (see Chapter 2), one might think that there is a great interdependency between laws. One might think that the nonlaw status of L_1 in U_2 might have to take several (logically independent) laws down with it, perhaps even some of the laws governing b's motion. My argument, however, does not threaten any plausible interdependency thesis. We surely want to acknowledge that there are worlds that partially overlap on their laws. Also, nothing in my argument requires that the only difference in the nomic structure of U_1 and U_2 be that L_1 is a law of U_1 and not of U_2. In these two worlds, there may be two entirely different networks of laws governing particle/field interactions. So, to challenge my argument, some very specific connection needs to be established between laws governing the motion of X-particles and particle/field interaction laws like L_1. Furthermore, even if that were done, the challenge could be easily avoided by changing the nature of the nomic disagreement between the two worlds. There is nothing terribly special about L_1. I could have considered the charge of the particles in the Y-fields, the behavior of the particles when in the presence of other X-particles, or several other variations. In sum, it is overwhelmingly plausible that there is a *sufficient* lack of interdependency among laws to permit some version of my argument to succeed.

There are some still more interesting questions about the possibility of U_1 and U_2 that center on the properties of being an X-particle and being a Y-field. 'X-particle' and 'Y-field' are made-up terms. They are not, at least not intentionally, taken from the pages of any science text. Though some may find this feature of my example troubling, it can't really present any serious problem; there is no reason why a case cannot include descriptions of the behavior of some merely possible particles and fields. Even so, for the most part, I use these made-up predicates just as a bit of shorthand. The argument works as well in nearly all respects if 'X-particle' is understood as an abbreviation for 'silver atom' and 'Y-field' is short for 'nonhomogeneous magnetic field'. Besides being easier to say and type, the advantage of going with the made-up terms is that their use discourages distracting questions about the actual behavior of genuine particles and fields. I do not want some self-proclaimed science whiz to be even tempted to say, for example, that it is an essential property of silver atoms that they have spin down in non-homogeneous magnetic fields. Such claims are merely distractions because there is nothing very special about the properties I fix on. Even if having spin down in nonhomogeneous magnetic fields is an essential property of silver atoms, not every lawful feature had by silver atoms is. (Necessitarians might think so, but their extreme position was set aside in Section 1.4b of Chapter 1.) So there would surely be analogous versions of my argument that were successful. Incidentally, to throw in a little trivia, no *true* scientific whiz would say such a thing about the essence of silver atoms. There actually are some silver atoms in nonhomogeneous magnetic fields that do have spin up, while others have spin down.[5]

There is, I suspect, something lurking behind the questions about X-particles and Y-fields that is very insightful. There is something about particle b and its Y-field that is somewhat mysterious. It is hard to see how b and that Y-field could be so similar in U_1 and U_2, having all the same nonnomic features prior to b's entrance into the Y-field, and yet b have spin up in U_1, but not in U_2. Doesn't there have to be something about b or something about that Y-field that explains this difference in b's behavior? Some reflection makes it clear that there does not. Suppose that X-particles and Y-fields are *fundamental* particles and fields, that they are some of the most basic building blocks of these two universes. Then, there would not be any further concrete facts about either b or the Y-field that would (or could) account for the difference in what goes on in the two worlds. At this elemental level, all that would (or could) account for this difference would be the difference in the laws governing X/Y interactions. Because of the laws governing its behavior, b behaves one way in U_1 and another in U_2; L_1 is a law of U_1 and not of U_2. This assessment of the situation is one that Humeans should find palatable. They both take laws to have explanatory force and also take the behavior of particulars to determine the laws. So, from a Humean perspective, the difference in b's behavior should be enough to account philosophically for the difference in laws, while the resulting difference in laws in turn should provide the scientific explanation for the behavioral difference between the universes.

5 In fact, my thought experiments have some things in common with the Stern-Gerlach experiment.

67

With the supposition that X-particles and Y-fields are fundamental in this sense, we get a very simple and quite convincing version of my argument.[6] But it is not an essential feature of my argument that X-particles and Y-fields be basic in this way. They need not be basic, so long as there is a corresponding disagreement in the laws governing the more basic structures that make up the X-particles and the Y-fields. Then these laws are what ultimately explain the difference in b's behavior in the two worlds. For example, all X-particles could be composed of three protons, two neutrons, and so many electrons. Then so long as the laws governing protons, neutrons, and electrons varied in the just right way between the two worlds, there would be no problem. In U_1, it could be a law that particles with three protons subject to a Y-field have spin up. In U_2, this would not be a law.

3.2. SOME CONCEPTUAL GEOGRAPHY: A LOOK AT CHANCE

Though not nearly as popular as Humeanism about lawhood, Humeanism about chance is another traditional approach to understanding nomic modality. Like Humeanism about lawhood, it presupposes a certain supervenience thesis, the thesis that no two possible worlds have propositions that agree on their nonnomic features, and that disagree on their chance. As you might expect, I call this presupposition *Humean supervenience about chance*. In this section, I argue that it is false. Indeed, it is much more obviously false than is Humean supervenience about lawhood. Of course, I realize that this section is not critical to this chapter's main themes. (In fact, those whose interests are narrowly focused on lawhood should feel free to skip to Section 3.3.) But, this auxiliary investi-

6 If we make this supposition, there might be an argument to the conclusion that these cannot be silver atoms in nonhomogeneous magnetic fields. There would be if there were an argument to the effect that silver atoms or nonhomogeneous magnetic fields cannot be fundamental. This is why earlier I said that *in nearly all respects* my example would be just as successful if 'X-particle' abbreviates 'silver atom' and 'Y-field' abbreviates 'nonhomogeneous magnetic field'. If silver atoms and nonhomogeneous magnetic fields can't be basic in this way, then X and Y can't be interpreted this way in the most convincing versions of the argument. In these versions of the argument, they could still be interpreted using the genuine scientific predicates for whatever are considered to be the most elementary sorts of things.

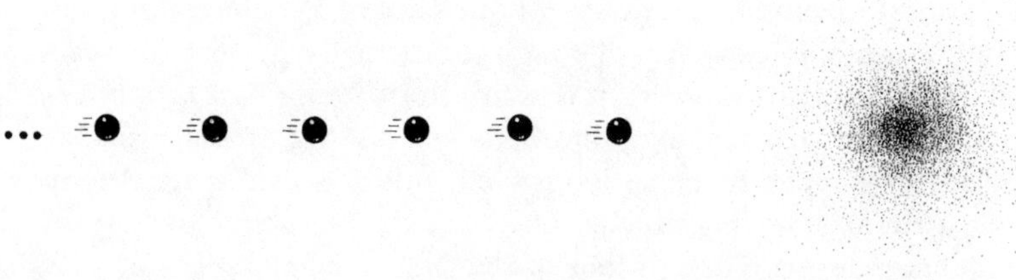

Figure 3.2

gation, in addition to its own intrinsic interest, has an interesting
ramification: With only a little effort, we can turn the argument for
the nonsupervenience of chance into an argument for the nonsupervenience of two other nomic concepts: causation and explanation.

Consider a possible world in which there are only five W-
particles, and each exists only for a short time. The first W-particle
to come into existence, particle b, has spin up. In fact, four of the
five W-particles have spin up; only one has spin down. With so few
relevant trials, the chance (just before b comes into existence) of b's
having spin up is undetermined. In one possible world, it may well
be that b has a ninety percent chance of having spin up. Yet, in another world, even one in nonnomic agreement with the first, it
could be that this chance is seventy percent. Indeed, given just the
nonnomic facts, b and each of the other W-particles could have almost any chance of having spin up. The only appealing constraint
is that if a W-particle in fact does have spin up, then it also has some
nonzero chance of having spin up. It would be a poor facsimile of
our concept of chance that tightly linked chances with actual frequencies. It is part and parcel of this concept that an entire range of
frequencies be copossible with an entire range of chances.

Using an argument that is similar to the argument of Section
3.1, the nonsupervenience of chance can also be defended in a more
rigorous fashion. Consider U_3. Unlike U_1, which contains only
five X-particles, it contains an immense number of X-particles,
perhaps infinitely many. These X-particles are all traveling in a line
one after the other toward a Y-field, the only such field that ever
exists in U_3. (See Figure 3.2.) Before a certain time t_0, only five

69

X-particles are subject to our Y-field. As they enter the field, the first two and the fourth and fifth acquire spin up; only the third does not. One important feature of our solitary Y-field is that it has a rather unstable existence. Though it is actually present for years and years (perhaps forever), it remains in existence past t_0 only because certain surrounding conditions are just right. Since the Y-field does happen to be so long-lived, millions of X-particles do pass through it. After time t_0, however, the frequency of upward spinners changes. Though four of the first five have spin up, only three out of the next five X-particles do. From then on, throughout the rest of time, this same pattern continues – seven out of every ten X-particles subject to the field have spin up. The behavior of X-particles in Y-fields is governed by a probabilistic law, namely:

L$_3$: All X-particles subject to a Y-field have a 70% chance of having spin up.

Besides the many X-particle/Y-field interactions just described, to keep the example suitably simple, I assume that not much else happens in U_3. The X-particles pass through the Y-field, they either get spin up or they don't, and then they proceed off in the same direction, never to encounter much of anything else.

Now consider a second possible world: U_4. It also contains those same X-particles, that same Y-field, and not much else. As they do in U_3, those particles travel in a line toward that one Y-field and pass through. Then, the X-particles continue on just as they do in U_3. Thus, U_3 and U_4 agree on *almost* all their nonnomic facts. Their only significant difference regarding these facts involves what goes on as each X-particle passes through the Y-field. Indeed, the only significant difference in their Humean facts involves the behavior of X-particles in Y-fields *after time t_0*. After t_0, in U_4, the next five X-particles subject to a Y-field *all* have spin up, and then it continues, throughout the rest of time, that nine out of every ten have spin up. There is a difference in the lawful nature of U_3 and U_4 that corresponds to this difference in the behavior of X-particles in Y-fields. In U_4, L$_4$ is a law:

L$_4$: All X-particles subject to a Y-field have a 90% chance of having spin up.

70

Though there is at least this much disagreement on their laws, we should suppose there is also some agreement between the two worlds. As I do about U_1 and U_2, I assume that U_3 and U_4 agree on the laws governing particle motion. For this argument, I also assume that they agree on their laws of field formation. There should be no doubt about the possibility of these two universes. They present no challenge to Humean supervenience about chance. The key laws, L_3 and L_4, reflect the pertinent frequencies as well as any Humean could ever demand.

It is natural to think that L_3's status as a law in U_3 does not depend on whether that one Y-field exists after t_0. That is, even if there were no Y-fields in U_3 after t_0, L_3 would still be a law. Yet it is just as natural to think that L_4's status as law in U_4 does not depend on whether Y-fields exist after t_0. L_4 would still be a law in U_4 even if there were no Y-fields after t_0. About both universes, if the circumstances hadn't been just so, then the one Y-field would not have continued to exist, and yet surely the laws would be unchanged. (Maybe that Y-field is created by a high-tech device that is extremely expensive to operate. For economic reasons, it may have almost been destroyed soon after its invention. If this contraption had lost its funding, the laws would not have been any different.) So, it seems there are really two further ways that our world could be. In one of these ways, the Y-field ceases to exist at time t_0 and yet L_3 is a law. The other way our world could be is similar, also having no Y-fields after t_0, but in it, L_4 is a law. Though these worlds have different laws, they need not have any distinguishing Humean features.

To make this argument a bit more precise via an appeal to principle (SC$\star$), let $U_{3\star}$ be the world that would result were Y-fields not to exist after t_0 in U_3. Let $U_{4\star}$ be the world that would result were Y-fields not to exist after t_0 in U_4. It is plausible to think that it is physically possible in both U_3 and U_4 that no Y-fields exist after t_0. The support for this claim of physical possibility is exactly parallel to the support for the analogous claim about U_1 and U_2. The one belonging to the present argument requires only that it not be a necessary condition of either U_3's or U_4's having the laws that it does that some Y-field exist after t_0. Surely, that requirement is satisfied. Since it is physically possible in U_3 that Y-fields not exist after t_0, and since L_3 is a law in U_3, it follows from (SC$\star$) that in

71

U_3, if Y-fields were not to exist after t_0, then L_3 would be a law. Thus, L_3 is a law of $U_{3\star}$. For similar reasons, L_4 is a law of $U_{4\star}$.

What about the nonnomic facts in $U_{3\star}$ and $U_{4\star}$? In addition to the nonexistence of Y-fields after t_0, there may have to be other changes to what goes on in U_3 and U_4 to accommodate this counterfactual supposition. What changes need to be made is determined by such factors as the applicable laws of particle motion, the applicable laws of field formation, and the events that occur before the formation of the Y-field. The changes apparently do not depend on facts about the direction of spin of the X-particles while they are in the field. Since we are supposing that U_3 and U_4 agree on their laws of particle motion and field formation, and since they agree on all the events leading up to the creation of the Y-field, it is plausible to think that the additional changes that need to be made to U_3 and U_4 result in two possible worlds that agree on their nonnomic facts.

Some mistakenly think that $U_{3\star}$ and $U_{4\star}$ contradict Humean supervenience *about lawhood*.[7] They think this because $U_{3\star}$ and $U_{4\star}$ agree on all their nonnomic facts and disagree on whether L_3 and L_4 are laws. While this is true, $U_{3\star}$ and $U_{4\star}$ do not contradict Humean supervenience about lawhood. They do not because they do not agree on all the nonnomic features instantiated by L_3 and L_4. L_3 and L_4 both have at least one nonnomic feature in $U_{3\star}$ that they lack $U_{4\star}$, and vice versa: L_3 is *true* in $U_{3\star}$ and *false* in $U_{4\star}$; L_4 is *false* in $U_{3\star}$ and *true* in $U_{4\star}$. To see my point from a slightly different perspective, notice that $U_{3\star}$ and $U_{4\star}$ clearly are consistent with the existence of a Humean analysis of lawhood. Consider the most naive of all the naive regularity analyses: P is a law if and only if P. This analysis is a completion of schema (S1) solely in terms free of nomic commitment. Yet, as far as L_3 and L_4 are concerned, it has the correct consequences in both $U_{3\star}$ and $U_{4\star}$. It appropriately implies that L_3 is a law in $U_{3\star}$ and not in $U_{4\star}$. It also correctly says that L_4 is a law in $U_{4\star}$ but not in $U_{3\star}$.

The proper lesson to be learned from the $U_{3\star}/U_{4\star}$ example is not a lesson about lawhood; it is a lesson about chance. Consider any one of those five particles that prior t_0 is subject to a Y-field in U_3 and U_4. Let it be f. In $U_{3\star}$, the chance that f has spin up is seventy

---

7 I make this mistake myself (Carroll 1990, pp. 214–215). Tooley (1987, p. 143) makes a similar error.

percent. In U_{4*}, the chance that f has spin up is ninety percent. Thus, these two worlds differ on their chance assignments to the proposition that f has spin up. Yet, as I argued, they also agree on all nonnomic facts. They are two worlds that agree on the nonnomic features of a single proposition P but also disagree on the chance of P. Therefore, they contradict Humean supervenience about chance.

As is true of our argument of Section 3.1, one nice feature of this argument is that it allows us to set aside many questions about possibility. The argument begins by supposing there are two possible worlds that, though they have different laws and different chances, have differences in the nonnomic facts that seem sufficient to ground these nomic differences; U_3 and U_4 are not a direct threat to Humean supervenience. Then, the counterexample is derived from the possibility of these two seemingly harmless and very ordinary universes. Of course, having seen where my argument ends up, some will still question the possibility of U_3 and U_4 in the same way that some challenge the possibility of U_1 and U_2. But I think it is pretty clear from my earlier discussion that this will be to no avail. As before, that there are so few things in the universes and that I require some partial agreement on the laws of U_3 and U_4 are very incidental to the argument, completely irrelevant to whether U_3 and U_4 are possible, or both. Especially if we add the supposition that these are fundamental particles and fields, concerns to the effect that there must be something intrinsic about the X-particles or the Y-field that accounts for the difference in the histories of U_3 and U_4 are shown to be misdirected by the fact that the explanation of the behavioral differences might be exhausted by their being governed by different laws.

Given all this, one might wonder why Humeanism about chance was ever an attractive position. I suspect that the story of its former charm is a familiar story, one that parallels the story I have been telling about the continuing attraction of Humeanism about lawhood. The epistemological importance of frequencies to probabilities led Humeans to think that there must be the corresponding reduction of physical probability to frequency. Thus was born the finite frequency interpretation, which merely identifies probabilities with frequencies. Simple counterexamples to this account spawned the many futile attempts to reduce probability in terms of some more sophisticated notion of frequency. As I have pointed out before, other philosophers, such as the phenomenalists and the behaviorists, have been led to seek reductions in a similar way. But, as is now well-known about the external world and the mental, as we learned in Chapter 2 about lawhood, and as has just become clear about chance, epistemological connections between two classes of concepts or propositions are no evidence that the corresponding reduction can be given.[8]

Doing a little more conceptual geography, we can use an example that is similar to the U_{3*}/U_{4*} case to undermine the supervenience of causation. Suppose that P, Q, and R are three states of affairs in close spatiotemporal proximity to one another. Also suppose that the chance of Q given P is ninety-eight percent and that the chance of Q given R is a mere one percent. It is surely consistent with these suppositions that P, but not R, causes Q. Perhaps not much else happens in this universe. Then, my discussion above suggests there is a world in nonnomic agreement with the world just described in which the chance of Q given P is one percent; and the chance of Q given R is ninety-eight percent. In this world, it could be that R causes Q though P does not. These two possible worlds contradict Humean supervenience about causation. They agree on all the nonnomic concepts instantiated by P and Q, but they disagree on whether P causes Q. The same two worlds are a counterexample to the supervenience of explanation. In the first world – the world in which the chance of Q given P is ninety-eight percent, and P causes Q – it could also be that P explains Q though R does not. In the second world – the world in which the chance of Q given R is ninety-eight percent, and R causes Q – it could be that R explains Q though P does not.

In Chapter 5, I return to supervenience issues about the causal relation. I again argue that causation does not supervene on the nonnomic concepts, but in a more interesting manner. I establish the significantly stronger thesis that causation does not supervene on the nonnomic concepts even when they are supplemented with lawhood, the counterfactual conditional, and chance.

8 Criticisms of reductive interpretations of physical probability are raised by Mellor (1971), van Fraassen (1980), Pollock (1990), and others. In general, philosophers have recognized that chance admits of no reduction. Even Lewis (1986, pp. 109–113, 127–129), with his strong Humean sympathies, despairs of reducing chance and instead focuses on associated epistemological questions.

3.3 VACUOUS LAWS AND THE VARIETIES
OF SUPERVENIENCE

We have now seen my arguments against the purest way for a realist about lawhood to carry out the positivist-inspired program. Insofar as we resist appealing to abstract entities, there is nothing that does the work that many hope would be done by a definition of 'law of nature' solely in terms free of nomic commitment. Not only is there no such definition, but two possible worlds may agree on the *concepts free of nomic commitments* exemplified by a proposition P and yet disagree on whether P is a law. Though the nomic/nonnomic distinction has limited significance, the two worlds apparently could even agree on all the *nonnomic concepts* exemplified by P and disagree about P's status as a law. As is clear, there is a reason these nonsupervenience conclusions are of great importance: They show that even if we were to weaken empiricist constraints in *certain* ways, there would still be no way to preserve realism about lawhood. For the sake of completeness, we should ask whether there are any *other* ways to weaken the constraints.

Expanding the legitimizing base to include more than all the nonnomic concepts might be suggested as one way of doing this. But, actually, this is not an option. Indeed, it would only worsen an earlier mistake. It would lead to the inclusion of some nomic concepts in the legitimizing base, and that would undermine what I consider to be the essence of the empiricist framework: to describe the otherworldliness associated with the nomic in *other* terms. (As I see it, this problem arises even when we consider expanding the base to include some concepts with nomic commitments. As I argue in Chapter 1, the modal character of lawhood is very clearly shared by all the concepts with nomic commitments.) So, rather than contemplating augmentation of the base, it makes more sense for us to consider whether there is some weaker sort of connection that might hold between it and lawhood. Of course, we also have to ask whether such a connection would address the original Humean suspicions that prompt the search for an analysis.[9]

9 My discussion of the varieties of supervenience owes much to the work of Kim (1984) and especially Shalkowski (1992). Though Kim does not directly discuss issues about laws in this article, I suspect that both he and Shalkowski would be prepared to accept Humean supervenience about lawhood, and in fact may see

Philosophers of mind and ethicists are enticed by two supervenience theses that have analogues for our metaphysical topic. Both analogues are weaker than Humean supervenience. Here is the first:

> *The First Weak Thesis.* No possible world has propositions that agree on their nonnomic features and that do not also agree on their lawhood.

Humean supervenience is stronger than this principle because there can be *intra*world agreement without *inter*world agreement. The U_{1*}/U_{2*} example makes this point clear. For all the reasons given earlier, it is a counterexample to Humean supervenience; U_{1*} and U_{2*} are two possible worlds that agree on the nonnomic features instantiated by L_1 though they disagree on whether L_1 is a law. But neither U_{1*} nor U_{2*}, at least insofar as they have been described, provides a counterexample to the first weak thesis. To challenge it, we need an intraworld comparison of propositions. U_{1*}, for example, would have to contain another proposition sharing all of L_1's nonnomic features that, unlike L_1, was not a law. But there are no good candidates. (L_2, the proposition that all X-particles subject to a Y-field have spin down, does not do the trick, because it is not in nonnomic agreement with L_1; L_1, though not L_2, is true in U_{1*}.) The second weak thesis is even more frail than the first.

> *The Second Weak Thesis.* The actual world does not have propositions that agree on their nonnomic features and that do not also agree on their lawhood.

To thwart this thesis one needs to show that there *actually* is a law and a nonlaw that agree on all their nonnomic characteristics.

Does either of these weak theses have any plausibility? They may have some initial plausibility left over from that thoroughly philosophical and yet hard-to-repress feeling that somehow the nomic concepts are less fundamental than the concepts free of nomic commitments. But, even if they do, there is a two-universe argument, which is very similar to two arguments given earlier in this chap-

their arguments against weaker forms of supervenience as preparing the way. While I agree that Humean supervenience is required by the Humean program, to my mind this just goes to show how wrong-headed the program is.

Figure 3.3

ter, that shows that at least the first weak thesis is false. It also raises some questions about the second weak thesis. Having already given two arguments of a similar structure, I shall only sketch the new argument. Before doing so, however, let me make two simple but important points. First, since the new argument undermines the first weak thesis, it must also frustrate Humean supervenience. So, it further supports the conclusions reached in Section 3.1. Second, be aware that an interesting difference between the new nonsupervenience argument and the structurally similar argument from Section 3.1 is the *source* of the nonsupervenience. In the earlier argument, the source is the fact that a single proposition can be true and a law in one world, but true and an accident in another. In the new argument, an additional source is the fact that a vacuous generalization can be a law.[10]

Consider another possible world: U_5. Like U_1, it contains just five X-particles. Like U_3, all the X-particles are traveling in a line toward a single Y-field. (See Figure 3.3.) The Y-field, the only

10 This example originally derived from an example discussed by Tooley (1977, p. 669; 1987, pp. 47–48, 67). In Tooley's example, there are ten fundamental types of particles and so fifty-five possible sorts of particle/particle interactions. Fifty-four of these types of interactions have been subject to scientific scrutiny, and a law has been discovered governing each. The world happens to be so arranged that the last two types of particles (X- and Y-particles) never interact. He suggests, and I agree, that it would be very reasonable to believe that there is some underived law governing this final sort of interaction. Apparently, no nonnomic considerations need determine what that law is. Putnam (1978, p. 164) advances a similar example. McGinn's (1981) article brought Putnam's discussion to my attention.

77

such field that ever exists in U_5, came into being because conditions near the Y-field were just right. In fact, the Y-field exists for just a very short time before the conditions change and it fades out of existence. During its existence, the five X-particles each pass through. As they do, they all have spin up. This behavior is governed by what should by now be a very familiar law, namely, L_1. A second possible world, U_6, has those same five X-particles, that same short-lived Y-field, and not much else. Just as they do in U_5, those particles travel in a line toward that one Y-field and pass on through before it dissipates. The particles continue on in just the way that they do in U_5. U_5 and U_6's only significant difference with regard to their nonnomic facts involves what goes on as each X-particle is in the Y-field. In U_6, unlike in U_5, on every such occasion, the X-particle acquires spin down, not spin up. Since it is not true, L_1 is not a law in U_6. We can suppose instead that L_2, the generalization that all X-particles subject to a Y-field have spin down, is. We should also assume that U_5 and U_6 agree on their laws that govern particle motion and field formation.

The rest of the argument is very straightforward. Let U_{5*} be the world that would result were Y-fields not to exist in U_5. Let U_{6*} be the world that would result were Y-fields not to exist in U_6. It is plausible to think that it is physically possible in both U_5 and U_6 that no Y-fields exist. Since this is so, and since L_1 is a law in U_5, it follows from (SC★) that in U_5, if Y-fields were not to exist, then L_1 would still be a law. Thus, L_1 is a law of U_{5*}. For analogous reasons, L_2 is a law of U_{6*}. Since L_1 and L_2 cannot both be laws of a single world, L_1 is not a law of U_{6*}. For the same reason, L_2 is not a law of U_{5*}. Both U_{5*} and U_{6*} are a counterexample to the first weak thesis. They each contain a pair of propositions, L_1 and L_2, that agree on all their nonnomic features. In U_{5*}, L_1 exemplifies lawhood but L_2 does not. In U_{6*}, L_2 exemplifies lawhood though L_1 does not. Thus, there is a possible world, indeed there are at least two possible worlds, containing propositions that agree on their nonnomic features and yet disagree on their status as laws.[11]

---

11 Besides undermining the first weak thesis, the U_{5*}/U_{6*} example also very simply undermines both Humean supervenience about the counterfactual conditional and Humean supervenience about at least some dispositions. Pick any of the X-particles in U_{5*} or U_{6*}, and give it the name 'e'. In U_{5*}, since it is a law that all X-particles subject to a Y-field have spin up, *if e were subject to a Y-field, then e*

The plausibility of the second weak thesis is more difficult to judge. Assessing its truth requires us to make a posteriori judgments about what the actual laws are. Not being a scientist, I do not have much to say about that. Nevertheless, the U_{5*}/U_{6*} argument does give us a cursory reason to be suspicious of the second weak thesis. Notice that these two possible worlds are somewhat *realistic*. For example, it is not much of a reach to think that there are actual events similar to the events of U_{5*}: that there are particles of some basic kind that are not subject to some fundamental kind of condition, though it is a law that all particles of that basic sort subject to conditions of that fundamental kind have some property. So it doesn't seem very farfetched to think there actually is a law and a nonlaw that agree on their nonnomic features. Of course, I don't really have much of an idea how likely it is that events similar to the events that take place in U_{5*} actually take place. As far as I know, there may be very few basic sorts of particles and very few fundamental kinds of conditions, in which case it may be very likely that particles of every basic sort have at one time or another been subject to every fundamental kind of condition. All of this just goes to show how preliminary my reasons are for being suspicious of the second weak thesis. I am definitely not prepared either to accept or to reject this claim.

The plausibility of the second weak thesis is a very insignificant matter. Even if it is true, it is clear that the first weak thesis, the stronger of the two, is much too weak. Humeans and others with empiricist leanings need a thesis saying what *determines, fixes,* or *grounds* facts to the effect that a given proposition is a law. So, clearly, they need to recognize some sort of *dependence* between a

---

would have spin up. In U_{6*}, since it is law that all such particles have spin down, *it is not the case that if e were subject to a Y-field, then e would have spin up.* Yet U_{5*} and U_{6*} agree about the nonnomic concepts instantiated by e's being subject to a Y-field and e's having spin up. Thus, the counterfactual conditional does not supervene on the nonnomic concepts. The nonsupervenience of a sample disposition follows on the coattails of this conclusion about counterfactuals. Let *spinupable* be defined thus:

x is spinupable if and only if x would have spin up if x were subject to a Y-field.

Particle e is spinupable in U_{5*}, but not in U_{6*}. As U_{5*} and U_{6*} nonnomically agree about e, they thwart Humean supervenience about spinupability.

suitably wholesome base and lawhood. As should be no surprise, dependence – even the noncausal dependence at issue here – requires for its instantiation that at least some sufficiently interesting counterfactuals be true. Hence, the thesis that is supposed to express this dependence, the thesis that is supposed to state how lawhood is fixed by the underlying facts, ought to have such counterfactual commitments. Yet, by staying clear of interworld claims, both the weak theses also avoid the desired counterfactual consequences.

To see my point, consider the plausible supervenience thesis that there is no possible world in which some bachelor and some non-bachelor are both unmarried males. (It is analogous to the first weak thesis.) Let us also consider some actual married male, m. This plausible supervenience thesis has nothing to say about possible worlds in which m has never been married. In other words, someone who merely accepts this thesis without accepting anything stronger leaves it open what such a world would be like. Were this thesis all we had to go on, we would have no reason to accept that if m had never been married, then m would be a bachelor. So this supervenience thesis does not establish a sufficiently strong dependency between being an unmarried male and being a bachelor. It does decide the truth of *some* counterfactuals. For instance, one consequence of this thesis is that if m were an unmarried male and a bachelor and n were also an unmarried male, then n would also be a bachelor. My point is only that it does nothing to establish the *required* counterfactuals. Analogously, if all one is prepared to endorse is the first weak thesis about lawhood (or, worse, the extremely feeble second weak thesis, which has no interesting counterfactual consequences), then one would not have grounded lawhood in the nonnomic base.[12]

---

12 Shalkowski (1992, p. 80) points out that there is a supervenience claim that avoids the charge of explanatory impotence just leveled against the two weak theses. This moderately strong thesis is still weaker than Humean supervenience. The first weak thesis says that no possible world has propositions that agree on their nonnomic features and that do not agree on their status as laws. The moderately strong thesis goes on to say that within every world each pair of propositions must be such that they *would* agree on whether they were laws if they *were* to have the same nonnomic features. Although this thesis has precisely the sort of counterfactual consequences that the two weak theses lack, this success comes at a great price. It achieves its added strength by employing a prohibited concept: the counterfactual conditional. Furthermore, the moderately strong thesis is too strong. It entails the first weak thesis, which is false.

3.4 ETHICS, MIND, AND THE LAWS OF NATURE

To be as fair as possible, and perhaps also trying to pique your interest, I have been writing as if the denial of Humean supervenience is rather daring. But, quite to the contrary, it is really Humeanism that is the daring, extreme position. And, this is hardly unique; after being impressed by the failings of phenomenalist reductions, we do not reject only phenomenalism. Rather, in agreeing that there are certain nonphenomenalistic possibilities, for example, our being brains in vats, we are in effect denying the supervenience of physical objects on pure appearances. Physical object propositions are recognized as being too rich to be fully shaped by perceptual-appearance propositions. Humean supervenience about the nomic is as extreme as phenomenalist supervenience about the physical. Conversely, the denial of Humean supervenience is, I believe, as innocuous as the denial of the supervenience of physical objects on pure appearances.

While my position takes on a favorable hue when we look at the problem of the external world, certain aspects of it take on an unflattering tint when we look at certain other philosophical issues. In particular, my position seems at odds with what are now popular positions in ethics and in the philosophy of mind. Partly motivated by empiricist concerns themselves, and partly moved by disappointing failures of reductionist programs, many philosophers now hold that our mental concepts supervene on the nonmental physical concepts, and many hold that our ethical concepts supervene on the nonethical natural concepts. Indeed, matters have gone so far that a denial to these positions is more likely to be ridiculed than it is to be taken seriously. Thus, we should ask: What is it that so distinguishes the nomic from the ethical and the mental? What is it about the nomic that permits my allegiance to the denial of Humean supervenience?

One factor that distinguishes the nomic from the mental and the ethical is its centrality, both in our thinking about the world and, assuming that thinking to be as least roughly right, in the order of the world: As was effectively argued in Chapter 1, nearly all our ordinary concepts have substantial nomic commitments. So, any world devoid of laws, and hence without any nomic concepts instantiated, is an *extremely* desolate world. Now, I am prepared to be convinced that the ethical and the mental are more central than is usually acknowledged. For example, perhaps x's being a person requires something to the effect that it is ethically proper to treat x with at least some respect; and that it is ethically wrong to treat x with no respect at all. And, perhaps there is a good argument to the conclusion that x's being red requires that there be people with enough mental abilities to have visual appearances. But, even if all that is so, it is still quite clear that ethical and mental commitments are not nearly as widespread as nomic commitments. For one thing, ever so many ordinary concepts, like the concept of being a table, are obviously devoid of mental as well as ethical commitments.[13] Yet these concepts just as obviously have nomic commitments. Turning to more philosophical considerations, it is also clear that ethical and mental commitments do not extend as deeply into our most central *metaphysical* concepts as does the nomic: Persistence and materiality have nomic commitments, but they do not have any mental or ethical commitments. All of this being so, a very central point is plain: In stark contrast to the very barren worlds that do not partake of the nomic, a world devoid of mentality or value, or both, might still be a reasonably rich world.

In footnote 11 of this chapter, I argue that nonsupervenience about lawhood directly leads to the denial of interesting supervenience positions about the counterfactual conditional and a certain disposition. But, because of the centrality of the nomic, there is no way to use my nonsupervenience conclusion to argue effectively against standard supervenience claims about the mental and the ethical. These traditional positions put plenty of nomic concepts both in the class of supervening concepts and in the subvening base. In ethics, the pertinent relationship is between the ethical and the nonethical natural concepts. The inclusion of nomic concepts among the latter is evidenced by familiar naturalistic analyses that implement the concept of *being a consequence of*. Their inclusion

13 Perhaps it isn't obvious that tablehood is devoid of mental commitments. Someone might think that for something to be a table it must have been *designed* or, at the very least, have a certain *function*, and this same person might also think that for something to have been designed or have that particular function there must be at least one mind. Though I suspect that this person would be mistaken in his or her thinking, it is not worth our while to investigate this matter any further. There are plenty of other examples of ordinary concepts with nomic commitments that do obviously lack mental commitments. Here are just a few: being gold, wetness, being a boulder, being a plant, being heated (or cooled), exploding, growing, eroding, and blooming.

in the ethical sphere is confirmed by the presence of value-laden dispositions like *being evil* or *being blameworthy*. The customary supervenience claims in the philosophy of mind relate the mental with the purely physical. *Causation, counterfactuals,* and *chance* are used in a variety of physicalist analyses of mental states, and the most familiar mental concepts like *belief* and *desire* are loaded with nomic commitments. Since the nomic does permeate these subvening bases as well as the supervening realms, no challenge could be raised to these positions based on my nonsupervenience arguments.

There is another factor that relevantly distinguishes the nomic from the mental and ethical. At the very least, this factor shows why my arguments against Humean supervenience cannot be easily transformed into arguments for other less plausible nonsupervenience positions. That factor is this: Unlike mental concepts and ethical concepts, nomic concepts are clearly applicable at the "atomic" level, i.e., at the level of fundamental, noncomplex, physical things. Each of my arguments begins with two worlds that, though they need not match perfectly with respect to nonnomic facts, do need to be in at least pretty close agreement. Now, if we weren't able to focus on the atomic level, or on some not much higher level, we couldn't be confident that these worlds would agree in these ways. In essence, then, the *atomic applicability of the nomic* permits me, in giving my nonsupervenience arguments, to isolate certain possible laws from the facts they could conceivably supervene on.

Here is a macroscopic analogue to my U_{5*}/U_{6*} argument that I hope makes this point clear. (Colin McGinn suggested it in conversation.) Consider a world where it is a law that all trees subject to a forty-mile-per-hour wind bend. In it, there are just five trees, all are simultaneously subject to one forty-mile-per-hour breeze, and each bends. When the wind dies, each tree returns to its original position. Now consider a second world that agrees with this first one on its history, right up until those five trees are subject to the wind. In the second world, when the gale blows, the trees do not budge. So, there is supposed to be much nonnomic agreement between the two worlds; the nonnomic differences are supposed to be confined to what goes on during and after that one wind. The argument would then continue by considering two more worlds: the ones that would result had no wind been present.

The preceding argument is not very convincing, and it wouldn't be any more convincing even if it were fully spelled out. The problem is that it is very hard to see how the starter worlds could agree on so much of their history. Making interworld comparisons, each tree and its counterpart would have to be composed of exactly the same kind of molecules, all arranged in precisely the same way. Yet, when subject to the wind in the first world, all the trees bend. When subject to precisely the same kind of wind in the second world, their counterparts do not. It is very hard to see how this could be the case given that whether a tree bends is clearly so dependent on its makeup.

In Section 3.1, I observed that a very convincing version of my U_{1*}/U_{2*} argument made the assumption that X-particles and Y-fields are fundamental. I also pointed out that this was not absolutely crucial to the argument. As I illustrated, X-particles can be composed of three protons, two neutrons, and however many electrons so long as there are low-level laws governing these more basic parts that account for the difference in b's behavior in U_1 as opposed to U_2. These laws also obviously have to be consistent with L_1 being a law in U_1. For the tree argument to succeed, there would have to be some analogous hypothesis of low-level laws that explain the difference in the trees' behavior and are consistent with its being a high-level law in the first starter world that all trees in forty-mile-per-hour winds bend. Since trees and winds are such high-level phenomena, no one should dare guess whether there could be such a consistent hypothesis of low-level laws.

All the same points apply to arguments for the nonsupervenience of the ethical on the natural that parallel my nonsupervenience proofs. Such an argument might begin by supposing that there was a possible world in which some fellow Smith enters some very simple choice situation, and despite knowing all the relevant consequences of his act, he chooses heinously. Surely, he might be an evil person in this world. Suppose there is a second world which agrees with the first on all its natural facts up until the time Smith enters that choice situation. Once in the situation, however, Smith does not choose the monstrous action but does something completely innocuous instead. It is surely possible that he is not evil in this world. (You can imagine how the argument would go from there.) The problem with this argument is that it is very hard to see how there really could be so much naturalistic agreement between the two initial universes. Making an interworld comparison, Smith and his counterpart would have to be composed of exactly the same kinds of molecules, arranged in precisely the same way. Yet, when subject to the choice situation in the *first* world he does *one* thing, and when subject to *precisely the same* (sort of) situation in the *second* world his counterpart does *another*. How could this be the case given that a person's decisions are so dependent on his or her makeup? Furthermore, this ethical analogue is really in much worse shape than the macroscopic analogue. We should not forget that lawhood and the other nomic concepts are members of the class of natural concepts. So the difference in Smith's behavior would have to be possible given the exact compositional agreement *plus* exact agreement on the laws of physics, chemistry, and biology. Hence, there is strong reason to think there could not be the required naturalistic agreement. (All the points made in this paragraph about the ethical supervening on the natural apply as well to the mental supervening on the physical.)

Therefore, there is ample reason to believe that the popularity of certain supervenience positions in ethics and the philosophy of mind is no indication that there is something wrong with my denial of Humean supervenience. Especially with regard to their centrality to the rest of our conceptual framework, there are fundamental differences between the nomic realm, on the one hand, and the mental and the ethical realms, on the other. These basic differences signal significant disanalogies about the pertinent supervenience issues. Just so, as is shown above, the nomic commitments of both our mental concepts and our nonmental physical concepts and the nomic commitments of both our ethical concepts and our nonethical natural concepts prevent interesting ethical or mental nonsupervenience positions from being consequences of the nonsupervenience of lawhood. So, there is no direct route from the failure of Humean supervenience to free-floating values or Cartesian disembodied minds. There is no indirect route either: The mental's and the ethical's lack of atomic applicability ensures that my arguments against Humean supervenience don't suggest plausible parallel arguments against the popular supervenience claims.

4

A realist perspective

The empiricism of, say, Locke or Hume states that every idea either originates in our phenomenal experience or is exhausted by component ideas thus originating. One descendant of this tenet is the logical positivists' criterion of cognitive significance: A sentence is cognitively meaningful only if it is verifiable. At the hands of A. J. Ayer (1936), Carl Hempel (1971), and other disciples of the Vienna Circle, this criterion was quietly transformed into a principle that makes the essence of cognitive meaning *translatability* into an empirical language. The surviving core of empiricism, what I have referred to as the *empiricist framework,* is roughly this:

> If there is some expression of English, call it '*F*', such that there is no necessarily true completion of '*x* is *F* if and only if. . .' that uses only suitably wholesome terms, then '*F*' must fail to describe reality.

What counts as suitably wholesome varies from one expression to the next; the analyzing vocabulary might have to include only nonmental physical terms if '*F*' is a mental predicate, or only nonethical natural terms if '*F*' is an ethical predicate.

Given this background, it is easy to see why someone convinced by the arguments in Chapters 1, 2, and 3 may feel forced to adopt some sort of *antirealism* about laws. After all, Chapter 1 shows that the concepts appropriate for a comforting definition of 'law of nature' are those without nomic commitments. Then, Chapters 2 and 3 show that not only is there no such *definition,* but lawhood doesn't even *supervene* (in any interesting sense) on these concepts. Thus, the empiricist framework points us down a well-trodden path to the land of antirealism. As the present chapter reveals, it is for just this reason that the framework must be abandoned. Sections 4.1 and 4.2 show that the road from irreducibility to antirealism is an avenue to disaster. Then, Section 4.3 scrutinizes an influential epistemological fear that most directly supports Humeanism but, in a slightly different form, also supports antirealism. Indeed, it is *the* major culprit behind the lingering define-or-decline attitude. Over the course of this fourth chapter, a sensible realist outlook is gradually confirmed.[1]

4.1 LAWLESS REALITY

Various rationales underlie the empiricist framework. As I just indicated, the primary one is epistemological. It infers from the failure to analyze an expression '*F*' that no knowledge that there are *Fs* arises *indirectly* from perception. If no knowledge that there are *Fs* arises *directly* from perception (as is clearly the case when the expression in question is something like '. . . is a law' or '. . . is morally wrong'), then there is no knowledge that there are *Fs*. The knowledge failure is then explained by the failure of '*F*' to describe reality. Having a similar structure, the reasoning behind the framework that is truest to its heritage is semantical. It moves immediately from the irreducibility of '*F*' to the conclusion that if '*F*' does not express a perceptually given concept (as again is clearly the case with certain pertinent expressions), then no concept is expressed by '*F*'. Yet another rationale meanders through some issues that sound more ontological than semantical or epistemological. Given that '*F*' is not analyzable in suitably wholesome terms, these so-called *arguments from queerness* contend that if there were any *Fs*, then they would be "entities . . . of a very strange sort, utterly different from anything else in the universe" (Mackie 1977, p. 38). These arguments conclude that, most likely, there aren't any things so radically queer as that.

There are several prominent defenders of some form of antirealism about lawhood (cf., Ayer 1963, Mackie 1974a, Ramsey 1978, Braithwaite 1953, Blackburn 1984 and 1986, and van Fraassen 1989). Though I am sure that these philosophers would all deny be-

---

1 There is some precedence in the recent history of philosophy for a realist antireductionism about lawhood. Prior to the 1970s, the authors who advocate an account closest to the position being advanced here are Kneale (1961, 1950, 1949) and Molnar (1974). These authors present arguments against naive regularity analyses. They also clearly hold that there are laws and that laws somehow involve some sort of irreducible necessity.

ing moved to their antirealism by arguments as simple as those sketched in the previous paragraph, what may have moved them there is a matter of little consequence. Indeed, I use those arguments primarily as a foil. By its being revealed just how outlandish nomic antirealism is, *all* arguments that move from irreducibility to antirealism immediately appear to be entirely devoid of substance. To that effect, we should now turn to consider briefly some further evidence for the centrality of the nomic. Then, in Sections 4.1b and 4.1c, I show how this centrality makes big trouble for the two primary forms of antirealism.

a. More on centrality

Because of some specific issues that come up below, in reaffirming the centrality of the nomic it will be especially useful to consider two concepts whose nomic commitments have not been discussed at length in any of my earlier chapters. The first is *reasoning* and the second is *believing*.

As I use the word 'reasoning', it does not describe any terribly demanding activity. Reasoning need not be rule-governed in any interesting sense, and it can be made up of ever so many atrocious assumptions and plenty of preposterous inferences. I do, however, want to distinguish reasoning from mere deliberation. The former, as opposed to the latter, always involves reaching some conclusion, coming to believe some proposition. Now suppose, contrary to fact, that my belief that it will rain tomorrow was not *caused* by any of my other beliefs, or by any of my recollective processes, or by any of my perceptual states. If you like, we can suppose that this belief was primarily the result of a bad bump on the noggin. Then, it is already pretty clear that I would not have reasoned to that belief. In case there are any doubters, let us push things a little further. Let's suppose not only that my belief was not caused in any of the usual ways, but also that it was *uncaused,* that it sustained no natural dependency on any other state of affairs. Suppose the atoms of my brain that realize my belief would have occupied their exact spatiotemporal position no matter what else went on before, during, or after the time I actually came to have the belief. It is absolutely clear that, were this the case, I would not have reasoned to my belief. (In fact, it's pretty clear that I wouldn't even *have* that belief. More on this in a moment.) So, even if I were wrong, even if the culmination of reasoning need not be accepted *on the basis of* or *because of* something like other beliefs or perceptual states or memory states, at the very least, it must be *based on* or *caused by* something.[2] What about the end state of reasoning? What about believing? According to a once fashionable position, I have a belief if and only if a kind of phenomenal incandescence attaches to one of my mental images or ideas. On this view, beliefs are the vivid ideas or the most irrepressible ideas or who knows what. Quite recently, this account of belief has been jettisoned for views that, while containing some mistakes themselves, are vastly more plausible. Even if one has doubts about *functionalism* as some sort of general solution to the mind-body problem, one of its underlying convictions is almost perfectly beyond doubt: To be a state of believing anything at all, a mental state must stand in certain counterfactual relations to, and in myriad potential and actual causal relations to, environmental input, other mental states, and bodily behavior. Even *logical behaviorism* contains a similar truism: To believe any proposition, one must have some disposition to behave. When taking our cue from these unobjectionable aspects of these two familiar programs in the philosophy of psychology, at least this much is clear: Suppose the atoms of my brain actually realizing my belief that it will rain tomorrow stood in no causal relations, and they lacked even the potential to cause anything. Then, even if arranged precisely as they actually were, those atoms would not realize any belief at all, and so they certainly wouldn't realize that particular belief.

Thus, reasoning and believing are two more examples of ordinary concepts with nomic commitments. This conclusion is some further support for, and a timely reminder of, one of my first chapter's chief lessons: Nearly all our ordinary concepts have nomic commitments. Reasoning and believing belong right alongside perception, persistence, tablehood, and materiality – four of Chapter 1's key examples of nomically committed concepts. The reminder is timely because it is the centrality of the nomic that does most of the work in my attempt to show why antirealism is untenable.

Though there is in essence one huge problem for all antirealisms, the exact nature of the trouble generated by the centrality of the

2 My manner of revealing the nomic commitments of reasoning is suggested by Unger's unpublished manuscript, "A Transcendental Argument". This paper is a much shorter version of the last chapter of his (1966) Oxford D. Phil. thesis *Experience, Scepticism, and Knowledge*.

nomic depends on the specific sort of the antirealism in question. So, in Section 4.1b, I consider the trouble centrality presents for *error theories*. The parallel problem for *noncognitivisms* is considered in Section 4.1c.

b. Error theories

Unlike noncognitivisms, which will be characterized more fully in a moment, error theories about a certain class of sentences do not fuss with the semantics of those sentences. The sentences in question are thought not to differ semantically from commonplace sentences about middle-sized physical objects; both sorts of sentences *attempt* to describe reality. Error theories qualify as antirealisms only because they maintain that the sentences in question, unlike ordinary sentences about middle-sized physical objects, necessarily fail in their attempt. Thus, all error theories about lawhood sentences maintain, for example, that when a physicist or anyone else says, 'It is a law that no signals travel faster than light', that person is saying something false. More generally, these error theories all deny that there is even one law of nature.

About error theories, the first thing to notice is this: If the error theorist accepts (as I do) that the instantiation of any nomic concept requires there to be at least one law of nature, then he resolutely *should not* believe that our universe is lawless. Since nearly all our concepts require for their instantiation that some nomic concept also be instantiated, and since this error theorist recognizes that the instantiation of any nomic concept requires that there be at least one law, he should also accept that if there were no laws, then there would be little else. So denying there are any laws would be tantamount to an overwhelming and evidently absurd nihilism – it would require admitting that there are no beliefs, that no one ever reasons, that there is no perception, that nothing survives the lapse of time, that tables do not exist, etc., etc.

Indeed, this error theorist is in quite a bind. As we saw in Section 4.1a, and as I just reiterated, in order for believing or reasoning to be instantiated at least some nomic concepts must also be instantiated. So, granting that the instantiation of any nomic concept requires there to be at least one law, for the error theorist or anyone else to believe any proposition at all, there must be at least one law.

90

Thus, like anyone else, the error theorist *cannot* correctly believe that our universe is lawless. For the error theorist to believe that there are no laws, there must be at least one law.[3] Similarly, the error theorist could not have reasoned to the conclusion that there are no laws unless there are laws. So, if, *per impossible,* he did correctly believe there are no laws, lacking any reason, his belief would be baseless.

It is pointless for the error theorist to reject the plausible claim that the instantiation of any of the nomic concepts requires there to be at least one law. Rejecting such a connection does not void the threat of nihilism. Lawhood is just one of the many nomic concepts, all of which may appear to have an otherworldly aura. What does our error theorist say about causation, the counterfactual conditional, and the rest? Depending on what is said, the error theorist either strays once again into nihilism or holds a rather peculiar and unmotivated position. *At one extreme,* the error theory can be extended to all the nomic concepts, denying that there is any causation, any true (nontrivial) counterfactual conditionals, and so on. But, then, the error theorist is back in the nihilistic soup; if no nomic concepts were instantiated, then there would be little else; in particular, there would be no beliefs and no reasoning.[4] *At the other extreme,* the error theory can be confined to lawhood, and realism endorsed with regard to all the other nomic concepts. But, like any finicky position that is error theorist about some, but not all, of the nomic concepts, this view is entirely *ad hoc.* What arguments could warrant antirealism about lawhood without challenging realism about, say, the counterfactual conditional? Furthermore, this sort of position likely would not threaten one of my most important conclusions. Since this sort of position upholds realism about *some* nomic concepts, and since the arguments of Chapter 3 show that my irreducibility results apply to nearly *all* nomic concepts,[5] the

3 Compare what Schiffer (1990b, p. 178) and Foster (1991, p. 19) have to say about the incoherence of eliminativism about propositional attitudes.
4 Furthermore, the threat of nihilism cannot be dodged by denying the conceptual connections from our many ordinary concepts to the nomic concepts. Lawhood has a relatively small, overt role to play in everyday thought and talk. So it is tempting to rebuff conceptual connections with lawhood. It is not so tempting, and indeed it is very clearly a mistake, to deny the conceptual connections between nearly all our ordinary concepts and the other nomic concepts.
5 See the last two paragraphs of Section 3.2 and footnote 11.

one exception being my unsurprising failure to extend these results to all dispositions, my refutation of the empiricist framework would still stand.[6]

c. Noncognitivisms

When one adopts a noncognitivism about a supposedly problematic group of sentences, one can see those sentences as containing a descriptive component. But what distinguishes any noncognitivism from a corresponding error theory is its holding that these sentences also contain a nondescriptive part. (It is this nondescriptive part that sets these sentences apart from mundane sentences about middle-sized physical objects.) Consider:

    (1) Elvis is about to sing.
    (2) Hooray! Elvis is about to sing.

---

6 Perhaps sensing the associated absurdities, Ayer and Mackie do not dwell on the skeptical aspect of their antirealisms. Instead, they play up claims to the effect that there are explanatory gains to be had from turning our attention to the analysis of certain *psychological* locutions. Here, Ayer characterizes his endeavor:

Now I do not wish to say that a difference in regard to mere possibilities is not a genuine difference, or that it is to be equated with a difference in the attitude of those who do the interpreting. But I do think that it can best be elucidated by referring to such differences of attitude. In short I propose to explain the distinction between generalizations of law and generalizations of fact, and thereby to give some account of what a law of nature is, by the indirect method of analysing the distinction between treating a generalization as a statement of law and treating it as a statement of fact (1963, pp. 230–231).

Similarly, Mackie (1974a) maintains that a central task for metaphysicians is to give an account of why we *take* some, but not all, generalizations to sustain counterfactuals. By themselves, these suggestions are relatively harmless. They have no special tie with antirealism. They could just as easily have been made by a realist in favor of mapping out the conceptual connections between certain sorts of mental state properties and our other concepts. (Given his attraction to a "projection strategy" (1984, p. 103), Stalnaker may be just such a realist.) Nevertheless, Ayer and Mackie seem to have false expectations regarding their recommendations. They seem to think that the analyses of the psychological locutions would provide the same sort of illumination as would be provided by a reduction of lawhood. But how could *this sort* of illumination be dispensed if – as it seems they must – the desired analyses contain *nomic* terms (cf., Peacocke 1980, p. 45)? Furthermore, it is a mistake to suggest that the analysis of the various psychological locutions has any greater importance than, say, the analysis of certain other psychological locutions or the mapping out of the connections among the nomic concepts.

Though (1) and (2) share a descriptive core, it is plausible to think that the latter includes something extra; (2), unlike (1), projects a noncognitive attitude – the speaker's approval of what the King is about to do. This projective element prevents (2) as a whole from being *believed* "in the strictest, most literal sense of the verb 'to believe' " (Schiffer 1990a, p. 602). Noncognitivists about lawhood sentences stretch this reasonable story about (1) and (2), letting essentially the same account apply to sentences like the following:

(3) No signals travel faster than light.
(4) It is a law that no signals travel faster than light.

They see sentence (4) (and other nonembedded lawhood sentences) as containing a nondescriptive part. Though they admit that everyone can believe that no signals travel faster than light, they also deny that anyone can believe (at least in the most literal sense of 'to believe') that *it is a law that* no signals travel faster than light.

By taking a suitably deflationary view of the predicate '. . . is true' and cognate phrases like '. . . is a fact', a noncognitivist will accept that (4) is true, say such things as that it is a law that no signals travel faster than light, and gladly admit that it is a fact that there are laws. So, we should ask: Have noncognitivists about lawhood sentences discovered a way to lessen the severity of antirealism? No, they have not; the problems originating from the centrality of the nomic merely take a different form. To be specific, far too much of our language would have to be projective. Unless one oddly limits noncognitivism solely to lawhood sentences, there are the many phrases apparently used to state nomic facts that would have to be treated in a noncognitivist fashion: 'it is physically necessary that . . .', 'there is a thirty percent chance that . . .', 'if it were the case that . . . , then it would be the case that_____', and so on. And, that is just the beginning. There are all the phrases apparently expressing concepts with nomic commitments: '. . . is a table', '. . . perceives_____', '. . . is a material object', '. . . believes_____', '. . . is reasoning', and so on. Were we to pursue noncognitivism, our view of the semantics of nearly all of natural language would be dramatically changed. One simple sign of the absurdity of the resulting semantics is the lofty number of distinct kinds of noncognitive attitudes that would need to be acknowledged. Presumably, since each has a different meaning, many (if

93

not all) of the supposedly noncognitive expressions would have to be treated as projecting a unique attitude. What reason do we have for thinking that these many kinds of attitudes exist? Though we ascribe all sorts of beliefs and *some* noncognitive attitudes (e.g., desires or approval), we ordinarily do not ascribe the plethora of different sorts of noncognitive attitudes apparently needed for the theory.[7]

There are a variety of other more familiar objections to noncognitivist theories. To mention just two, there is *Frege's point* (Geach 1965) about embedded projective sentences, and there are questions about the required nonunivocality of the verb 'to believe'. Many of these objections are more familiar, in part, because they apply as well (or as poorly) to noncognitivism about ethical terms as they do to noncognitivism about nomic expressions. When contrasted with the trouble brought on by the centrality of the nomic, however, these better-known problems begin to look like minor technical glitches.

d. Conclusions

The utterly decisive problem for all nomic antirealisms is that they originate in a merely apparent division, one antirealists perceive between certain supposedly problematic sentences and other unproblematic sentences. For noncognitivists, the proposed explanation of the split is that the supposedly problematic sentences, unlike the others, contain a nondescriptive component. For error theorists, the suggested explanation of the split is that the supposedly problematic sentences, unlike the others, necessarily do not succeed in describing any genuine aspects of reality. Nevertheless, once reminded of how central the nomic really is, it is hard even to see the initial division. The antirealists' unproblematic sentences,

---

7 Continuing to observe certain parallels, we should also notice that noncognitivism faces incoherences on a par with those faced by error theories. They are not *precisely* the same incoherences. No part of noncognitivism commits the noncognitivist to believing there are no laws. (In fact, the sentence 'There are no laws' would probably be treated in the same way that 'There are laws' is, as something that *can't* be believed in the most literal sense of 'believes'.) Still, since no one believes anything at all unless there is at least one law, one believes noncognitivism only if there is at least one law. Since it is part and parcel of noncognitivism that no one (including the noncognitivist) literally believes that there are laws, one can correctly believe noncognitivism only if his belief corpus is incomplete.

our ordinary sentences about middle-sized physical objects, are as chock full of nomic commitments as nearly all the others. Nomic antirealism collapses under the pressure of centrality.

By this point in the book, and by this stage in the history of philosophy, it is easy to see where the epistemological and semantical routes from irreducibility to antirealism go wrong. As most now agree,[8] the semantical argument depends on a simplistic hypothesis about the origin of our ideas. As Section 4.3 will make very transparent, the epistemological argument is grounded in a similarly crude epistemological picture.

Despite how clear it has become that they must be unsound, arguments from queerness are a bit harder to diagnose (or even understand!). This added difficulty may stem from the fact that they often appear to be something they are not. They often appear to be ontological concerns, concerns about what sorts of *entities,* especially what sorts of *facts,* one permits in one's ontology. But this cannot be what ultimately drives these arguments. To see my point, notice that no serious ontological anxieties should ever arise about facts – to say P is a fact is just a slightly roundabout way of saying P. There is a minor ontological problem about facts brought on by the apparently valid inference from 'P is a fact' to 'There are facts', but this problem arises for *any* sentence of the form 'P is a fact', even if the contained sentence 'P' is a mundane sentence about middle-sized physical objects. The force that some find in standard queerness arguments doesn't really involve ontological issues at all. The worry behind these arguments is that if there really were a fact to the effect that P is a law (or to the effect that x is morally wrong or what have you), then it would have to be just too different from most of the facts that we take to be unproblematic. If this is the real concern behind these arguments, then their big mistake when applied to the nomic rests in the assumption that some deep difference divides the supposedly problematic nomic concepts and our most familiar unproblematic concepts. On the contrary, and as I've said before, nearly all those secure and commonplace concepts are loaded with nomic commitments.

In a final effort to give antirealism a fair shake, in the next section I will consider Bas van Fraassen's reasons for his recently offered error theory.

8 Wilson (1986, pp. 85–87) is a notable exception.

4.2. VAN FRAASSEN'S ANTIREALISM

It is popular to maintain that there is some close connection between there being some good (or warranted) inductive reasoning and there being laws of nature. This perfectly sober thought, however, is often supported by a highly controversial picture of induction. Here are some remarks by David Armstrong, John Foster, and Fred Dretske that indicate the picture I have in mind:

On my view, we have a pattern of inference which runs observed instances→law→unobserved instances (Armstrong 1983, p. 56).

When rational, an extrapolative inference can be justified by being recast as the product of two further steps of inference, neither of which is, as such, extrapolative. The first is an inference to the best explanation – an explanation of the past regularity whose extrapolation is at issue. The second is a deduction from this explanation that the regularity will continue or that it will do so subject to the continued obtaining of certain conditions. . . . A crucial part of the inferred explanation, and sometimes the whole of it, is the postulation of certain laws of nature – laws which are not mere generalizations of fact, but forms of (objective) natural necessity (Foster 1983, p. 90).

The only way we can get a purchase on the unexamined cases is to introduce a hypothesis which, while *explaining* the data we already have, *implies* something about the data we do not have. . . . [T]he generalization can be confirmed, but only by the introduction of a law or circumstance (combined with a law or laws) that helps to explain the data already available (Dretske 1977, p. 259).

As is evident, this view of induction is one that gives a prominent role to lawhood and to *inference to the best explanation* (IBE). As is also evident, the three authors also believe there are many very ordinary and very good reasons to believe in laws. If they didn't, they couldn't uphold their view of induction while also maintaining that an appropriately large portion of our inductively held beliefs are rational.

In its briefest and simplest form, van Fraassen's key argument for his error theory is this: Since there is no reason to believe there are laws, one ought to believe there are no laws.[9] Though there is a

---

9 Though the textual evidence is hardly conclusive, that this is his primary argument is suggested by the introduction of part two of *Laws and Symmetry* (p. 130) and a key passage (pp. 180–181) to be discussed below. Van Fraassen does say things like "do not rely on such a concept as law without inquiring whether there is anything that could play that role" (p. viii), which might lead one to think that

subargument (discussed below) for this argument's solitary premise, much of the premise's support derives from van Fraassen's severe criticisms of the idea that lawhood plays a crucial role in the formation of ordinary inductively formed beliefs. He also disparages all epistemologies that adopt IBE as a basic inference rule.

To some extent, I agree with his criticisms. I allow that, as boldly stated by Foster, Dretske, and Armstrong, the law-driven view of induction is mistaken. An example employed by van Fraassen makes this point clear:

> I am told that the ten coins I am about to be shown came either from Peter's pocket or from Paul's; that Peter's contained ten dimes and fifty nickels, while Paul's contained sixty dimes. The first seven to be put before me are dimes (1989, p. 136).

Here, with the background beliefs that (i) the coins are equally likely to come from Peter's pocket as from Paul's and that (ii) the coins are chosen randomly from whatever pocket is the source, my probability that the last three coins are dimes has been raised by my observation of the first seven coins. Yet, where are the laws? It is not a law that all ten coins are dimes, it is not a law that all the coins came from Paul's pocket, and it is not a law that all the coins in Paul's pocket are dimes. Nor do I believe that any of these are laws. Of course, Armstrong, Dretske, and Foster might restrict their views to *suitably basic* cases of induction. But, if these cases are supposed to include cases carried out by typical nonscientists, these authors still have overestimated the role of laws and lawhood in our reasoning. Most of us have never formed any belief involving lawhood and have never believed any laws. We all, however, have many inductively confirmed beliefs.

Despite agreeing with these criticisms, I believe there may be something to these authors' conceptions of induction. Start by considering a plausible (and very weak) epistemological thesis: For S to

he must be trying to impugn the *concept* of lawhood. But, the overall structure of his book counts against this interpretation. If the concept of lawhood was in question, it would be odd for him in part two of his book to go on to consider at length potential reasons for believing in laws. If he didn't think there was a concept of lawhood, how could he inquire into its epistemology? I think van Fraassen believes there is a concept of lawhood, something that is meant by 'is a law'; he just doesn't believe that anything could instantiate it. In any case, if he does want to place any weight on some sort of semantical argument, he needs to say how it differs from old-fashioned empiricist arguments.

be inductively warranted in believing some rather ordinary matter of fact P, S must have evidence of some sort of connection between P and S's evidence for P. So, in van Fraassen's case, for me to believe justifiably that the coins still to be shown me are all dimes, I must have evidence for some connection between the first seven being dimes and the proposition that the remaining three are dimes. Obviously, I do; I have evidence that all the coins came from Paul's pocket and evidence that all the coins in Paul's pocket were dimes. In this case, the connection is an accidental one. In other relevantly similar cases, the tie may also be accidental. But, at least in many more basic cases, cases where roughly there is more limited background evidence, it is plausible that S must have evidence for some sort of nonaccidental connection between P and the evidence for P. In fact, something Dretske says may be close to the truth. At least for this range of cases, it may be that we must have reason to "introduce a hypothesis which, while *explaining* the data we already have, *implies* something about the data we do not have" (1977, p. 259).

In trying to resurrect something of the picture of inductive reasoning endorsed by Dretske and the others, I have altered that picture in three key respects. First, I have explicitly restricted it to a certain, vaguely delineated, range of cases. Second, laws and lawhood fade from the picture; the relevant nonaccidental connection between the evidence and the conclusion need not be a law itself, and it need not be a hypothesis to the effect that some generalization is a law. Third, the cognizer needn't even believe that this nonaccidental connection obtains; it suffices that she merely have evidence of its existence. What results form my alternations is a view that does not overintellectualize induction. Furthermore, though I hold that in the relevant range of cases the investigator must have evidence for a suitably explanatory connection, this does not commit me to IBE as "the true rock on which epistemology must build" (van Fraassen 1989, p. 131). As I just said, the connection between P and the evidence that P need not even be believed. If the investigator does happen to believe that the connection obtains, it needn't be because she believes that the connection seems to explain the evidence better than any other available hypothesis; it is enough that the connection *in fact* be so explanatory. Indeed, supposing a cognizer reasons from P to Q, and supposing that this inference is one that is rational only if Q seems to explain P, then this explanatory relation may hold only *because* the evidentiary one does. In other words, I don't even take my mild explanatory constraint to illuminate what it is to be a reason. As far as I am concerned, *P*'s being a reason for *Q* may be more basic than *Q*'s seeming to explain *P.*

I realize that, despite my alterations, this is still a lot to swallow. Nevertheless, if I am right about this, van Fraassen is in trouble. Remember that his primary argument for antirealism begins with the premise that there is no reason to believe there are laws. If I am right, the rationality of certain suitably basic cases of induction does depend on there being reason to believe certain nonaccidental propositions, many of which are nomic propositions. And, if there is reason to believe any nomic proposition, then there is also reason to believe that there is at least one law. So van Fraassen's premise looks doubtful. Furthermore, even setting my controversial suggestions aside, we can cause some serious trouble for van Fraassen by focusing on some other less questionable connections between induction and the nomic. For example, as I see it, the rationality of any particular inductive inference depends on the reasoner's not believing that there are no laws. If you believe there are no laws, then you ought not to believe based on induction (or in any other manner) that the sun will rise tomorrow. After all, for anything to rise it must exist at two different times; it must persist. If you believe there are no laws, then you ought not to believe that Descartes believed in God, because if there were no laws, then there wouldn't be any beliefs. To put my point strongly, nobody can believe there are no laws and also come rationally to believe much of anything else.[10]

Returning to van Fraassen's key argument, he must have something more to say in support of the premise that there is no reason to believe there are laws; he couldn't have merely defended it against positions like the positions of Armstrong, Dretske, and Foster. He does. His subargument for the faltering premise begins innocuously enough with the assumption that any reason for be-

---

10 This is obviously a bit too strong. Van Fraassen believes that there are no laws, and yet it is also quite clear that he has many rationally held beliefs, and many inductively confirmed beliefs. We have ways of isolating certain extraordinary beliefs, either in a rather cerebral fashion by denying certain conceptual connections – like connections linking lawhood to the other nomic concepts – or in a more ordinary fashion by ignoring the grave implications of the bizarre belief, as does the solipsist who most of the time acts and thinks just like the rest of us.

lieving in laws must be a reason that is based on data. It continues with the claim that *P* and *P*'s being a law always fit the data equally well. Thus, according to van Fraassen, the data could only support that *P* is a law (in addition to *P*) in virtue of the fact that *P*'s being a law (though not *P* alone) *explains* the data. He continues:

So the question: *Do laws explain?* has to be a substantive question, which must be answered, with substantive reasons for the given reply. But it is a question which we have no way of answering, without a previous account of what laws are (1989, p. 181).

Van Fraassen argues that none of the extant analyses of lawhood succeed in this task. He also claims:

If we make it definitional or analytic that laws explain, or explain if they be real, then we have automatically removed their explanatoriness from the list of reasons for their reality (1989, p. 181).

In short, the argument is this: Since any reason to believe in laws depends on lawhood being explanatory, and since this conviction can't be sustained in a way that permits it to underlie an inference to the reality of laws, there is no reason to believe in laws.

I think there are all sorts of reasons to believe in laws. One very good sort is a reason to believe that some specific proposition is a law. For example, my evidence that it is a law that no signals travel faster than light is evidence that there are laws. Furthermore, since it is much weaker than any claim to the effect that some specific proposition is a law, the thesis that there are laws also has some independent support: namely, that there are many generalizations that just miss qualifying as laws (e.g., excellent approximations like Newton's gravitational principle). Finally, there is another connection between induction and lawhood that van Fraassen overlooks. As I suggested in Section 4.1, if there were no laws, there would be no beliefs and no reasoning at all, and so obviously there would be no beliefs confirmed via inductive reasoning. To the extent that we do have reason to believe that we have ever believed anything or that we have ever reasoned, there is evidence of laws. Being an inductively confirmed belief is another one of our many concepts with a nomic commitment.

I am willing to admit that in some indirect fashion the reasons to believe in laws cited in the previous paragraph (and elsewhere) may have something to do with the fact that *P*'s being a law is sometimes explanatory in ways that P itself is not. For example, it may be true that my evidence would not have confirmed my belief that it is a law that no signal travels faster than light if this proposition's being a law didn't explain or at least seem to explain my evidence. So, my most serious doubts about van Fraassen's argument surround his contention that lawhood is not explanatory. His support of this claim has two parts. One part says that it couldn't be a definitional or analytic feature of lawhood that it be explanatory, and yet its explanatoriness still underlie an inference to laws.[11] But why is that? I am tempted to hold that it is analytic that if P is a law, then P's being a law explains P. I also take it that this would be one perfectly natural way to maintain that it is analytic that laws explain. I just don't see, however, how the analyticity of this thesis prevents it from underlying an inference to laws. Despite what van Fraassen says, it remains plausible to think that someone would have reason to believe that P is a law if she had evidence for a certain hypothesis H and also believed that if P were a law, then P's being a law would suitably explain H (provided, of course, that she had no other evidence against P's lawhood). The other part of van Fraassen's argument suggests that he thinks that lawhood is explanatory only if there is a successful account of laws. Since I agree wholeheartedly with his conclusion that there is no such account, a conclusion I would put by saying that lawhood is irreducible, my unsurprising complaint here is that there is no apparent reason to think that reducibility is a necessary condition of explanatoriness.

There is much that I agree with in *Laws and Symmetry*. Van Fraassen's criticisms of reductive analyses, especially the non-Humean reductive analyses discussed in my first appendix, are devastating.

---

11 There is a very opaque analogy offered by van Fraassen (p. 181) in support of this step:

Imagine the dialogue: 'Bachelors are single men – that is analytic.' 'Yes, but are there any?' 'You had better believe it – they couldn't very well remain single if they didn't exist, could they?'

I have very little idea how this analogy is supposed to apply. Van Fraassen seems to be worried about an inference merely from the proposition *that laws explain* to the conclusion *that there are laws*. Clearly, that is a bad inference, but it has little to do with the analyticity of the proposition that laws explain. It merely results from moving from the proposition that all *Fs* are *Gs* to the proposition that there are *Fs*. Furthermore, I see no reason to think that anyone who came to believe that there are laws based on lawhood's explanatoriness need commit this trivial mistake.

My resistance to error theories, and my distrust of arguments from irreducibility to antirealism, no doubt derive from an orientation that he does not share. As I say in Chapter 1, and as should have been clear all along, my interest is the concept of lawhood underlying the commonsense practice employing the other nomic concepts and our many other concepts with nomic commitments. So my *starting point* is the connections between lawhood and our other concepts. But these connections are exactly what any error theorist must reject to begin to make his position plausible.

4.3 THE ARGUMENT FOR HUMEANISM

In Chapter 2, I discuss the impact of an influential epistemological fear that arises from asking how we know of a proposition that it is a law. The fear essentially stems from an argument questioning the source of our knowledge involving lawhood. In short, the argument contends that no approved sources produce such knowledge unless Humeanism is true. At the end of Chapter 2, I quickly dismiss the argument for Humeanism because of obvious analogies with two skeptical arguments once advanced in support of two false metaphysical positions: phenomenalism and behaviorism.[12] The influence of the Humean argument, however, has been *so* overwhelming that it warrants further discussion. In undertaking a more careful assessment of the argument, we will eventually be led to a deep and difficult epistemological problem not uniquely associated with my position on lawhood. As this is not a book on general matters of epistemology, I discuss this problem only to the extent necessary to put the argument for Humeanism in perspective.

a. The two arguments

Without any drastic oversimplifications, the argument for Humeanism can be regimented as follows:[13]

---

12 For the sake of brevity, in this chapter I do not extend my discussion of the argument for behaviorism.
13 See Kitcher (1989, p. 460), Earman (1986, p. 86), Swartz (1985, pp. 67–78), Rescher (1969, p. 184), and Popper (1959, p. 433). Blackburn (1984, pp. 158–159 and scattered about) seems to have something like this argument in mind. Braithwaite (1953, p. 11) and Nagel (1961, p. 52) offer very informal epistemo-

(1) At least some of us know of a proposition that it is a law.
(2) All (nonanalytic) knowledge arises either directly or indirectly from perception.
(3) No knowledge of a proposition that it is a law arises directly from perception.
(4) If Humeanism is false, then no knowledge of a proposition that it is a law arises indirectly from perception.

---

(5) Humeanism is true.

The Humean and I are both strongly committed to premises (1) and (2). These assumptions stand quite well on their own. Usually, premises (3) and (4) receive some additional support, which we should now consider very carefully.[14]

One traditional kind of support for premise (3) is a partly psychological assumption. According to this assumption, all knowledge arising directly from perception is knowledge of *pure appearance propositions,* propositions to the effect that we are appeared to in such and such ways. Given this assumption, when in the presence of a red object, I cannot even know directly by perception *that it is red;* all I can know in this manner is *that I am appeared to redly.* There is another traditional source of support for the third premise. Some philosophers that deny that all direct perceptual knowledge is knowledge of pure appearance propositions still accept that all such knowledge contains only concepts that have a corresponding sensory appearance. With this assumption, though I can know directly by perception that a nearby object is red, I still cannot have perceptual knowledge of lawhood, since there is no *appearance of lawhood,* no look or feel of lawhood, that is part of anybody's sensations, at least not in the way that color appearances are. Finally, there is a less traditional reason to think that we have no perceptual knowledge of lawhood. Lawhood is just too recondite to be known directly by perception. We are no more likely to find perceptual

logical worries about positions with some similarities to mine. Unfortunately, their worries are so informal that it is difficult to tell exactly what their worries are. I am indebted to Swartz (1985, pp. 70–71) and to Armstrong (1983, pp. 107–108) for many of these references.

14 The variation of the argument for Humeanism that most directly supports antirealism takes the failure of Humeanism as a premise, and concludes that no one knows of a proposition that it is a law. In other words, (1) is replaced by the negation of (5), and (5) is replaced by the negation of (1).

knowledge of lawhood than we are to find perceptual knowledge of kinetic energy or of being Mesolithic.

The support for the fourth premise of the argument for Humeanism is just what you might expect: The only apparent way that any knowledge can arise indirectly from perception is through a series of *good* inferences from perceptual beliefs; and, since Humeanism is false, it is not clear how any of the relevant knowledge could arise in this way. In contrast, if Humeanism is true, and especially if some naive regularity analysis is correct, indirect knowledge involving lawhood is relatively unproblematic. According to the epistemological picture motivating naive regularity analyses, we first believe a universal generalization based on a straightforward inductive inference. We observe many *Fs*, see that they are all *Gs*, and on that basis come to believe that all *Fs* are *Gs*. Then, no further perceptual or inductive support is required. We simply consider the essential features of the generalization itself and determine whether it is lawlike. If it is, we make a deductive inference to the conclusion that it is also a law. Other Humean analyses receive some apparent support from the argument, although not as much. Defenders of Humean analyses that appeal to nonessential features of a proposition (other than its truth) face an extra epistemological task; they need to say how we know whether that nonessential feature applies.

Regimenting the argument for phenomenalism, the similarities are manifest:

(1′) At least some of us know something about physical objects.
(2′) All (nonanalytic) knowledge arises either directly or indirectly from perception.
(3′) No knowledge about physical objects arises directly from perception.
(4′) If phenomenalism is false, then no knowledge about physical objects arises indirectly from perception.

(5′) Phenomenalism is true.

The support for (3′) overlaps with some of the traditional support for (3). Because of the partly psychological assumption that all perceptual knowledge is knowledge of pure appearance propositions, not only is none of our perceptual knowledge about a proposition being a law, none of it is knowledge about physical objects. The support for (4′) exactly parallels the support for (4); it is initially

104

hard to see how any knowledge about physical objects could arise from a series of good inferences if physical object propositions do not reduce to pure appearance propositions.

My discussion at the end of Chapter 2 made the following simple point: Since little has been more obvious in the recent history of philosophy than that phenomenalism is false, the argument for phenomenalism's similarities[15] with the argument for Humeanism greatly diminish the appeal of the latter. Though I find this reason enough to reject the argument for Humeanism, I shall now try to say exactly where this argument goes wrong. It should come as no surprise that my guide will be some of the well-known replies to the argument for phenomenalism. Curiously, it turns out that, despite their similarities, the two arguments may go wrong for slightly different reasons. I urge the reader to be patient. Before getting to the best reply to the argument for Humeanism, some time is spent sifting through a couple of interesting, but more limited, replies. The more limited replies contain many grains of truth that help to dull the initial glow of the Humean argument. Furthermore, it is only by appreciating their limitations that the need for what I see as the best reply can be fully comprehended.

b. Direct realism

In contrast to the psychological picture that has sense impressions producing beliefs of pure appearance propositions from which we then infer material object propositions, Thomas Reid suggested that our sensations directly produce material object beliefs.[16] One attraction of this reply is that it eliminates all concerns about the nature of the inference to physical object knowledge; according to the Reidian picture, there is no such inference. Another attraction is

15 Of course, the analogy is not exact. For example, the first premise of the argument for phenomenalism is more general than the first premise of the argument for Humeanism. The former concerns knowledge of any *physical object* having *any ordinary property*, whereas the latter is about any *proposition* having *one single property*, namely, lawhood. Clearly, this difference is irrelevant to the conclusions I want to draw based on the similarities between the two arguments. More interesting differences, which are discussed in the text, involve the support for (3) and (3′).

16 See Reid's *An Inquiry into the Human Mind* (1970 [f.p. 1813]). As the title of this section suggests, this reply is sometimes known as *direct realism*. It has been adopted by Armstrong (1961) and others.

that it suggests a less intellectual picture of belief formation. Despite what some have maintained, it is doubtful that, in ordinary perceptual situations, very many people believe *any* pure appearance propositions. Prima facie, it is only upon careful reflection – reflection often prompted by epistemology teachers – that we ever form any pure appearance beliefs. Denying that all perceptual knowledge is knowledge of pure appearance propositions also has a moderately important result for the argument for Humeanism: It undermines one traditional source of support for the argument's third premise. This consequence is only moderately important, because premise (3) still has the two other sources of support. As I said, some philosophers sympathetic to Reid's point still accept that all perceptual knowledge contains only concepts that have a corresponding sensory appearance. Others, including me, accept the third premise simply because lawhood is too recondite. Evidently, this is one point where the analogy between our two arguments breaks down. The Reidian reply is extremely damaging to the argument for phenomenalism, but it only dents the argument for Humeanism.

There may, however, be a roundabout way of extending the Reidian reply. It begins by denying that all perceptual knowledge is comprised only of concepts with a corresponding sensory appearance. Though this denial is not *required* to undermine the argument for phenomenalism, some of the same considerations that make Reid's point attractive carry over reasonably well. Then, while it is still implausible to think that lawhood is part of any of our perceptual knowledge, it is not implausible to think that other less abstruse nomic concepts are. So, for example, even if there is no appearance of causation, we may still have perceptual knowledge of causation in certain distinctive cases. Upon being in the presence of, say, one billiard ball striking another, one might come to know directly from perception that the collision caused the ball to move. A host of background beliefs would surely play some role in the formation of this belief, as they do in the formation of all beliefs. What I am suggesting is that the observer need not make an *inference* from any other beliefs to the causal knowledge.[17] It is also

17 That causation can be known directly by perception has been closely associated with the work of Anscombe (1971). Armstrong (199?) apparently wants to adopt a stronger position than the one I find attractive, holding not only that causation can be known noninferentially, but also that there is something like a sensory

plausible to think that some knowledge involving certain other key concepts arises a little less directly from perception. For example, suppose that upon bending a wooden slat at noon, someone comes to know directly that it is flexed at noon. She can then deduce that it is *flexible* at noon. Or again, a cognizer may come to know directly that *a* is red and that *b* is yellow. Then, she can make a good deductive inference to the subjunctive conclusion that if *a* were red, then *b* would be yellow. I recognize that these are special cases. It is much harder to see how anyone could know a subjunctive with a false antecedent and a false consequent, or how anyone knows of a slat, not flexed, that it is flexible. But this does not undermine the point I am about to make. My suggestions about knowledge of causation and these other concepts call premise (4) of the argument for Humeanism into question. The irreducibility of lawhood only suggests that it is impossible to analyze lawhood *in solely nonnomic terms;* as far as my arguments go, there could be an analysis of lawhood using some nomic terms. If there is, then the gap between perceptual knowledge and our knowledge involving lawhood could be bridged by a deductive inference from our perceptual knowledge of causation or our slightly less direct knowledge of some other nomic concepts.

Though I find this extended Reidian reply deserving of further investigation, it probably does not tell the whole story. This reply may garner an undue appearance of plausibility from the common thought that the nomic concepts are more or less interdefinable. But, as will become clear in Chapter 5, this familiar idea is actually quite doubtful. Thus, I doubt there is a *sufficiently interesting* nomic analysis of lawhood, one that could deductively bridge the gap between knowledge of lawhood and the more easily obtained nomic knowledge. In addition, this extended Reidian reply suggests that an analysis of lawhood (albeit nonreductive) has a direct and central role in our coming to know of a proposition that it is a law. On the contrary, the only interesting analyses of lawhood not trivially mistaken, be they reductive or not, are complicated beasts, and hence are not the sort of thing that plays any serious role in our reasoning. Furthermore, in a plausible and suitably basic case of knowledge involving lawhood presented at the end of this section,

impression of causation. Fales (1990) agrees with Armstrong on this point but goes still further, maintaining that our concept of causation originates in our phenomenal experience. For criticisms of Fales's arguments, see Carroll (1992).

it is clear that the subject does not make a deductive inference to her belief of a proposition that it is a law.

c. Inference to the best explanation (IBE)

Another well-known, but less promising, reply to the argument for phenomenalism maintains that knowledge about material objects arises from pure appearance propositions via an inference to the best explanation (cf., Goldman 1988; Vogel 1990). I find this reply less promising than the Reidian reply for a couple of reasons. For such an inference to take place, the inferred belief must *seem to explain* the propositions from which it is inferred *better* than any competing hypothesis, and it is not clear that ordinary physical object beliefs do so; evil genius and brain-in-the-vat hypotheses have many explanatory virtues. Furthermore, depending on how the position is filled in, depending on exactly what an IBE is supposed to be, the IBE reply *may* imply an excessively intellectual picture of belief formation, not only in assuming that all perceptual beliefs are beliefs of pure appearance propositions, but also in the suggested nature of the inferences. At one extreme, it would suggest that upon being faced with an assortment of pure appearance beliefs, each of us *consciously* considers many competing hypotheses and *consciously* judges which best explains the sensory data. But nothing like this goes on except in the mind of the occasional misguided philosopher. And, even if it *never* went on in *anybody's* mind, there would still be ever so much knowledge of the external world.

The IBE reply is as credible, if not more credible, when applied to the argument for Humeanism. It is plausible to think that for some *P*, a belief that *P* is a law seems to explain the content of the beliefs from which it was inferred (e.g., the belief of *P* itself and/or various counterfactual beliefs). There is also *less* danger that treating inferences to lawhood as inferences to the best explanation would overintellectualize anything; discovering what the laws are is a somewhat sophisticated and demanding task. So maybe some knowledge involving lawhood does arise via an IBE. If it has even once, then the fourth premise of the argument for Humeanism is false. Nevertheless, this reply has certain limitations. I agree with John Earman (1984, p. 199) that such an inference to lawhood would be unlike more paradigmatic inferences to the best explanation. Furthermore, though the danger of overintellectualizing may not be *as bad* as it was when our concern was with the formation of material object beliefs, it may still be bad enough. How serious the threat is again depends on exactly what an IBE is supposed to be. If one requires much conscious reasoning, then it is at least psychologically unrealistic to suppose that knowledge involving lawhood is *typically* obtained in this manner. In that case, the IBE reply would not be a terribly revealing response. We would like our response to the argument for Humeanism to say something about knowledge involving lawhood generally.[18]

d. Chisholm's realism

It was Roderick Chisholm (1977, pp. 126–127) who offered the reply to the argument for phenomenalism that, to my mind, suggests the most promising and revealing reply to the argument for Humeanism. Thinking that physical object knowledge arises by an inference from pure appearance propositions, he needed to say how this could be the case even if physical object propositions do not reduce to pure appearance propositions. But he also believed that these inferences do not conform to any of the approved sorts of inductive or deductive inferences. Undaunted, he had the good sense to deny that all the good forms of inference had been approved. According to Chisholm, some inferences to physical object beliefs simply make up another class of good inferences, a class that has not received much attention.

Though Chisholm's reply to the argument for phenomenalism is superfluous if one accepts the Reidian reply, something like his approach is needed for the argument for Humeanism. We philosophers too often exaggerate our own ability to identify the good kinds of inferences. I can see no reason to assume, as the Humean apparently does, that the only good nondeductive inferences must take the form of either a simple enumerative induction or an infer-

18 If even a tacit transition from one set of beliefs to another satisfying certain minimal explanatory constraints could be an IBE, then this reply may not be all that different from the one I favor. You may recall that, in Section 4.2, I even proposed a minimal explanatory constraint on certain sorts of ordinary inductive inferences. As 'inference to the best explanation' is *ordinarily* understood, however, my constraint is not sufficiently strong to qualify these inferences as IBE's.

ence to the best explanation. It is not as if there have been any clear successes in characterizing the nature of even these inferences. In this general area, the only clear successes have been in work on deductive *logic,* and it is not even clear that this work has very much to do with the nature of deductive *inference* (cf., Harman 1986, pp. 1–20; Goldman 1986, pp. 81–89).[19] In sum, being in the epistemological dark, as we are, it would be presumptuous to assume that all the good inferences conform to the small group approved by Humeans. Frequently, knowledge of a proposition that it is a law does arise via an inference from perceptual knowledge despite the irreducibility of lawhood. Premise (4) of the argument for Humeanism is false. That we cannot show it to be false by classifying the fundamental inferences with any of the approved kinds of inductive or deductive inferences is no great surprise.[20]

There are a variety of ways to persist in arguing that I am faced with some serious skeptical problem. For example, one might argue that, given the irreducibility or nonsupervenience of lawhood, there must be something the matter with an inference to the conclusion that *P* is a law, since nothing *could prove me wrong.* This particular argument clearly breaks down. There are many things that I might come to know that would contradict a conclusion of the form that *P* is a law; I might come to know that *P* is false, or I might come to know some counterfactual proposition that contra-

---

19 As I see it, logic is a mathematical investigation of the relationships between propositions, statements, sentences, or something of that ilk. A theory of inference would specify the conditions under which certain sorts of mental state transitions are rational (or give rise to knowledge). Of course, deductive logic is relevant to the formulation of any theory of deductive inference. My point is only that the well-known advances in deductive logic should not be mistaken for successes in stating a theory of deductive inference.
20 My agreement with Chisholm does need to be tempered. As I imply above, I do not accept his assumption that all perceptual knowledge is knowledge of pure appearance propositions. In addition, he goes on to suggest that there is a kind of logic of perceptual inference, or at least a set of epistemological rules describing good perceptual inferences. I do not believe that there is an analogous set of rules characterizing the inferences leading to knowledge of a proposition that it is a law. Indeed, I doubt that these inferences are rule-governed in any interesting sense; the rules (if they exist) play no role in our reasoning. For these reasons, it is probably misleading to speak of *inferences* at all. What I contend is that there are certain *belief transitions* that cannot be identified with any of the approved sorts of deductive or inductive inferences. Nevertheless, if these belief transitions are of the right sort, they do give rise to knowledge of a proposition that it is a law.

110

dicts that P is a law.[21] In general, I suspect that additional episte-mological concerns of this sort also rest on mistakes. Nevertheless, what may lie behind any remaining feeling that some skeptical problem exists for my position is an argument that is taken up in Chapter 6. As I demonstrate in that final chapter, it is possible to describe certain hypothetical situations in which – given my real-ism about lawhood – P could be a law and yet there also would be little or no evidence either for or against P's lawhood. In an impor-tant sense, one *can't* know P is a law in such situations. I deny, how-ever, that this reveals any problem for the nonsupervenience of lawhood, or any other aspect of my position. In fact, as I argue in Chapter 6, in a distinctive way, it supports my overall stance.

e. Almost anything goes

What may worry some about my response to the argument for Hu-manism is that it leaves me open to a further concern. Because of the epistemological posture embodied in my reply, some may worry that *anything goes*. There are many inferences that do not fall under any of the approved sorts of inductive or deductive inferences and that are also *bad* inferences, ones that *do not* culminate in knowl-edge. For example, suppose that Brown has few, if any, back-ground beliefs about the chance of life on Mars. He has heard the term 'Martian' used and knows what it means, but he is agnostic about whether Martians exist. In fact, he is pretty much an astro-

---

21 Though I do not discuss it in the text, I have heard another epistemological con-cern that takes off from the *causal impotence* of lawhood. Lawhood is causally im-potent in that for all P and all Q, P's being a law does not cause Q. The natural contrast here is with physical object propositions. Ordinary physical object facts are part of the causal nexus, and – in particular – do cause human cognitive states. For example, one cause of my believing that there is a computer in front of me is the fact that there is a computer in front of me. Supposedly the causal impotence of lawhood makes it mysterious how our beliefs involving lawhood could be knowledge. I find this concern far less troubling than the argument for Humeanism. It is difficult to say exactly what the problem is that is brought on by lawhood's causal impotence. (It has proved difficult to formulate a plausible causal constraint on knowledge that is not terribly *ad hoc*.) But, if there really is a problem, it is clear that it is not brought on by the irreducibility of lawhood. None of the reductive analyses considered in this book, and certainly no other remotely plausible reductive analyses of lawhood, have the consequence that lawhood is causally potent. Furthermore, insofar as there is a problem, it also arises for nearly all nonskeptical theories of value, modality, and mathematics. There is no epistemological problem of peculiar interest to us stemming from lawhood's causal impotence.

111

nomical ignoramus. One evening, upon experiencing a bright light on the horizon, he forms the belief that there is a bright light out there. Based on this belief, he infers there are Martians. Now, surely, without a rich set of unusual background beliefs about Martians and bright lights, Brown's inference is a terrible inference. He does not know there are Martians. Indeed, Brown would lack this knowledge even if, surprisingly, his belief turns out true.

This further concern adds an interesting twist to our discussion. Whereas at first the fear was that anti-Humeanism prevented us from having certain sorts of knowledge, now the concern is that other sorts of knowledge come too easily. The Reidian reply to the argument for phenomenalism faces a similar added challenge. Not every perceptual belief, not even every true perceptual belief, constitutes knowledge. For instance, true perceptual beliefs that are not knowledge can arise in the midst of a drug-induced hallucination. So, just as I apparently need to say what the difference is between *good* and *bad* inferences, a Reidian apparently needs to say what the difference is between *good* and *bad* perceptual processes. Indeed, analogous concerns can be raised about any psychological processes putatively giving rise to knowledge. Therefore, the Humean's further concern is just one part of a much more general worry about the difference between good and bad belief-forming processes. This is the deep and very difficult epistemological problem forecast at the beginning of this section; indeed, it is *the* central problem in epistemology. The plausibility of my position on lawhood clearly does not depend on my providing a solution. In order to revive the argument for Humeanism, the Humean must show that there is something *about my position on lawhood* that prevents this problem from being solved. Clearly, this has not been accomplished.

Although I am not able to specify the conditions under which a belief constitutes knowledge, I can cite several important features of Brown's inference that distinguish it from ordinary inferences to knowledge of lawhood. At least some of these features are certainly *relevant* to the difference between good and bad belief-forming processes, and so provide a formidable obstacle to any attempt to argue that my anti-Humeanism prevents me from acknowledging such obvious instances of irrationality as Brown's belief in Martians. For example, beliefs involving lawhood occur in accordance with an established *belief-forming practice* to which we have all been exposed. This practice has given rise to a *coherent, resilient,* and largely *irre-*

sistible corpus of beliefs. Contributing to these three features of the corpus of beliefs is the fact that the practice – by its own lights – has permitted many successful *predictions*. Brown does not form his belief in Martians according to any established belief-forming practice. Furthermore, any corpus of beliefs that might be formed in accordance with such a practice (if there were one) would surely lack the coherence, resilience, and irresistibility accompanying our nomic belief-forming practice. Support for these brief speculations about the difference between good and bad belief-forming processes comes from the problem of the external world. It is plausible to think that the reason that only some true perceptual beliefs constitute knowledge also has to do with our exposure to an established belief-forming practice. The beliefs formed according to this practice form a corpus of beliefs that is coherent, resilient, and largely irresistible. It is one that by its own lights permits successful predictions to be made.

f. A case of knowledge

To reinforce my earlier discussion, I conclude this final portion of Chapter 4 by presenting a plausible case of a person's coming to know of a proposition that it is a law. This would be a simple task except that most knowledge involving lawhood arises either from the testimony of others or via a deductive inference from some prior knowledge already involving lawhood. Humeans, however, have not worried about our ability to acquire knowledge of lawhood in either of these ways. Nor do they fret about our ability to gain such knowledge based on prior knowledge involving other nomic concepts. What worries the Humean is how knowledge of a proposition that it is a law arises from *scratch*. Beware that in trying to describe a case of lawful knowledge that even approximates a case from scratch, I have bent over backward to meet the Humeans on their own terms. The plausibility of my realism certainly doesn't depend on my providing such an example. After all, no real-life investigators begin to test a claim of lawhood ignorant of all nomic facts. If we could explain how new data in conjunction with the nomic information we already have warrant conclusions about what the laws are, then surely that would be more than enough. We would have "met all the epistemic demands that it is reasonable to impose on such claims" (Woodward 1992, p. 188).

113

Let us suppose that Jones is interested in the conditions under which X-particles have spin up. Starting out, she has few, if any, relevant nomic beliefs. She begins by subjecting one X-particle – particle b – to a Y-field and determines that it has spin up. She observes other X-particles outside of Y-fields, many have had spin down, and all of these particles have acquired spin up upon entering a Y-field. She repeats her experiments many times with other X-particles. Throughout her investigations, every X-particle in a Y-field that she sees has spin up. Being a good scientist, Jones varies the experimental conditions – she varies the source of her X-particles, she puts two X-particles in a Y-field (at one time), she subjects some of the X-particles to a Z-field before putting them in a Y-field, and she has created the Y-fields used in her experiments six different ways. Jones eventually forms the belief that all X-particles subject to a Y-field have spin up – she believes L_1. Several factors encourage this belief. First, there is the usual enumerative induction – Jones has seen many X-particles in Y-fields, and each has had spin up. Second, she has taken note of the great variety of conditions under which the experiments transpired. Third, L_1 has the virtue of simplicity – it is at least simpler for her than some other hypotheses; for example, the hypothesis that all X-particles subject to a Y-field either have spin up or are made of maple syrup. Fourth, L_1 has a certain amount of strength for Jones – it permits her to deduce, what are for her, interesting conclusions. Fifth, L_1 does not contradict anything else Jones believes. Only because there is all this going for it, Jones believes L_1. Surely, if this generalization is indeed true and the situation is otherwise fairly ordinary, she *knows* L_1.

At some point in her experiments, perhaps concurrently with her coming to believe L_1, Jones forms some counterfactual beliefs. For example, on one afternoon, she may have had a large sample of X-particles. She may have planned to subject each member of the sample to a Y-field, but became bored halfway through. Knowing that the remaining X-particles came from the same source as those already tested, and knowing that they have many other similarities with the tested particles, Jones believes that the next X-particle in the sample – particle c – *would* have spin up if it *were* subject to a Y-field. Again, many elements foster her belief. There are all the considerations that led her to believe L_1. There are the similarities

114

between particle c and the X-particles already tested. The counter-factual has certain virtues of simplicity and strength, and it does not contradict anything else Jones believes. Only because there is all this going for it, she comes to believe the counterfactual. Surely, if its true and the situation is otherwise normal, then Jones knows the counterfactual.

Jones's counterfactual belief about particle c together with her other beliefs make plausible other counterfactual beliefs, and many of these share the same important form. For example, she has reason to believe the counterfactual that if c were subject to a Y-field, then L_1 would (still) be true. She also believes that if particle b were subject to a Z-field and then put in a Y-field, then L_1 would be true. She believes that if b and c were subject to a single Y-field, L_1 would be true. In sum, for a wide range of propositions P, Jones believes that if P were the case, then L_1 would be the case. As a result, Jones forms the belief that L_1 is a law of nature. It may be that there are some other factors contributing to this belief involv- . ing lawhood. It has some of the same virtues of simplicity and strength as her belief of L_1 and as her counterfactual beliefs. It also does not contradict any of her earlier beliefs. Assuming that L_1 really is a law and that the situation is otherwise normal, it is plausible to think that Jones knows that L_1 is a law.[22]

22 Roy Sorensen has pointed out (in conversation) that Jones's knowledge, insofar as it really is knowledge, may depend on antecedently held, less salient, nomic beliefs. He feels that she must have prior nomic beliefs, perhaps beliefs involving lawhood or physical possibility, that permit her to form beliefs as to what are appropriate variations of the experimental conditions. It is not enough that Jones *in fact* has performed many appropriate variations; otherwise, her ensuing beliefs involving lawhood and the subjunctive conditional are arrived at too *accidentally* to be knowledge. Though my opinion is not terribly strong, I am inclined to think Sorensen is mistaken. So long as Jones has no beliefs to the contrary, no beliefs implying a proposition to the effect that the variations performed are somehow inappropriate, then it seems to me that she does know what I say she does. We do not want to overintellectualize scientific practice. In any case, even if Sorensen is correct, his point does not challenge my claim that the example is a case in which the relevant knowledge arises from scratch. Even he does not think that these less salient nomic beliefs must qualify as *knowledge* for Jones to have her nomic knowledge. So long as the background beliefs are sufficiently rational, Jones knows that L_1 is a law. Though Woodward (1992, pp. 208–210) understands knowledge of lawhood in a way that would make him sympathetic to much of my description of Jones's reasoning (and so I find much of his discussion supportive), he not only agrees with Sorensen but wants to go a step further, apparently requiring that the less salient nomic beliefs constitute knowledge.

This example reinforces my reply to the argument for Humeanism. Without contradicting the irreducibility of lawhood, I have described a person who ultimately believes of some proposition that it is a law without basing her belief on any prior nomic knowledge – Jones gains the belief that L_1 is a law from scratch. Given the commonsense practice employing lawhood, and especially given how we naturally think of laws as nonaccidental, it is very plausible to think that her belief qualifies as knowledge. Incidentally, it is important to remember that Jones's case is nothing like a typical case. We usually draw nomic conclusions based on prior nomic knowledge. Furthermore, I do not mean to suggest, even for those rare cases when someone does start from scratch, that anything like the slow and meticulous procedure followed by Jones is required. I wanted a case in which it was especially plausible that knowledge involving lawhood is acquired.

Let us leave the discussion of epistemology, and return to doing some conceptual geography, charting the connections that exist between the nomic concepts, sometimes saying what those connections are, and more often showing where the connections must be absent. Beginning in the next chapter, our focus is causation.

5

Causation

According to the Laplacean picture, it is as if God created our universe by specifying the initial conditions and the laws of nature. Then, given the Supreme Being's specifications, the entire history of the cosmos, *every fact,* was completely determined. Within this picture, causal facts receive no special treatment. Once the laws and the initial conditions are set, then so are such truths as that my striking the match caused it to ignite.[1] Because it depicts the causal facts as fixed in this way, we can think of the Laplacean picture as at least suggesting that lawhood (when taken together with certain particular facts) has important *causal entailments.* Ignoring other parts of the picture (like its portrayal of our world as deterministic), we should wonder if the particular suggestion about the relationship between lawhood and causation is accurate. Does being a law

---

1 The verb 'to cause' can apparently be predicated of objects, events, and many other sorts of things. For convenience, I have chosen to focus on sentences that apparently relate two states of affairs:

   (a) John's striking the match caused the match's igniting.

As I see it, however, sentences that ostensibly relate states of affairs can be paraphrased using the sentential connective 'because'. For example, sentence (a) is equivalent to:

   (b) The match ignited because John struck the match.

It also seems that sentence (a) is equivalent to:

   (c) John's striking the match caused the match to ignite.

For expository reasons, I assume as much, feeling free to move back and forth between constructions like (a) and (b), and this noun-infinitive form. None of what follows turns on the positions just adopted. Three recent discussions of the nature of the causal relata are Bennett (1988), Mellor (1987), and Lewis (1986, pp. 241–269).

117

of nature guarantee the presence of any causal truths? What about closely related nomic concepts? Does chance or the counterfactual conditional have causal repercussions?

Let us draw a distinction that parallels Chapter 1's distinction between the nomic concepts and the nonnomic concepts. Let the *causal* concepts be the ones that have both extremely direct and very obvious connections with causation. Here I primarily have in mind causation itself and its very close nomic cousins like production, bringing about, and (causal) explanation. The *noncausal* concepts include the three nomic concepts mentioned toward the end of the previous paragraph (i.e., lawhood, chance, and the counterfactual conditional) as well as all the nonnomic concepts. Some dispositions belong on one side of the causal/noncausal line, and some belong on the other. There certainly are some complex dispositions (e.g., being disposed to cause fires) that belong on the side with causation. More ordinary dispositions, having less obvious and less direct connections with causation, are more at home with lawhood, chance, and the counterfactual conditional. Naturally enough, this new terminology has both some pluses and some minuses. Its primary advantage is that it permits certain key issues about causation to be formulated in a way that parallels the way certain important issues were raised in earlier chapters about lawhood. Its primary disadvantage is that it is potentially very misleading. Because of the label 'noncausal', one could easily think that the noncausal concepts have no conceptual ties with causation. That, however, is one of the issues still to be addressed. Just as it turned out that the bulk of our nonnomic concepts have nomic commitments, it could turn out that most of our noncausal concepts have causal commitments. If they do, then the causal/noncausal distinction just drawn would turn out to be a *mere* convenience that marks nothing of any metaphysical importance.

As this chapter develops, it should become clear that nearly all of the noncausal concepts do have causal commitments, and among the many that do are the key noncausal nomic concepts: lawhood, chance, and the counterfactual conditional. In fact, causation exhibits centrality among the noncausal nomic concepts in much the same way that the nomic concepts exhibit centrality among our nonnomic concepts. With regard to our total conceptual apparatus, causation is at the center of the center. We might have expected this had we paid a little closer attention to some examples from earlier chapters. My many illustrations of the centrality of the nomic typically also illustrate the centrality of causation. For example, the nomic commitment of *persistence* revealed in Chapter 1 is also a causal commitment. As I say there, no material entity exists at two different times unless there is an entity that exists at one of those two times that is *causally* linked to an entity that exists at the other time. Analogously, the previously revealed nomic commitment of *reasoning* is also a causal commitment. As I point out in Chapter 4, we have reasoned only if the resulting judgment is *caused* by other mental states.

Though causation is pivotal to our conceptual framework, we should be careful not to overestimate the conceptual ties between it and our noncausal concepts. The ties are not so strong as to permit an identification of causation with any concoction composed solely of noncausal notions. Indeed, as I see it, the Laplacean picture is misleading insofar as it suggests that the laws together with the surrounding conditions *fix* the causal facts. Just so, in this chapter I argue for an overall view about causation's relationship to the noncausal that is similar to my overall view regarding lawhood's relationship to the nonnomic. In particular, I defend an analogous nonsupervenience thesis: the proposition that there are at least two possible worlds agreeing on all the noncausal features instantiated by P and Q though they disagree on whether P causes Q.[2] I call this thesis *the independence of causation*.[3] This nonsupervenience thesis is

2 This position is also defended by Woodward (1990), very briefly by Foster (1979), and to some extent by Tooley (1984, 1987, 1990). (Not surprisingly, Tooley advocates a platonistic account of causation. It is not nearly as developed as his platonistic account of lawhood, but I reject it for similar reasons. My criticisms of his account of lawhood can be found in Appendix A.) Though they do not explicitly draw all of the same conclusions, Scriven (1971) and von Wright (1974, 1975) present examples with many important similarities to those I use to establish the independence of causation. Ducasse (1969 [f.p. 1924]; 1974 [f.p. 1926]) and Anscombe (1971) are both well known for insisting that laws are not conceptually prior to causation, but Ducasse would probably have denied the independence of causation. He offered an arguably nonnomic analysis of causation (1974, p. 116). Anscombe may have been more sympathetic (see p. 1).
3 Please don't read anything into this grandiose name. The independence of causation could simply have been called *the nonsupervenience of causation*. But, I wanted to be sure that it was distinguished from the weaker nonsupervenience claim about causation made at the end of Section 3.2. The difference between these two

at odds with much of the recent literature; many do accept that causation is reducible to noncausal concepts. In doing so, they manage to adopt a position that has the virtue of being weaker than the stance demanded by empiricist scruples; their favored analyses, far from being couched solely in terms free of nomic commitment, typically invoke nomic terms. But, as the arguments of this chapter show, they do not go far enough.

In Section 5.1, before giving three separate arguments for the independence of causation, I start the chapter off with a look at the causal commitments of the noncausal nomic concepts. While taking this look, I also introduce three simple, yet highly influential, noncausal analyses of causation.[4] In their primary role, the analyses serve as an illustrative focus, helping to reveal what it is about causation that prevents its supervenience on the noncausal base. In their secondary role, these analyses – and their susceptibility to a few basic counterexamples – provide some separate support for the conclusion that causation does not reduce to noncausal concepts. Of course, a much more thorough argument for this result that did not first establish the independence of causation would include a whole series of counterexamples to each of the analyses, and to each of the many natural ways of revising them. This argument would do for analyses of causation what my second chapter does for analyses of lawhood. As this is not a book mainly about causation, I won't be nearly that thorough. Still, we should keep in mind that the irreducibility result is significantly weaker than the independence of causation. It may hold even if, much to my surprise, independence does not.

claims concerns the size of the relevant subvening bases. In Chapter 3, the relevant base included only the nonnomic concepts. In this chapter, the relevant base has been expanded to include the noncausal nomic concepts as well. Actually, 'the independence of causation' is a poor name for this chapter's nonsupervenience thesis. Independence is really a two-way street: If F is independent of G, then F does not depend on G and G does not depend on F. But, as I have stated it, the independence of causation is a one-way thoroughfare.

4 There are at least two familiar sorts of analyses of causation that I do not discuss: manipulability theories and transference theories. The former are associated with the work of Collingwood (1940), Gasking (1955), and von Wright (1971). Defenders of the latter include Aronson (1971) and Fair (1979). These theories have had less impact on recent philosophy than the analyses discussed in the text. To my mind, they provide much less reason for thinking that causation is analyzable in purely noncausal terms. For an excellent critical discussion of transference theories, see Ehring (1986).

5.1 THE CAUSAL COMMITMENTS OF NOMIC DEPENDENCIES

To uncover (at least in a rough way) the causal commitments of the key noncausal nomic concepts, I devote much of this section to a discussion of the counterfactual conditional's conceptual ties with causation. By focusing on this conditional, it is possible to present similar thoughts about chance and lawhood more briefly.

There is an initially plausible principle that, if it were true, would reveal a causal commitment of the counterfactual conditional. It says that for all states of affairs P and Q, if (i) P obtained, (ii) Q obtained, and (iii) if P had not obtained, then Q would not have obtained, then P and Q were casually connected or P and Q had a common cause or P and Q had a common effect.[5] Since this principle is rather unwieldy, and since similar principles will be offered below, it will be helpful to introduce a little more terminology. Let us say that two states of affairs *belong to a single causal network* if and only if they were causally connected or had a common cause or had a common effect. Then, using this terminology, and giving our principle an appropriate name, we have

> *The One-Way Principle for the Counterfactual Conditional.* If (i) P obtained, (ii) Q obtained, and (iii) if P had not obtained, then Q would not have obtained, then P and Q belong to a single causal network.

All the principles and analyses to be discussed in this chapter should be understood as applying only when P and Q are distinct states of affairs. They should all begin with the restriction that P and Q are not identical. I don't make this restriction explicit in the text merely for convenience.

Perhaps tacitly finding the one-way principle enticing, some are also tempted by a stronger two-way tenet:

> *The Counterfactual Analysis.* P caused Q if and only if (i) P obtained, (ii) Q obtained, and (iii) if P had not obtained, then Q would not have obtained.[6]

---

5 I am invoking some standard jargon: P and Q were causally connected if and only if either P caused Q or Q caused P; they had a common cause if and only if there is an R such that R caused P and R caused Q; they had a common effect if and only if there is an R such that P caused R and Q caused R.

6 Lewis (1986, pp. 159–213), Pollock (1984, pp. 148–171), and Swain (1978) all defend more sophisticated counterfactual analyses of causation.

Of course, this analysis is very simplistic. It is always just a starting point for those who actually end up defending some counterfactual analysis of causation. For instance, it is almost always thought to need revision because causation is usually taken to be transitive, and counterfactual dependence usually is not. There are also some problems (discussed in a moment) that apply as well to the one-way principle. To my mind, none of these commonly raised issues seriously threaten a counterfactual reduction of causation. Some have limited ramifications, because the analysis is easily revised so they no longer apply. Others simply are not nearly as compelling as they first appear. My discussion should be more revealing if we stick with the simple biconditional displayed above, not cluttering it with technical clauses or subtle provisos.

Though I ultimately reject the counterfactual analysis, I am sympathetic to the one-way principle. It is threatened *only* by some of the problems mentioned in the previous paragraph and, as mentioned, these problems aren't devastating. Here is a sampling of those difficulties. According to the received view about counterfactuals, any subjunctive conditional with an impossible antecedent is true. So, on this view, everything counterfactually depends on every necessarily obtaining state of affairs, and hence the one-way principle absurdly implies that every necessarily obtaining state of affairs belongs to a single causal network with every other obtaining state of affairs. Or, suppose that Q counterfactually depends on P. Then, as a matter of logic, it follows that for any R, Q counterfactually depends on the disjunction of P and R. But, it looks like we would be hard-pressed to accept, as the one-way principle requires, that Q and the disjunction of P and R belong to a single causal network. On a related note, many will be troubled by our one-way principle's implication that many *negated* states of affairs (e.g., my not running a four-minute mile) are causes or effects. Finally, consider this well-known example:

When Socrates expired in the Athenian prison, Xantippe became a widow. The onset of Xantippe's widowhood was determined by the death of Socrates. As we might say, Xantippe became a widow in consequence of, as a result of, or in virtue of Socrates' death (Kim 1974, pp. 41–42).

Of course, had Socrates not died, Xantippe would not have become a widow. But, despite this counterfactual dependence, and the relations that do hold between Socrates's dying and Xantippe's becoming a widow (e.g., the in-consequence-of relation), some believe that the causal relation does not relate them. Some even take this strong conclusion another step, denying that Xantippe's becoming a widow has any causes at all (cf., Kim 1974, p. 49).[7]

If these issues present deep problems for the one-way principle, then they also present serious problems for the counterfactual analysis. But, as I have said, I want to set them aside. In part, this is because *some* of these problems seem to me not to be terribly serious. For example, about the Xantippe case, I just don't see how Xantippe can become a widow *as a result of* or *in consequence of* Socrates's death, but not become a widow *because* of Socrates's death. And, I am not at all troubled by the result that negated states may be causes and effects. After all, though the corresponding sentence might be an uninformative thing to say, isn't my not running a four-minute mile at least one cause (among many others) of my lack of athletic fame? In any case, even if I am wrong, these supposedly noncausal connections between things like Socrates's death and Xantippe's becoming a widow or my not running a four-minute mile and my lack of athletic fame are still a lot *like* causation. They are still thoroughly modal, thoroughly nomic, and thoroughly directed determinations. They are so much like causation that they couldn't threaten the one-way principle (or the counterfactual analysis) in any manner that is particularly pertinent to this book.

There are a couple of other reasons for setting these less serious problems aside. First, these problems all seem to have something to do with subtle questions about what sorts of things can be causally related. Since this chapter is on the causal relation, not its relata, a detailed discussion of the objections would be quite tangential.[8] Second, there simply is not enough riding on the one-

---

7 Strictly speaking, to use Kim's example against the one-way principle for the counterfactual conditional, one must also be prepared to hold that the two pertinent states of affairs do not have any common effects. Even if that's not a very tempting thing to say about this example, one can easily imagine other cases for which it is plausible. For example, we need only add to the original case that Xantippe's becoming a widow has no effects. Perhaps the universe comes to a sudden end just after Xantippe becomes a widow.

8 Indeed, some may already be wondering what all the commotion is about. Most philosophers focus on *events* as the causal relata. Not having much in common with paradigmatic events (e.g., a wedding), necessarily obtaining, disjunctive, and negated states of affairs are conveniently excluded from these philosophers' consideration.

way principle to justify any additional discussion of these problems. The principle will help us to identify what causation brings to our conceptual framework over and above what is delivered by the other nomic concepts. But, for these purposes, we could even rely solely on a vague, but still informative, restriction of the principle. If we restrict our attention to run-of-the-mill, *eventlike,* states of affairs, then counterfactual dependence has at least the causal commitment required by the one-way principle.

Turning our attention away from the counterfactual conditional, and turning it toward chance, let us say that P *raises* the chance of Q if and only if the conditional chance of Q given P is greater than the unconditional chance of Q. Then, this kind of probabilistic dependence appears to have some causal commitments that are identical in form to the causal commitments of counterfactual dependence.

> *The One-Way Principle for Chance.* If (i) P obtained, (ii) Q obtained, and (iii) P raised the chance of Q, then P and Q belong to a single causal network.

As is true of the one-way counterfactual principle, there is an influential sort of analysis of causation that is made somewhat enticing by the sensible reflections that make the one-way principle for chance tempting. One very simple instance of this sort follows:

> *The Probabilistic Analysis.* P caused Q if and only if (i) P obtained, (ii) Q obtained, and (iii) P raised the chance of Q.[9]

Not surprisingly, there are some minor concerns about the one-way probabilistic principle and the probabilistic analysis that appear to center on questions about the causal relata. (For example, one negated state of affairs can raise the chance of another.) I shall continue to ignore these relatively minor sorts of issues.[10]

What about lawhood? Introducing a little more terminology, I shall say that P is *lawfully sufficient* for Q if and only if it is physically necessary that if P obtains, then Q obtains. Employing this concept, we do well to consider

9 More sophisticated probabilistic analyses have been offered by Salmon (1980), Suppes (1970), Humphreys (1989), and others.

10 As it turns out, however, there is also a more interesting and more pertinent reason for rejecting this one-way principle. It is given in Section 5.3. As we'll also see in that section, there is another very similar principle that can be sustained.

The One-Way Principle for Lawhood. If (i) P obtained, (ii) Q obtained, and (iii) P was lawfully sufficient for Q, then P and Q belong to a single causal network.

Again setting aside the relata problems, we can move quickly to consideration of a corresponding analysis. Following the pattern we have before, you would expect to see the proposal that

P caused Q if and only if (i) P obtained, (ii) Q obtained, and (iii) P was lawfully sufficient for Q.

This analysis, however, is pretty pathetic. In fact, it is too obviously false to serve even the modest illustrative role I intend for it. After all, in an ordinary situation, my striking a match would cause it to light even though my striking it would not be lawfully sufficient for its lighting. We can, however, formulate a more interesting analysis that still is stronger than the one-way principle for lawhood. Just so, one might take a cause to be part of a larger condition, one whose parts jointly suffice for the effect. This is the intuition behind

The Subsumption Analysis. P caused Q if and only if (i) P obtained, (ii) Q obtained, and (iii) P was lawfully sufficient in the circumstances for Q.[11]

There are serious problems in saying more precisely what it is for P to be lawfully sufficient *in the circumstances* for Q. After all, not just any part of a more encompassing condition lawfully sufficient for an effect causes that effect. But, the rough idea is simple enough: My striking the match is lawfully sufficient in the circum-

11 My discussion of the subsumption analysis owes much to Scriven (1971, p. 52). Given such a simple formulation, it would be inappropriate to associate this particular statement of this account (or any of the analyses discussed in this section) with any philosopher. Nevertheless, all of the following authors defend an analysis that can appropriately be taken to be *some form* of the subsumption analysis: Braithwaite (1927, p. 470), Pap (1962, p. 255), Mackie (1974b, pp. 29–58), Taylor (1963, p. 298), and – on behalf of Hume – Beauchamp and Rosenberg (1981). Some of these philosophers defend what are often called *necessary and sufficient conditions analyses*. It may be unfair to take them to be defending a subsumption analysis, since these analyses are often spelled out in terms of the counterfactual conditional rather than lawhood or physical necessity. Incidentally, Kim (1973) provides a careful and extremely useful discussion of the subsumption approach.

stances for its lighting because the circumstances do in fact include oxygen being present, the match being dry, etc.[12]

In line with the three one-way principles, I believe that the noncausal nomic dependencies between two states of affairs P and Q guarantee (or at least guarantee that there is a chance[13]) that P and Q are causally connected or have a common cause or have a common effect. But, as I see it, the noncausal nomic dependencies between P and Q need not determine anything further about how P and Q are causally related. So, I stop short of those who take the next step and advocate causation's supervenience on the noncausal concepts or, worse, advocate its reducibility to those concepts. At first glance, this may seem like a very small thing that can be left out by the noncausal nomic concepts. On the contrary, as I shall argue, it is exactly the sort of thing that can make a very big difference with regard to what other parts of our conceptual apparatus are instantiated.

Just to whet your appetite, let us think once again about one of our more mundane concepts. In Chapter 1, I suggested the following as an approximate truth about *tables:* For something to be a table, it must be capable of supporting other things. This showed very clearly that tablehood at least has some nomic commitments. But, as we can now see clearly enough, it also shows that it has causal commitments: The notion of support that is being appealed to here has an obvious one. After all, for it to be the case that x supports y, x must in some way *cause* y to continue to occupy some spatial position (or some range of spatial positions) relative to x. It is not enough for y merely to be in that position (or range of positions). Nor is it enough for x and y to occupy their relative positions because of some common cause. If the world were either of *these* ways, then x *wouldn't* support y; x might not be capable of supporting *anything at all*. The difference between causing, on the

12 Even setting aside the problems about the causal relata, the probabilistic analysis and the subsumption analysis, like the counterfactual analysis, are usually just starting points for investigations of causation. They are in obvious need of refinement. As I recommended with the counterfactual analysis, rather than build in the standard revisions, we should leave these two analyses as they are. I want to investigate the most basic intuitive support for the analyses, not to have to worry about sticky details.
13 The need for this parenthetical hedge is discussed at the end of Section 5.3. It stems from the interesting objection to the one-way principle for chance also alluded to in footnote 10.

Before   After

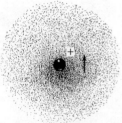

Figure 5.1

one hand, and, on the other hand, merely belonging to a single causal network is absolutely critical to whether one thing supports another. Evidently, this seemingly small difference is also absolutely critical to whether anything is a table. Thus, it's beginning to look as if what can be left undetermined by the instantiation of the noncausal nomic concepts may matter very, very much.

5.2 LAWFULLY EQUIVALENT EPIPHENOMENA

Suppose some source emits particle c. Further, as happens about half the time in such cases, the emission immediately creates a Y-field enveloping c. At the same time, the emission causes c to have spin up. Then, c's having spin up has no further effect on c – that causal chain ends. The other chain continues: Because it is subject to a Y-field, c acquires positive charge. (See Figure 5.1.) What makes this case especially interesting is the presence of two laws: It is a law that something is subject to a Y-field if and only if it simultaneously has spin up, and it is also a law that something is subject to a Y-field if and only if it immediately gets positive charge. In this first example, c's having spin up and c's having positive charge are *lawfully equivalent epiphenomena*.

Though it doesn't present any problem for any of the one-way principles,[14] this case clearly presents problems for two of our three analyses. Consider the subsumption analysis. Since c's having spin up was *lawfully sufficient* for c's having positive charge, it trivially

14 Dropping my helpful terminology, the one-way principles all have the following consequent: P and Q were causally connected or P and Q had a common cause or P and Q had a common effect. The epiphenomena case just given makes it

follows that the former was *lawfully sufficient in the circumstances* for the latter. Since these states of affairs also obtained, the analysis has the untoward consequence that c's having spin up caused c's having positive charge. Matters are exactly analogous concerning counterfactual dependence. It is plausible to think that if c hadn't had spin up, then it wouldn't have had positive charge.[15] (After all, if c hadn't had spin up, it wouldn't have been in a Y-field.) So, the counterfactual analysis has the same mistaken consequence as the subsumption analysis.

In response, proponents of subsumption-style analyses may claim to have been misrepresented. In stating the subsumption analysis, I do not distinguish between *causal* laws and *noncausal* laws. These philosophers may insist there should be a specific appeal to causal laws within the subsumption analysis. But this is a rather weak response. It doesn't suggest a way to revise the analysis; simply insisting on an appeal to causal laws falls far short of offering an alternative formulation. In addition, it is not clear what a causal law is supposed to be. On the *natural* understanding, the concept of a causal law is a concept that includes the concept causation. For instance, on this understanding, one causal law is, say, the law that exposure of an X-particle to a Y-field *causes* it to have positive charge. This understanding, however, is unsuitable for those hoping to state the subsumption analysis in a way that appeals to causal laws. On the natural understanding, to be a causal law is

clear why this consequent needs its second disjunct. The primary example from Section 5.4 will make it clear why the first disjunct is needed. What about the third disjunct? It is needed because there are cases of *lawfully equivalent overdeterminers:* Suppose that P was lawfully necessary and sufficient for R and that P also caused R. In addition, suppose that Q, which is simultaneous with P, was also both lawfully equivalent to R and a cause of R. Then, P and Q might stand in all the relevant nomic relationships without being causally connected or having a common cause. They would, however, have a common effect. A case of lawfully equivalent overdeterminers (which doesn't happen to demonstrate why the third disjunct is needed) is discussed in footnote 18 of this chapter.

15 Indeed, this follows from the fact that c's not having spin up is lawfully sufficient for c's not having positive charge, the plausible assumption that c's not having spin up is physically possible, and our principle (SC) from Chapter 1. Remember that (SC) states that for all P and Q, if P is physically possible and physically necessitates Q, then Q would be the case if P were the case. Though he does not explicitly discuss lawfully equivalent epiphenomena, Lewis's discussion of epiphenomena (1986, p. 170) suggests that he would deny that c's having positive charge counterfactually depends on the c's having spin up. I defend (SC) in Appendix B.

to be a causal proposition that is a law. But, for a proposition to be a law, it must be true. So, given the natural understanding, any analysis of causation appealing to causal laws would tell us that the truth of causal propositions depends on the truth of causal propositions; such an analysis would be guilty of a vicious circularity. Perhaps there is some other interpretation of 'causal law' that avoids this problem, but we need to know what it is. Until we do, this sketchy response should be set aside. (In the remainder of this chapter, I stick with the natural understanding, taking causal laws to be laws that include the concept causation.)

There is another idea for dealing with lawfully equivalent epiphenomena. The starting point is the thought that there must always be some mechanism spatially and temporally linking the cause and the effect. With this in mind, one might maintain that P causes Q only if there is a causal chain of spatiotemporally contiguous states between P and Q, or P and Q themselves are spatiotemporally contiguous (cf., Nagel 1961, p. 74; Beauchamp and Rosenberg 1981, pp. 171–200; Bennett 1988, p. 46). The hope would be that our analyses would escape my counterexample if supplemented with this further necessary condition. This hope, however, is clearly misplaced. Obviously, there is no problem about the spatial contiguity of the states of affairs in my example; insofar as it is natural to assign them spatial location, they all are right around particle c and inside of that Y-field. I was a bit vague about when c acquires spin up and when c gets positive charge. Still, as far as the counterexample is concerned, it doesn't matter when these states obtain. They can be as temporally contiguous as you like – they can even be simultaneous – without diminishing the effectiveness of the example. Furthermore, it is a mistake to rule out the coherence of *action at a distance,* i.e., causation between spatially or temporally separate states of affairs for which there is no mediating causal chain. The classical conception of gravitation suggests such a possibility, and there even have been coherent scientific theories proposed for which the *only* action is action at a distance.[16]

What about the probabilistic analysis? The impact of our case on this analysis depends on the chance of c's having positive charge.

16 I owe this point to Suppes (1970, pp. 85–87). His example is Boscovich (1966 [f.p. 1763]). For further philosophical discussion of Boscovich's theory, see Campbell (1976, 86–94).

Suppose that this probability was one hundred percent. In fact, assume that our case of lawfully equivalent epiphenomena takes place in a deterministic world. Then the chance of every obtaining state of affairs is one hundred percent at all times. With this assumption, the probabilistic analysis at least appears to do better than the other two analyses. Since it already was as high as it could be, c's having spin up did not raise the chance of c's having positive charge. Thus, the analysis correctly recognizes these epiphenomenal states for what they are, implying that c's having spin up did not cause c's having positive charge. Nevertheless, it has this desired consequence only because of one of its severe limitations. According to this analysis, since the probability of c's having positive charge was one hundred percent, this state of affairs was uncaused. Indeed, since the chance of every obtaining state of affairs is one hundred percent at all times, our analysis implies that no states of affairs are causally connected in this or any other deterministic universe.[17]

When actually defended, the probabilistic analysis is always revised to deal with more ordinary cases of epiphenomena, cases not involving lawfully equivalent states of affairs. The revision requires that the cause raise the chance of the effect *when background factors are held fixed;* that is, the analysis is usually revised so that in any case of epiphenomena where P and Q are both caused by R, a necessary condition of P's causing Q is that the conditional chance of Q given the conjunction of P and R be greater than the conditional chance of Q given R. Clever though it may be, this familiar move is relatively inconsequential. If the probability of Q was one hundred percent, then – so long as the chance of R was greater than zero – the probability of Q given R was also one hundred percent.

Our example reveals the first of three ways in which causation is independent of the noncausal nomic concepts. This can be seen by recognizing that along with there being cases of lawfully equivalent epiphenomena, there are also cases of *lawfully equivalent cause and effect.* Indeed, our original example of lawfully equivalent epiphenomena includes one such case. In this case, c's being subject to a

---

17 Otte (1981, p. 176) raises a problem for Suppes's (1970) probabilistic analysis of causation involving epiphenomena. For additional discussions of the problems for probabilistic analyses involving zero and one probabilities, see Humphreys (1989, pp. 81–86) and Lewis (1986, p. 178). Otte's work (p. 180) also led me to see the significance of lawfully equivalent epiphenomena for all attempts to analyze causation.

Y-field is lawfully equivalent to and causes *c*'s having positive charge. Another very useful example parallels, but is not identical to, our epiphenomena case. Suppose that the emission of particle *c* immediately creates a *Y*-field surrounding *c*. At the same time, the emission causes *c* to have spin up. As you might expect, these two effects are lawfully equivalent. In fact, we may suppose that the noncausal laws are as they were in the original case. In this parallel example, however, *c*'s being subject to that *Y*-field has no further effect on *c*. In particular, it does not cause *c*'s having positive charge. Instead, *c* has positive charge because *c* has spin up. In this example, *c*'s having spin up and *c*'s having positive charge are lawfully equivalent cause and effect.

We see that at a crucial point in my description of the original case, I had an important choice. Having specified the sequence of states and the noncausal laws, another fact was yet to be specified. On the one hand, it could have been that *c*'s having spin up did not cause *c*'s having positive charge; these two states of affairs could have been lawfully equivalent epiphenomena. This is how the critical causal fact was specified in the initial example. On the other hand, it could also have been that *c* had positive charge because *c* had spin up. Then, *c*'s having spin up and *c*'s having positive charge would be lawfully equivalent cause and effect. This is how the critical causal fact was specified in the more recent parallel example.[18] (Of course, this is just the sort of choice that our one-way principles leave open. It is only the full analyses that say that the nomic dependencies close out all but one of the causal hypotheses.) Since there are these two worlds in noncausal agreement about *c*'s having spin up and *c*'s having positive charge, the independence of causation follows.

Placing the two key cases in direct contrast to one another may make the reader uneasy. The differences between these cases begin to look "purely verbal"; there do not seem to be any *real* or *substantial* differences between (i) the initial example where *c*'s having spin up and *c*'s having positive charge are lawfully equivalent

---

18 There is really a third relevant possibility. It could be that *c*'s having spin up does cause *c*'s having positive charge, though it is also true that *c*'s being subject to a *Y*-field causes *c*'s having positive charge. *c*'s having positive charge would be both lawfully and causally overdetermined. In his arguments for the irreducibility of causation, Scriven (1971, pp. 61–62) emphasizes overdetermination cases and deemphasizes epiphenomena cases (in his terms, cases involving a "pathognomonic symptom" (p. 52)).

epiphenomena, and (ii) the more recent parallel case where these two states of affairs are lawfully equivalent and causally connected. It will be well worth our while to take a few paragraphs to discuss this uneasiness; those afflicted by it may experience it again when I present my two remaining arguments for the independence of causation.

The same kind of uneasiness could attend almost any interesting nonsupervenience argument. Indeed, it may have accompanied my arguments about lawhood in Chapter 3. But, any feeling of uneasiness that might have accompanied those earlier arguments was much less evident, and consequently much less disturbing. In part, this difference is a result of lawhood being much less *isolated* in Chapter 3 than causation is in this chapter. With the nonsupervenience of lawhood, it is really the nonsupervenience of all (or nearly all) the nomic concepts that is at issue; causation, explanation, chance, the counterfactual conditional and at least some dispositions fail to supervene on the nonnomic facts just as does lawhood. As a result, the other nomic truths of the worlds establishing the nonsupervenience of lawhood, especially those worlds' counterfactual truths, are extremely helpful in getting a handle on how lawhood is instantiated in those worlds. With the independence of causation, however, it is really not much more than the nonsupervenience of causation that is at stake. So, there is much less to give us a grip on the causal facts in the key examples. Furthermore, because of lawhood's special connections with the counterfactual conditional, the structure of Chapter 3's nonsupervenience arguments is different from the structure of the arguments given in this chapter. In Chapter 3, in giving each nonsupervenience argument, we were able to begin with two worlds not contradicting the supervenience of lawhood, and then "move" to the nonsupervenience worlds. This may have helped to minimize any feeling of uneasiness about the nonsupervenience worlds. In this chapter, this sort of indirect approach is not readily available.

While I acknowledge the uneasy feeling that arises when the initial epiphenomena example and the parallel cause and effect example are placed side by side, this uneasiness shouldn't be given any weight in our theorizing about causation. The uneasiness arises from the fact that these two examples in combination highlight a feature of causation that we don't often have to confront. But it is also a feature we pretty much have to acknowledge. Let me explain.

132

Our typical causal judgments are about what might be called *secondary* causation. For many of our true causal judgments, the causation is between states of affairs that are neither spatially nor temporally close to each other. Oftentimes, there are even some *go-betweens* (e.g., sound waves, strings, or electric pulses) that almost seem to *carry* the causation from the cause to the effect. When there are such intermediaries, we have one sort of case of secondary causation. Even when our true causal judgments are about causes and effects that are in close proximity, say a case where one billiard ball strikes another, there are typically other more basic objects and events that are responsible for the more macroscopic causal truth. With the billiard balls, it's the atoms of the first billiard ball doing something to the atoms of the second billiard ball. When there are such underlying causally related states of affairs, we have a second sort of case of secondary causation. Regardless of whether our concern is with an instance of the first or second kind of secondary causation, we naturally think of the further causal facts about the go-betweens or the further causal facts about the underlying states of affairs, or both, as what are responsible for or constitute the secondary causation.

That our typical causal judgments are about secondary causation is at least part of what accounts for our thinking of causation as something very substantial, and as not the sort of relation that could be acting in the way I say it does in the two examples constituting my first argument for the independence of causation. Nevertheless, it doesn't take too much careful thought to realize that it couldn't be necessarily true that all causation is like this. We must also admit the possibility of *primary* causation. We cannot legislate a priori that there is no causation between contiguous states of affairs that consist of certain fundamental entities exemplifying certain basic physical properties. As a result, we must admit that there could be causation between two contiguous states of affairs though there is no underlying causation and no mediating causal chains that account for it.

The possibility of primary causation is a possibility that, on an abstract or theoretical level, most of us are willing to admit. But, when theorizing in this way, it is easy not to notice what primary causation would be like. It really would be bare or insubstantial in ways the causation we usually encounter is not. My first argument for the independence of causation puts this intangibility on display.

133

When the two examples are placed side by side as an argument for the independence of causation, one realizes that there can't be much of anything that accounts for where the causation lies in the initial example where c's having spin up and c's having positive charge are lawfully equivalent epiphenomena, or for where the causation lies in the parallel case where these two states of affairs are lawfully equivalent and causally connected. In the initial epiphenomena example, nothing accounts for why c's being subject to that Y-field, rather than c's having spin up, caused c's having positive charge. In the parallel case, nothing accounts for why c's having spin up, rather than c's being subject to that Y-field, caused c's positive charge. Still, there is nothing wrong with the two key examples. They do establish the independence of causation. To maintain a sober view of how our own world might be, to allow for the seemingly real possibility that there are true atoms with truly basic physical properties standing in unmediated causal relations, we must be willing to admit the possibility of primary causation.[19]

5.3 PROBABILISTIC CAUSATION

My second argument for the independence of causation involves causation's *behavior in chancy situations*. The argument begins with a description of a certain subatomic barrier: In some ways, this barrier behaves deterministically. For example, it is a law that if an electron strikes a barrier of this sort, then the electron is annihilated. It is also a law that particles emerge from this sort of barrier only if an electron has just been destroyed – at least one annihilated

---

19 In a way, my reply to the fear that there are only "verbal" differences between the initial epiphenomena example and the parallel case of lawfully equivalent cause and effect is similar to the reply I give to the insightful concern considered at the end of the first section of Chapter 3 about the genuine possibility of U_1 and U_2. As you may recall, this concern questions how particle b and its Y-field could be so similar in U_1 and U_2 – agreeing as they do on their nonnomic features prior to b's entering its Y-field – and yet b have spin up in U_1 and not in U_2. There, I pointed out that b could surely be a fundamental particle and its Y-field could surely be a fundamental field whose differences in behavior in U_1 and U_2 are explained by nothing else besides the basic laws of nature in these two worlds. Thus, in U_{1*}, but not U_{2*}, there is a fundamental law of nature governing the behavior of b and its Y-field. Here, in my cause and effect example, but not the original epiphenomena example, there is as fundamental a causal connection linking c's having spin up and c's having positive charge.

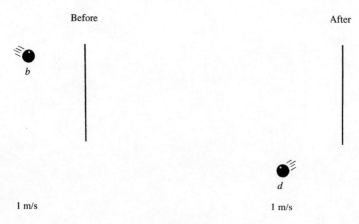

Before   After

b

1 m/s   1 m/s

Figure 5.2

electron for every emerging particle. Finally, it is a deterministic
law that any emerging particle has the speed of a just-destroyed
electron. In other ways, the barrier acts indeterministically. Here is
one unimportant example of its indeterministic behavior: Though
new particles usually emerge from the barrier shortly after an electron collision, they don't always.

Before completing my description of the barrier, let's consider
one possible interaction. Suppose that electron *b* is heading southeast, toward the barrier, at a speed of one meter per second. A collision takes place, *b* is destroyed, and then shortly thereafter a new
particle, particle *d*, is heading southwest, away from the barrier.
(See Figure 5.2.) The governing deterministic laws require that *d*
have a speed of one meter per second. What is a little unusual about
the barrier is that it works a little like a two-way mirror. When an
electron strikes it, there is a chance that the emerging particle (if
there is one) will travel away from the barrier in the direction that
the original particle would have traveled had it been reflected by
the barrier. There is an equally good chance that any emerging particle will travel away from the barrier in the very same direction
that the incoming particle was traveling; in other words, along the
line that the incoming particle would have traveled had it passed
through the barrier. Thus, in the case just depicted, though what
actually happened was that *d* emerged heading southwest, there
was a chance that another particle, particle *e*, would emerge heading southeast.

135

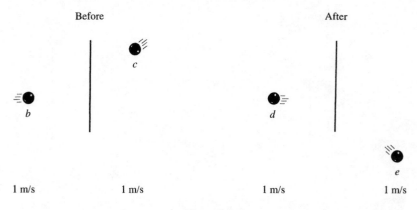

Before   After

c

b d

e

1 m/s   1 m/s   1 m/s   1 m/s

Figure 5.3

Though there are more interesting cases to discuss, even this first case is a problem for the subsumption analysis. Despite the obviously indeterministic nature of the barrier, it is clear that b's striking the barrier with a speed of one meter per second heading southeast caused d's emerging with that same speed heading southwest.[20] Yet, because of the accompanying indeterminism, b's striking the barrier was not lawfully sufficient, not even in the circumstances, for this effect. The attending circumstances could have been exactly as they were up to the time of the collision and it be the case that d not emerge at all. So, the subsumption analysis has the result that b did not cause d. This analysis is not prepared to handle even the simplest cases of chancy causation.

As I indicated, there's a further feature of the barrier. As I'll now specify, this feature is that the barrier works in much the same way even when two incoming particles simultaneously strike opposite sides of the barrier. In illustration, let's consider a pair of double-particle collisions. Suppose two electrons, b and c, both come in with a speed of one meter per second; b heading east, c heading southwest. Then, d emerges with b's speed heading west, while e emerges with c's speed heading southeast. (See Figure 5.3.) If this

20 In all the cases discussed in this section, my concern is with whether b's striking the barrier with such and such velocity causes d's emerging with so and so velocity. Since it is a bore to type, and an even greater bore to read, something like 'b's striking the barrier at a speed of one meter per second heading southeast caused d's emerging at a speed of one meter per second heading southwest', I will almost always shorten this down to 'b's striking the barrier caused d's emerging'

136

Before   After

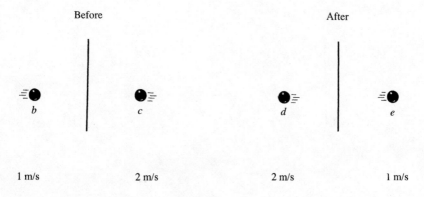

1 m/s   2 m/s   2 m/s   1 m/s

Figure 5.4

were the case, then we would not hesitate to draw some specific
causal conclusions: for example, that *b* caused *d*. For our second
two-particle collision, suppose *b* and *c* both come in perpendicular
to the barrier. Traveling at different speeds, they still strike the barrier simultaneously. In this case, *d* emerges with *c*'s speed and direction; while *e* emerges with *b*'s speed and direction. (See Figure
5.4.) Again, it would be very natural to draw some causal conclusions; for instance, that *c*'s striking the barrier caused *d* to emerge,
while *b*'s striking the barrier did not. Though I won't go through
the details, like our first simple case, these two double-particle
cases present a counterexample to the subsumption analysis.

At last we are ready for the key case, the case that presents problems for all three analyses. Suppose two particles strike the barrier
with exactly the same speeds traveling in opposite directions. Before the collision, *b* is heading east with a speed of one meter per
second; *c* is heading west with the same speed. At precisely the
same time, the two particles strike the same spot on opposite sides
of the barrier. After the collision, particle *d* is heading west at one

or even to '*b* caused *d*'. Keep it in mind that I am employing this rhetorical device. Otherwise, confusion will surely occur. Were I not employing it, b*'s striking
the barrier* and b*'s striking the barrier with such and such velocity* would be two
different states of affairs. As such, they could stand in distinct counterfactual,
lawful, and probabilistic relations. Incidentally, it is merely for convenience that
I always ask whether any causal connections hold between *b* and *d*. In most of
the cases discussed in this section, there are many causal hypotheses worthy of
consideration.

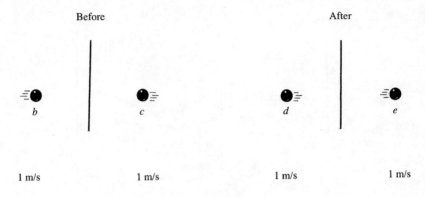

Before   After

b   c   d   e

1 m/s   1 m/s   1 m/s   1 m/s

Figure 5.5

meter per second; particle *e* is heading east at the same speed. (See Figure 5.5.) As seems quite certain, this key example admits of two completely distinct, and perfectly coherent, further specifications. One is that *it is b's striking the barrier that causes d's emerging*. Another, equally good, is that it is only *c*'s striking the barrier that does so, in which case it would be true that b's *striking the barrier does not cause d's emerging*. That these are both genuine possibilities is a natural conclusion to draw based on the conspicuous symmetry of this case and given our judgments in the other double-particle cases.[21]

In thus admitting that it is possible that *b* causes *d*, and that it is also possible that *b* does not cause *d*, we welcome trouble for our three analyses. Consider first the world in which *b* caused *d*. Since *b*'s striking the barrier is not lawfully sufficient in the circumstances for *d*'s emerging, the subsumption analysis mistakenly implies that *b* did not cause *d*. The counterfactual analysis fares no better: If *b* had not struck the barrier, then *d* might still have emerged, and thus it is not the case that if *b* hadn't struck the bar-

---

21 My argument resembles arguments given by Woodward (1990, pp. 214–216), Tooley (1987, pp. 199–202), Foster (1979, pp. 169–170), and Scriven (1971, pp. 62–64). Woodward's, Tooley's, and Scriven's arguments are much more abstract than mine, for the most part stating only the probabilistic connections that need to hold between the states of affairs. Foster's argument, like mine, is more specific. The primary advantage that my argument has over his is that it does not essentially involve any action at a distance. For no very good reason, some may be bothered by this aspect of his argument. Incidentally, my example also has certain similarities with Mackie's candy machine example (1974b, pp. 42–43).

138

rier, then *d* wouldn't have emerged.[22] So, this analysis also mistakenly implies that *b* did not cause *d*. The probabilistic analysis is undermined by the possible world in which *b* didn't cause *d*. Because *b*'s striking the barrier raised the chance of *d*'s emerging, about this world, this analysis incorrectly says that *b*'s striking the barrier *did* cause *d*'s emerging.

These two possible worlds work so well in combination against the three analyses because together they constitute an argument for the independence of causation. The first is a world in which the barrier is governed by the laws described, the relevant counterfactual and probabilistic connections hold in the way described, and *b* caused *d*. The other is a world in which this barrier is governed by the laws described, the relevant counterfactual and probabilistic connections hold in the way described, and yet *b* did not cause *d*.[23]

22 This is the one spot in the text where I reluctantly rely on a standard assumption about subjunctive conditionals. It is clearly true about this case that if *b* hadn't struck the barrier, then *d* *might* have emerged. It is usually assumed that this conditional is equivalent to its not being the case that if *b* hadn't struck the barrier, then *d* *wouldn't* have emerged. I rely on this equivalence to move from the clearly true *might*-conditional to the not-so-obvious negation of the *wouldn't*-conditional. It's this negation that is needed to show that *d* doesn't counterfactually depend on *b*. If the standard equivalence assumption is false, as Stalnaker (1984, p. 143) contends, then the barrier example may not establish the independence of causation from the counterfactual conditional. Of course, the barrier example would still succeed in other ways. It would still show the independence of causation from both lawhood and chance. It would also still undermine the overall position of philosophers who adopt a counterfactual analysis and the usual equivalence thesis.

23 Maybe there are infinitely many kinds of barriers. At one extreme, there are the *pure direction reflectors*. They never produce a new particle on the opposite side of the barrier, the side away from the incoming particle. So, were particle *b* to strike this kind of barrier heading southeast (as the lone incoming particle), there would be no chance of any new particle emerging with that same direction; any new particle that did emerge would have to emerge heading southwest – that is, in the reflected direction. At the other extreme, there are the *pure direction preservers*. They ensure that any emerging particle emerges on the other side; they never produce the new particle on the same side as the incoming particle. Between these two extremes is a continuum of other kinds of barriers, including our original sort of perfectly symmetric barrier that gives an equal chance to a new particle coming out either side. Now, in the key case, if the barrier were a pure direction reflector, then the causal connections would be determined: *b*'s striking the barrier would cause *d* to emerge. If the barrier were a pure direction preserver, the causal connections would also be determined: *c*'s, but not *b*'s, striking the barrier would cause *d* to emerge. Nevertheless, whenever the barrier is neither a perfect direction reflector nor a perfect direction preserver, we have an argument for the independence of causation. About all these cases, it is plau-

There are aspects of my general description of the barrier that are in line with the three one-way principles from Section 5.1. For example, in the case where there was only one incoming particle, d's emerging is lawfully sufficient for some particle's having just been destroyed, and these two states of affairs are also causally connected. I bring up the one-way principles because the probabilistic one is undermined by certain chancy situations. James Woodward (1990, p. 217) and Michael Tooley (1990, p. 229) describe a nonsupervenience example in which one state of affairs raises the probability of another though the states need not belong to a single causal network: Suppose that Q had some chance of obtaining spontaneously, of obtaining without being caused. Yet P might still have made Q more likely. Given that P and Q both did obtain, there seem to be two equally good possibilities. There is the possibility that P *caused* Q. But there is also the possibility that, though P raised the chance of its occurrence, Q *occurred on its own*. It is this latter possibility that presents the problem for the one-way principle for chance. In this situation, P raised the chance of Q. Yet, since Q was uncaused, P and Q could not have had a common cause. Since it is also true that Q did not cause P, it is also true that P and Q were not causally connected. Since P needn't have any effects at all, P and Q might have had no common effects.

I believe that this example shows that the one-way principle for chance cannot be exactly analogous to our one-way principles for lawhood and the counterfactual conditional. Still, we can accept a very similar, but weaker, principle for chance:

> *The Revised One-Way Principle for Chance.* If (i) P obtained, (ii) Q obtained, and (iii) P raised the chance of Q, then there was some chance that P and Q belong to a single causal network.

Not only is this revision weaker than the original, it attributes a much weaker sort of causal commitment than do any of our other one-way principles. Take, for instance, the one-way counterfactual

---

sible to think that it is possible *that* b *causes* d and that it is possible *that* b *doesn't cause* d. Indeed, in all these cases, not only are both hypotheses possible, both even have some nonzero chance of obtaining.

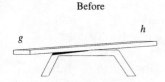

Before

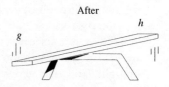

After

Figure 5.6

principle. According to it, a counterfactual dependence between obtaining states of affairs P and Q requires that P and Q belong to a single causal network; so, in particular, it requires that there was at least some *causation* in the world. The revised principle for chance, however, says that a probabilistic dependence between two obtaining states of affairs only requires that there be a certain *causal truth:* For P to raise the chance of Q, there must be some *chance* that P and Q belong to a single causal network. So, unlike lawful and counterfactual dependence, there can be probabilistic dependence without any actual causation whatsoever.

5.4 INSTANTANEOUS CAUSATION

Causation's *directionality* is what determines which of any two causally connected states is the cause and which is the effect. My final argument for the independence of causation stems from the directionality of causation. One noteworthy feature of the argument is that the two possible worlds differing on their causal facts and agreeing on all noncausal facts are such that, in one world, one state of affairs causes a second state of affairs while, in the other world, that second state of affairs causes the first.

Standard attempts to explain directionality invoke temporal considerations. One way to do this is to add to one's favorite analysis a necessary condition requiring that the time of the cause *be prior to* the time of the effect. But this would be a mistake. There are cases of causation between simultaneous states that would be ruled impossible by such a condition. For example, suppose there is a perfectly rigid seesaw (Figure 5.6) – when one end of the bar moves up or down, the other end moves in the opposite direction simultaneously. Also, suppose that I push down on side g and side h ascends. Then g's descending may instantaneously cause h's ascending.[24] It is no objection to this example to point out that such a perfectly rigid seesaw is physically impossible. It may well be: That there is a perfectly rigid seesaw moving in this way does contradict the generalization that no signals travel faster than the speed of light, and that generalization may be a law of nature. But an analysis of causation must be *necessarily* true; true in all possible worlds, not just the physically possible ones.

Some may find it hard to believe that for a single time t, g's descending at t causes h's ascending at t. Though they may be perfectly willing to admit that for some δ, g's descending at $t-\delta$ (t minus δ) causes both g's descending at t and h's ascending at t, they may deny the further claim of instantaneous causation. But it is hard to see what could motivate this denial. Very few arguments have actually been raised against the possibility of this sort of causation. Those who reject it usually want to defend some particular analysis of causation, and recognize that the possibility of causation between simultaneous states of affairs means trouble for their analysis. About this present case of instantaneous causation, I suppose that some might worry that the notion of a perfectly rigid seesaw is somehow incoherent. But, if they do, then their worry is misguided. I am merely assuming that the bar and fulcrum are perfectly solid, that they are completely inflexible. You can't bend them. You can't even dent them. The bar and fulcrum need only have one further significant feature, one that goes right along with their being perfectly solid: Whenever one side of the bar is raised or lowered, the other side moves simultaneously in the opposite direction. In any of this, wherein does there lie any incoherence?

Various considerations actually recommend the attribution of instantaneous causation. For one thing, without it, we would have to admit that action at a distance takes place in this situation. Side g's descending at $t-\delta$ would cause side h's ascending at t, but not *by* having any effect on g at time t. Nor would g's descending at $t-\delta$ cause h to ascend at t by causing any part of the bar between g and h to move at t. There would have to be a spatial skip in the causal chain between what went on at side g prior to t and what went on at side h at t. Whatever one feels about the *possibility* of action at a

24 Von Wright (1974, pp. 63–68; 1975, p. 108) presents an example involving a valve with a top that simultaneously closes as the bottom opens, and vice versa. This example has all the same key elements as my seesaw example. I started thinking about seesaws and instantaneous causation after reading Brand (1980).

distance more generally, it is rather unnatural to think it occurs in this situation. For another thing, denying that g's descending at t causes h's ascending at t is at odds with the many legitimate intuitions motivating our three analyses. For instance, consider the counterfactual analysis. (The same point could be made using any of our analyses.) If g hadn't descended at t, then h would not have ascended at t. So, without an additional condition ruling out the possibility of instantaneous causation, this analysis would imply that such causation is present. Thus, even by the lights of the counterfactual analysis, the causation should be there. Finally, there is just a strong intuition that g is *doing something* to h at time t. After all, were I to bump g sideways at t, h would swivel at t. If there were a laser splicing through the bar that completely severed the bar exactly at time t, h would move differently. How could any of this be the case if there were no causal connection between g and h at time t?

An alternative way to use the directionality of time to account for the directionality of causation is to require that the time of the cause *not be later* than the time of the effect. This condition does not exclude the possibility of instantaneous causation. But it also does not thwart all directionality problems. In fact, it does not allow our three analyses to avoid further directionality problems with the seesaw case just described. For example, consider the subsumption analysis. With the added necessary condition, it does appear to have the consequence that g's descending instantaneously causes h's ascending – g's descending appears to be lawfully sufficient in the circumstances for h's ascending. That's not the obstacle. The trouble is that h's ascending appears to be lawfully sufficient in the circumstances for g's descending. So, this analysis has the mistaken result that h's ascending causes g's descending. The counterfactual analysis and probabilistic analysis go wrong for much the same reason. Even with the additional necessary condition under consideration, all three analyses mistakenly say that the seesaw case is a case of *mutual causation* – that g's descending causes h's ascending, *and vice versa*.[25]

---

25 There may be another problem with invoking temporal considerations to account for the directionality of causation. Temporally backward causation may be possible. Both requiring that the time of the cause be prior to the time of the effect and requiring that the time of the cause not be later than the time of the effect rule out the possibility of temporally backward causation. But I shall set

143

Nearly everyone agrees that this is not a case of mutual causation. Some agree because they believe that all putative cases of mutual causation are impossible. Such a commitment can stem from a basic intuitive commitment to the asymmetry of the causal relation or from a desire to preserve the transitivity and irreflexivity of this relation (cf., Frankel 1986, p. 362). Others, myself included, agree that this is not a case of mutual causation for less general reasons. Consider our seesaw once again. Suppose that I push down on g with half the force used in the original example. As I do this, someone else lifts up on h, applying the same amount of force that I do, just in the opposite direction. (Since there are two forces, each of half the magnitude of the force applied in the original example, the seesaw moves exactly as it did before.) In the new example, it is somewhat plausible to think that at a time shortly after we have stopped pushing and lifting (and the seesaw is still moving), g's descending causes h's ascending, and vice versa. That h's ascending causes g's descending is part of the explanation of the motion of g, which is not explained just by the force I exert on g. When there are not two pushes, however, the hypothesis of causation from h to g does no work. As I am pushing on one end of the seesaw and the other end is left untouched, it is clear that the casual flow is completely in one direction; the hypothesis that there is causation from h to g is entirely superfluous.

There is a third standard attempt to account for the directionality of causation, one not appealing to temporal considerations. The general idea is that causation has a "circumstantial" character (Ehring 1982, p. 764). According to this idea, it is how states of affairs fit into the surroundings that determines which of two causally connected states is the cause and which is the effect. More specifically, this attempt to account for the directionality of causation plays on the following asymmetry. In most ordinary cases of causation, there are states of affairs that cause the effect and that are not causally connected with the cause. Assuming that causation is transitive, nothing that causes the cause fails to be causally connected with the effect. For example, if I strike a match and it lights, there are states that cause the match to light that do not cause me to strike

this problem aside. Given the especially controversial nature of backward causation, I have chosen not to use it in my arguments for the independence of causation.

the match. Yet, everything that causes me to strike the match also causes the match to light.

When most directly combined with any of our three analyses, this attempt to account for directionality takes those analyses as analyzing causal connection – instead of causation – and then would offer the following analysis of causation:

> P caused Q if and only if (i) P and Q were causally connected, and (ii) there is a distinct state of affairs R such that R caused Q, and R did not cause P.

As illustration, consider how this proposal would be combined with the counterfactual analysis. Suppose that I strike the match, the match lights, and surrounding conditions are normal. Then, my striking the match was *causally connected* with the match's lighting, because I struck the match, it lit, and if I had not struck the match, then it would not have lit. My striking the match *caused* the match to light, because those two states were causally connected and because there is a third state of affairs that caused the match to light but does not cause my striking the match.

As is obvious, this shot at capturing the directionality of causation is circular. Everyone taken with the circumstantial character of causation recognizes the need to develop one's account of directionality in some noncausal fashion. But, as is well known, simply replacing the word 'caused' by the phrase 'was causally connected with' does not suffice. Allowing for slight corrections in grammar, the resulting proposal would be:

> P caused Q if and only if (i) P and Q were causally connected, and (ii) there is a distinct state of affairs R such that R was causally connected with Q, and R was not causally connected with P.

The well-known problem is that there are usually side effects of the cause that are not causally connected with the effect. For example, suppose my striking the match had a side effect: It caused my finger to be scratched. Then, my finger's being scratched was causally connected with my striking the match and was not causally connected with the match's lighting. So, the proposal under consideration would falsely imply that the match's lighting caused me to strike the match. Attempts to remove the circularity must be much more sophisticated. I, for one, doubt that any of these more sophisticated attempts will succeed. We are trying to make good on an idea that forces us to provide a characterization of causation using only the nonnomic terms and noncausal nomic terms. Among other things, this requires an account of directionality, and that, after all, was the original problem. We evidently have made little progress in accounting for the directionality of causation.

My third argument for the independence of causation, which I am now ready to advance, is more complicated than the arguments offered in Sections 5.2 and 5.3. (It has a structure somewhat reminiscent of the arguments in Chapter 3 for the nonsupervenience of lawhood.) Consider one possible world, U_7, consisting only of that familiar seesaw and some entity to supply the force pushing (or pulling) down on side g. After the force occurs, the entity immediately goes out of existence. Let s be a time just after the entity goes out of existence, a time when g is descending. In U_7, side g's descending (at s) instantaneously caused h's ascending; h's ascending did not cause g's descending. Now consider a second world whose history overlaps with the first. It begins at some time before s, but after the force-supplying entity has gone out of existence. This world is otherwise in agreement with the first world. Let this new world be U_{7*}. U_{7*} is a *terminal segment* of U_7. It is plausible to think that in U_{7*}, g's descending instantaneously caused h's ascending; h's ascending did not cause g's descending. U_{7*} is one of the worlds constituting my third argument for the independence of causation. I still need to describe the other half of the example. Consider a possible world, U_8, consisting only of the seesaw and some entity that lifts (or pushes) up on h with a force equal to the force pushing down on g in U_7. The force-supplying entity goes out of existence in U_8 at exactly the same time that the force-supplying entity goes out of existence in U_7. In U_8, it is plausible to think that h's ascending (at s) instantaneously caused g's descending; g's descending did not cause h's ascending. Let U_{8*} be the terminal segment of U_8 that begins its history at the same time as U_{7*}. In U_{8*}, h's ascending instantaneously caused g's descending, and not vice versa.

U_{7*} and U_{8*} appear to be in close agreement. The seesaws are the only things that exist in the two worlds, and they move in exactly the same way at exactly the same time. The laws of the two worlds are the same. Relevant counterfactuals seem to agree: If g hadn't descended, then h wouldn't have ascended; if h hadn't ascended, g

146

wouldn't have descended. The probabilistic relations between the two states may be identical. (The worlds may be deterministic. Then, the chance of all obtaining states of affairs would be one at all times.) There are no noncausal characteristics of our two states of affairs accounting for the causal differences in $U_{7\star}$ and $U_{8\star}$. $U_{7\star}$ and $U_{8\star}$ are my final argument for the independence of causation.

5.5 CAUSAL COMMITMENTS CONFIRMED

My three arguments for the independence of causation affirm the speculations of Section 5.1: (i) The noncausal nomic dependencies between two states of affairs P and Q guarantee that, or at least guarantee that there was a chance that, P and Q belong to a single causal network. But, also: (ii) These dependencies need not determine anything further about how P and Q were causally related. Why (ii) holds should be perfectly clear from my earlier discussion, but it may not be as clear what about my arguments sustains thesis (i).

The support for (i) derives from our one-way principles. Focusing first on the argument of Section 5.2, it should be pretty clear how the original case of lawfully equivalent epiphenomena supports the one-way principle for lawhood. There are lawful dependencies all over the place and the corresponding causal networks required by the principle. For example, b's having spin up is lawfully sufficient for b's having positive charge, and it is also the case that these two states of affairs had a common cause: b's emission from the source. The support is just as straightforward for the counterfactual principle. Particle b's having positive charge counterfactually depends on b's having spin up, and – as I just said – they also had a common cause. Interestingly enough, as this case is presented in Section 5.2, it does not directly support (or weaken) either our original one-way principle for chance or the revision offered in Section 5.3. But that's only because, to make this case work as a counterexample to the probabilistic analysis (even given the standard refinements of that analysis), I assumed that all obtaining states of affairs have a one hundred percent chance at all times. Suppose instead that before b acquires spin up, the chance of b's having positive charge was seventy percent. So, b's having spin up raised this chance from seventy percent to one hundred percent. Just as is required by the original one-way principle for chance, these states belong to a single causal network; they had a common cause. The reader is welcome to search out aspects of the barrier example and the seesaw case that also support the three one-way principles. There are plenty of them. Here's one: In all the versions of the seesaw example, *h*'s ascending counterfactually depends on *g*'s descending, and in all these cases, these two states of affairs are also causally connected.

Given that the noncausal nomic dependencies between *P* and *Q* guarantee that, or at least establish that there was a chance that, *P* and *Q* belong to a single causal network, there is the appearance that only an insignificant morsel can be left undetermined by the noncausal nomic concepts. On the contrary, as I hinted at the end of Section 5.1, what is left over is exactly the sort of tidbit that can determine what sorts of things there are.

To see this, contrast two hypothetical cases involving our concept of *perception*. In the first example, I am standing directly in front of a burning lantern and, as usually happens in such a case, the glow of the lantern causes a familiar kind of visual image. In the second case, due to the presence of what might be called a *Gettier demon*, the glow doesn't cause the sensation. This demon is a mischievous relative of Descartes's nemesis who sees to it that humans end up with lots of (justified) true beliefs in very peculiar ways. In our second case, the glow of the lantern and my visual image are both present, just as they were in the first case, but the glow does not give rise to the image; they are merely the result of a common cause, that dastardly demon. Even if we suppose that in the second case there are all sorts of nomic dependencies between the glow and the image, *it is only in the first case that I have perceived the lantern's glow*. In the second case, I am the victim of an elaborate hoax; if I perceive anything at all, it is something along the causal chain leading to my visual image, not the lantern's glow.

Let's consider a very different example that also illustrates what can be left out by the noncausal nomic concepts. In Chapter 1, I suggested the following as an approximate truth about *materiality*: For something to be a material object, it must be impenetrable by a sufficiently wide range of (other) material things. Obviously, any such impenetrability has counterfactual and dispositional commitments. Less obviously, but, just as truly, it also has causal commitments: For an entity to be impenetrable, that entity itself must be disposed *to cause* a sufficiently wide range of objects that may collide with it to be stopped without penetrating it (too much or too far). If the entity in question merely has a disposition to be such that objects would not penetrate, perhaps because of the presence of something else that perfectly envelops it, that's perfectly consistent with its being ethereal. Thus, the difference between being a cause and merely being part of a single causal network is a difference that matters quite a lot.

At the beginning of this chapter, I introduced some terminology. I said roughly that the *noncausal* nomic concepts are those nomic concepts other than causation itself, explanation, and their most obvious neighbors in our conceptual space. The others are the *causal* concepts. We can now see very clearly that this verbal distinction corresponds to no significant distinction among our concepts; it is merely some convenient but misleading terminology. The centrality of causation to the noncausal nomic concepts, and the centrality of all nomic concepts to the rest of our conceptual framework, show that *on the ordinary use of the term 'causal'*, nearly all our concepts are *thoroughly causal;* they couldn't be exemplified without there being at least some causal truths. The only interesting exceptions, the only concepts without causal commitments, are the concepts that lack nomic commitments altogether.

The centrality of causation goes some distance toward explaining both why the various popular analyses of causation have some initial plausibility, and why they ultimately must fail. Since so many of our concepts do have substantial causal commitments, it is easy to think that the instantiation of some of these concepts like lawhood or chance or the counterfactual conditional could perfectly fix what the causal facts are. (Indeed, that is what is incorrectly suggested by one aspect of the Laplacean picture.) But, the nonsupervenience arguments of this chapter show that, in the end, this can't be right. Having realized that, and keeping in mind some obvious parallels with my earlier discussions of lawhood, the centrality of causation, far from supporting the analyzability of causation, actually bolsters my belief in the independence of causation. Twice now, where we have found centrality of a metaphysical concept, we have also met a corresponding lack of supervenience. This sort of discovery first occurred in Chapter 3 with respect to lawhood and its failure to supervene on our nonnomic concepts. Apparently, this very same sort of discovery has occurred once again, this time with respect to causation and its failure to supervene on the noncausal concepts.

6

The limits of inquiry

The arguments of Chapters 1 through 5 establish that lawhood and causation are subject to principles that, in a certain obvious respect, are perfectly parallel:

> *The Nonsupervenience of Lawhood.* There are at least two possible worlds agreeing on the nonnomic concepts instantiated by some proposition *P* and disagreeing on whether *P* is a law.

> *The Independence of Causation.* There are at least two possible worlds agreeing on the noncausal concepts instantiated by two states of affairs *P* and *Q*, and disagreeing on whether *P* causes *Q*.

In expressing these parallel doctrines, I employ some specialized terminology with which the reader, by now, should be familiar: The *nomic concepts* are the concepts with direct and obvious connections with lawhood. Key examples of the nomic concepts include lawhood itself, causation, and counterfactual dependence. The *causal concepts* are the nomic concepts with extremely direct and very obvious connections with causation. They are pretty much exhausted by causation itself and (causal) explanation.

Despite my arguments, I am sure that some remain unconvinced. Why is that? Stubbornness and other obviously objectionable reasons aside, I suspect that one minor obstacle is a concern stemming from a thesis I call *the supremacy of science.* It maintains that science will in a certain sense be *complete* – that scientists will discover or, in some strong sense of 'capable', are capable of discovering every fact there is.[1] Some may argue that my examples

---

1 This view is thoroughly entwined with the Laplacean picture. Thinking way back to Chapter 1, you might recall that the epistemological vision associated with this picture is that it is merely a matter of time and effort before all phenomena are embraced by science's laws.

supporting the nonsupervenience of lawhood and the independence of causation suggest that there are unknowable facts, and hence that science will be *incomplete*. Finding this absurd, these philosophers reject those examples, and as a result withhold assent from one, or perhaps both, of my key principles. As I shall argue, there is little that is compelling about this argument from the supremacy of science. Still, discussion of the argument will be useful because it will encourage some concluding reflections on both (i) the *epistemological sensitivity* of my metaphysics, indicating another interesting source of support for my position, and (ii) the *supremacy of philosophy*, which also is often presupposed but with considerably less justification than the corresponding thesis about science.

As it applies to the examples supporting the nonsupervenience of lawhood, the argument from the supremacy of science begins by noticing that some of the possible worlds described in Chapter 3, like U_{5*}, are *realistic*. (U_{5*} is the possible world in which there are X-particles, but no Y-fields, and it is a law, L_1, that all X-particles subject to a Y-field have spin *up*. The possible world in nonnomic agreement with U_{5*}, namely U_{6*}, also has X-particles and also lacks Y-fields, but it is a law, L_2, that all X-particles subject to a Y-field have spin *down*.) They are so realistic, the argument claims, that it is likely that there is a proposition P such that the nonnomic features *of the actual world* do not determine whether P is a law. So, for example, according to the argument from the supremacy of science, it is likely that events similar to the events of U_{5*} *actually* occur. It is likely that there are particles that are not subject to some kind of field, though it is a law that all particles subject to fields of that kind have some property. If such events do occur, and there really is a P such that the actual nonnomic facts about P do not favor either P's being law or P's not being a law, then it is hard to see how scientists, or anyone else, will discover whether P is a law. The argument concludes that my examples supporting the nonsupervenience of lawhood absurdly suggest that the science will be incomplete.

This argument works in the same way against the independence of causation. It begins with the observation that some of my examples supporting independence, like the barrier example, are pretty realistic. In the barrier example, two incoming electrons b and c strike the barrier perpendicularly on opposite sides of the barrier at the same time traveling at the same speed. Two new parti-

151

cles, *d* and *e,* emerge from the barrier. As this case is described, there seems to be a pretty good chance that *b* caused *d* and an equally good chance that *b* did not cause *d.* So, in one possible world, it is the case that *b* caused *d.* Though in another possible world in noncausal agreement with the first, *b* did not cause *d.* The argument from the supremacy of science contends that it is likely that there are events similar to those in the barrier example that actually occur. This is not to say that it is likely that there actually are barriers that interact with electrons in just the way described. Rather, the thought is that it is likely that there are actual situations *akin* to the barrier example, perhaps sharing its probabilistic structure. So, the concern is that there are states of affairs *P* and *Q* such that their actual noncausal features do not determine whether *P* caused *Q.* Suppose there are. How could scientists, or anyone else, figure out the causal truth about *P* and *Q*?

Why is the result that science will be incomplete viewed as absurd? It is so viewed, in large part, because of the great reverence we naturally bestow upon the sciences. (We'll eventually have to consider whether such reverence, insofar as it is appropriate, really warrants the supremacy of science.) But, the result that science will be incomplete may be viewed as absurd for another reason. The nonsupervenience of lawhood and the independence of causation are a priori philosophical theses. From the a priori arguments that support these a priori claims, the supremacy argument seems to derive an a posteriori conclusion – that science will be incomplete. *That* is especially disturbing. Philosophers not engaged in any empirical research ought not to be telling scientists how successful their theories can be. If the incompleteness of science follows from an a priori philosophical argument, then so much the worse for that argument. Fortunately, though my two nonsupervenience principles are a priori theses, the conclusion that science will be incomplete doesn't follow validly from the arguments supporting those principles. Even if not obvious at first glance, the argument from the supremacy of science contains an important a posteriori premise that, while perfectly compatible with the philosophy I've been advocating, certainly is no part of my philosophical position. The contained a posteriori premise is this: that at least some of the worlds I describe in support of the two nonsupervenience principles are *realistic,* that it is likely that certain sorts of events *actually* take place.

The a posteriori nature of the argument from the supremacy of science is disconcerting. I have no idea how likely it is that events similar to the events that take place in either U_{5*} or the barrier example will actually take place. Consider again the argument as it applies to the nonsupervenience of lawhood. Not being much of a physicist, I have no idea how likely it is that there is a certain sort of particle that has never been subject to a certain kind of field, though there is a law governing the behavior of that sort of particle when subject to that kind of field. As far as I know, there may be very few sorts of particles and very few kinds of fields. In that case, it may be very likely that particles of *every* sort have, at one time or another, been subject to every *kind* of field. But also, as far as I know, that may not be so.

Knowing that I am a philosopher and not a scientist, I shall not attempt to assess the a posteriori premises of the argument. Instead, I'll do something that's philosophically a lot more relevant to our discussion: In an attempt to make things difficult for myself, I shall suppose that the a posteriori premises of the argument from the supremacy of science are true. I'll suppose that there is a P such that, because conditions similar to the conditions in U_{5*} obtain, the actual nonnomic facts do not determine whether P is a law. Indeed, for convenience, I'll suppose that *exactly* what happens in U_{5*} happens in the actual world – that there are X-particles and Y-fields, that no X-particle is subject to a Y-field, and yet that it is a law, L_1, that all X-particles subject to a Y-field have spin up. I shall make analogous assumptions about the actual world and one possible completion of the barrier example. I shall assume that there actually is a barrier of the sort described in Chapter 5 – that b and c simultaneously and perpendicularly strike this barrier on opposite sides with equal, but opposite, velocities, and that, nevertheless, it is true that b's striking the barrier caused d to emerge.

In some sense, it *does* follow from these suppositions that science is, and will remain, incomplete. The evidential basis is too impoverished for the discovery of the pertinent nomic facts and causal facts. The available evidence does not favor that L_1 is a law or that it is not. It does not favor that b caused d or that b did not cause d. Still, an important question remains unanswered: Is this incompleteness reason to withhold assent from one of my nonsupervenience principles? I think not. Let me amplify on this thought.

153

If science is incomplete in this way, then we should not find this deficiency threatening. Indeed, and after all, there are a great many ways, each of them unremarkable and unworrisome, that our world could be such that scientists will not discover every fact. For example, conditions might not be right for the existence of beings of sufficient intelligence or sufficient sensory ability to discover every fact. For instance, suppose the laws and initial conditions were such that no intelligent beings ever exist. Atomic particles simply move about the universe colliding with each other, but nothing even capable of intelligence ever results. Then, not only would science be incomplete, it would be nonexistent. The world might also be such that only beings as smart as chimpanzees ever exist. They might be capable of something we might we willing to identify as a rudimentary science, but their science certainly would not be complete. This possibility, in turn, points to another more humbling possibility. In certain highly relevant ways, maybe we are like the chimps. Perhaps, only beings of much greater intelligence than us could advance an exhaustive science. If so, and if it turns out that no such beings exist, then, again, there'll never be a complete science.

Someone sympathetic to the argument from the supremacy of science may not be satisfied with this flurry of cases. While it does show that there are ways the world could be that would prevent science from being complete, and while it does show that this is in no way objectionable, it is not clear that the flurry of cases redeems the nonsupervenience of lawhood or the independence of causation. The limitations supposedly implied by the examples that support these two principles arise, it might be claimed, in a more troubling way. These limitations clearly do *not* arise because we are not sufficiently intelligent or because we lack requisite sensory abilities. They seem to arise because of the way the external world is, because of the way the world is independent of us.

Fortunately, there are other, more pertinent, examples. In these examples, the incompleteness of science arises in roughly the same way as does the incompleteness that, to make things difficult for myself, I am supposing is implied by my arguments for my two nonsupervenience principles: For example, it might be that a certain sort of particle existed only many millions of years ago, long before any intelligent beings evolved. These particles may have

154

entered into few interesting causal interactions, and hence may have had little effect on the way the universe turned out. Having no inkling of these particles, or any way of gaining an inkling of them, it's highly unlikely that scientists will discover any facts about them. So, science will be incomplete. The world would have been so arranged as to preclude the discovery of these facts. Similarly, it might be that certain particles exist in only distant regions of the universe, regions where no humans exist, and no other intelligent life exists. These particles may enter into few causal interactions, and hence may have had little effect on those parts of the universe with which humans are familiar. Having no knowledge of these particles, and having no way of gaining any information about them, scientists would not discover any facts about them. So, science would come up short. Again, the world would have been so arranged as to preclude the discovery of certain facts.

Here's a third example. Suppose that there's a certain event that's both uncaused and also that's at least very largely inefficacious. Then, science would not even acknowledge that event – in a pretty strong sense of 'could', no scientists could even discover that it occurred. As one last example, there's this: Scientists might want to know what happens on a certain date at a certain time as a result of a specific chancy astronomical process. They know that the result will be a quick flash of light, but they do not know what its intensity will be. They are paying close attention, monitoring their instruments very carefully, as the time approaches. When the time comes, the source supplying their instruments with electricity goes out, and they do not measure the intensity of the light. As a result, they will never know its intensity. They cannot discover what the result of the chancy process was at that time. Even if they could do so, recreating the conditions just prior to the blackout will not help. Since the process was chancy, there would be no way of knowing whether the new result matched the original result.

These four examples are particularly relevant to the question whether the argument from the supremacy of science poses a threat to either the nonsupervenience of lawhood or the independence of causation. The incompleteness in the examples is not due to any intellectual or perceptual shortcoming. Given the conditions, no amount of intelligence, and no added sensory capabilities, would help. Yet the resulting incompleteness is not particularly worrisome. It is also interesting to note about these cases that if they had been different in minor ways, then the undiscovered facts could have been discovered. For instance, if the electrical blackout had occurred a minute later than it did, then the scientists could, and almost certainly would, have discovered the intensity of that flash. Or, if conditions had been more conducive to the uncaused event being efficacious in ways that would have made it come under human observation, then someone could have discovered that it occurred.

In the four examples, the incompleteness is very similar to the incompleteness supposedly implied by my arguments for the nonsupervenience of lawhood and the independence of causation. As I said, the latter incompleteness seems to be a result of the way the "inanimate" world is. It is not due to any lack of intelligence or any lack of perceptual faculties. Furthermore, this incompleteness shares the other interesting feature of the four examples that we've recently noted: If history had been different in minor ways, the undiscovered facts would have been discoverable (and, in many cases, they'd even have been discovered). For example, if history had been just a little different, if several X-particles had gotten into a Y-field, then the undiscovered fact that L_1 is a law would be perfectly discoverable. Similarly, had things been a little different, if – for example – b had not struck the barrier at exactly the same time as c, and had d still emerged just after b was destroyed, then the unknowable fact that b caused d could have been known.

Thus, given certain ways the world could be, once we've made certain significant a posteriori assumptions, it's no (unwelcome) problem that science will be incomplete. And, as emphatically noted, the argument from the supremacy of science clearly has significant a posteriori premises. Now, as you'll recall, I've set aside the question of whether those premises are actually true. (If they're false, then the argument from the supremacy of science never gets off the ground.) But, even supposing that the premises *are* true, the argument *still doesn't* mean any trouble for the nonsupervenience of lawhood or the independence of causation. Despite first appearances, and despite the reverence with which philosophers have viewed science, it's clear that there are many ways the world could be that would preclude scientists from discovering every fact. What the truth of the a posteriori premises would mean is, simply, that one of those many ways had actually obtained.

Indeed, as I am inclined to think, the consequence that we wouldn't know whether L_1 was a law, and that we wouldn't know whether b caused d, are *attractive* features of my position. It shows that my position on lawhood and causation is an *epistemologically sensitive* approach. Certain other positions, notably many of the Humean positions (discussed in Chapter 2) and the positions analyzing causation using only noncausal terms (discussed in Chapter 5) are not sensitive in this way. Incorrectly, they suggest that we *could* know the "hidden" facts. Rather than shape my metaphysics so as to make our knowledge of lawhood and causation enticingly simple, I've respected the genuine epistemological limitations that can befall certain attempts to determine whether these concepts apply. It would be extremely presumptuous of us to think both that we are so endowed and that our world is so arranged as to permit knowledge of every fact. The various examples discussed in this chapter show that we may not be intelligent enough to discover every fact, that we may not have the requisite sensory abilities to discover every fact, and that events in the external world may occur in such a way as to prevent us from discovering every fact.

It would be as presumptuous to think that we can give an analysis of every philosophically interesting concept. Instead, the nonsupervenience of lawhood and the independence of causation require us to admit certain *philosophical limits*. In regard to one such limit, the nonsupervenience of lawhood suggests that a certain traditional sort of answer to the problem of laws is impossible: In terms free of nomic commitment, there is no way to specify the difference between laws and accidentally true generalizations. In regard to another philosophical limit, the independence of causation implies not only that an account of causation in solely nomic-free terms is impossible, but also that accounts using only noncausal terms are impossible. Empiricists see these limits as serious *limitations,* and question either the legitimacy of the respective concepts or the legitimacy of arguments forcing the restrictions upon us. But that, as I have argued, is a mistake. In fact, we should probably extend *at least* my antireductionism, if not (analogues of) my nonsupervenience theses, to a wide variety of philosophical issues.

Consider *necessity.* Evidently, some claims are necessary, and others are contingent. It is necessary that all bachelors are single, and it is contingent that I am married. But what is it to be a nec-

157

essary truth? This question has proved difficult to answer at all satisfactorily. Of course, there's the temptation to seek a necessarily true completion of:

P is necessary if and only if. . . .

But, as many philosophers' experience has shown, no such completion is illuminating. On the one hand, if we don't restrict the analyzing vocabulary, then there are necessarily true completions; for example,

P is necessary if and only if the negation of P is not possible.

But such completions are unilluminating – the terms invoked in the analysans are too similar to those in the analysandum. On the other hand, however, a nonmodal analysis of necessity is almost certainly as unrealistic a hope as a nonnomic analysis of lawhood, or as a noncausal analysis of causation.

Are there topics with a structure even *more similar* than the topic of necessity to the issues surrounding laws and causation? There may well be. Most likely, they are topics about concepts that are very central to our conceptual framework. For example, consider the concept of *materiality*. The atoms making up my desk are material objects – the empty spaces between them are not. But, what is it to be a material object? Like the parallel question about necessity, this question is very difficult to answer. Much as before, the natural temptation is to seek a necessarily true completion of:

x is a material object if and only if. . . .

I doubt, however, that there is any proper completion that is very illuminating: Empty spaces and matter can share many properties – position, size, shape, duration, divisibility. The most plausible *distinguishing* features seem to involve materiality itself, or some close cousin like solidity. So, it might well turn out that materiality is irreducible, and that there isn't any interesting way of saying what it is to be a material object.

Pushing matters a bit further, I must admit to finding a corresponding nonsupervenience position also to be at least somewhat tempting. In conversation, Peter Unger has speculated that there could be two possible worlds, one full of perfectly solid atoms moving about in perfectly empty space, and another full of little pockets of empty space moving about in a material plenum. In the first world, there are atoms, tiny material objects; in the other, the little pockets are immaterial. But, as it seems, nothing need distinguish these two worlds except facts about how materiality itself, or about how certain very closely related concepts like being an atom, or being solid, are instantiated.

An irreducibility thesis about *persistence* is also appealing, as is even a nonsupervenience thesis. Some authors (cf., Armstrong 1980, pp. 76–77; Shoemaker 1984, p. 243) have discussed the possibility of a perfectly homogeneous disk, or sphere, an object that might be spinning at any one of an infinite number of different speeds. That it could be spinning at one speed rather than another, and hence that one part of the object could be at one place rather than another, might show that persistence facts don't sueprvene on nonpersistence facts. (This is apparently the view adopted by Saul Kripke in his lectures on identity and time.)[2]

Obviously, I've not said anything here that establishes nonsupervenience claims about either persistence or materiality. But these are two of the places I'd begin to look for conclusions analogous to the nonsupervenience of lawhood and to the independence of causation. In this regard, my thinking is partly influenced by the fact that the concepts in question exhibit a centrality similar to the centrality exhibited by the nomic concepts. After all, a world without material objects, not even an infinitely large material plenum, is an extremely desolate world. And, a world without any persistence would be just about as bleak.

In those instances where there's no analysis of a concept, or when a certain sort of nonsupervenience holds for a concept, we must resist the empiricist urge to conclude that there is something wrong with the concept, or that there's something wrong with the arguments leading to the irreducibility thesis or to the nonsupervenience thesis. Suppose that certain of my speculations can be developed more fully. For example, suppose that extremely pow-

2 Something similar might hold for identity at a single time. Some have very plausibly held that there could be one world containing nothing but two qualitatively identical spheres, *c* and *d,* and another where those two spheres have merely swapped positions. If so, the facts of the matter about which is *c* and which is *d* would seem not to supervene on any suitably different concepts.

erful arguments are developed that favor antireductionism about necessity, or even that favor nonsupervenience about materiality or about persistence. On the basis of this development, it would be extremely rash to conclude that *there are no material objects* or that *nothing survives the lapse of time,* and almost as rash to conclude that *there are no necessary truths.* It would also be a mistake to conclude immediately that the extremely powerful arguments must, somehow, be unsound. Rather, it may be that what we ought to do is recognize the irreducibility, or the nonsupervenience, and then move on to other matters.

The so-called limits implied by irreducibility, and by nonsupervenience, are not unlike the limits that arise in science. About some cases of irreducibility, the limits could conceivably be due only to certain problems with us. It may be, for example, that they result from our lack of (sufficiently high) intelligence. But, especially about limits that concern nonsupervenience, I doubt that that's the correct explanation. More likely, these limits arise because of absolutely impersonal factors. They arise in ways analogous to how external factors can force scientific incompleteness. For some reason or other, certain of our central concepts developed in such a way that they can't be defined, and can't even be explained, in any very interesting manner. But, however any of that may be, I believe that there *are* physical objects, and that there *are* necessary truths, and that things *do* persist, and that there *are* laws of nature, and that the eruption of Mount Vesuvius *did* cause the destruction of Pompeii. All these beliefs of mine, which I'm sure you share with me, are completely consistent with lawhood being the rich commonsense concept embodied in the Laplacean picture, and with causation being the rich concept so prevalent in everyday thought and talk. Just so, I'd never even begin to presume that we are so richly endowed, and that the world is so neatly arranged, as to allow us to discover every fact or, for that matter, to allow us to provide the most perspicuous analysis of every philosophically interesting concept.

Appendix A:

Nomic platonism

Seeing themselves as opposing the Humean tradition, and convinced by arguments like those given in Chapter 2 (and, to some extent, by demonstrations something like those given in Chapter 3), certain philosophers have felt that an appeal to universals or possible worlds would be of tremendous benefit to their investigation of laws of nature. As these *nomic platonists*[1] see it, if we are willing to recognize necessary connections in nature, or other ways our world could be, then realism about laws can be upheld. David Armstrong (1983, 1988, 1993, 199?), Michael Tooley (1977, 1987), Fred Dretske (1977), and Robert Pargetter (1984) are four of the most prominent nomic platonists. As is indicated by the many references scattered throughout my book, I have great sympathy for many of their contentions. Indeed, I agree that one should endorse realism about the nomic, and I concur that Humeanism is not viable. Where I disagree is on two crucial points. First and foremost, I reject the reductionist tendencies that many of them frequently exhibit. Second, even setting the issue of reductionism aside, some of the specific positions that they adopt are untenable. In particular, Armstrong gives an analysis that, though it can be construed in a nonreductive fashion, is still subject to counterexample. In Section A.1, via a critical discussion of the work of Armstrong, Dretske, and

1 Some of the philosophers whose work is discussed in this appendix would object to being characterized as *platonists*. For example, Armstrong defends a theory of universals that, in a certain sense, is not platonistic; he denies that there are any uninstantiated universals. I use the word 'platonist' merely to acknowledge the ontological richness of the positions discussed. Armstrong prefers the term 'realist', but it encourages confusion of the ontological issue about what entities exist and the semantical debate between realists and antirealists. In a similar spirit, some authors may object to my characterizing possible worlds and universals as *abstract*. Though this terminology is somewhat unfortunate, nothing of any importance is at stake. I simply need a term encompassing all the entities that disturbed the positivists and philosophers like Nelson Goodman.

Tooley, I evaluate the chances of giving a reduction of lawhood via an appeal to universals. As representative of analyses appealing to possible worlds, Section A.2 assesses a simple analysis of my own invention and, more important, Pargetter's work. Finally, in the concluding and very brief Section A.3, I generalize a bit on my earlier conclusions, advocating a somewhat cynical, but I hope enlightening, thesis about the relationship between ontological issues and the problem of laws.

A.1 UNIVERSALS, LAWHOOD, AND REDUCTION

As I just indicated, Armstrong, Dretske, and Tooley all invoke universals in their investigations. Nevertheless, despite some glaring agreement, there is some important disagreement between these authors. It is not even perfectly clear to what extent each intends to offer a reductive analysis of lawhood. So, just before exhibiting what their positions have in common, and long before offering criticisms of their accounts, some time should be spent determining what each is up to.[2] We should also restrict our attention to nonprobabilistic laws. Dretske does not address the issue of probabilistic laws. Armstrong and Tooley do tackle this issue, but they seem to think that all suitably basic probabilistic laws include a probability concept relating two properties, and have the form: The probability of an F being a G is equal to r. This curious feature of their positions at least introduces complications, and may even

---

2 There are some important disputes between universalists that I do not discuss here. One turns on the nature of the invoked universal. There is a growing group of philosophers who hold that the modality-supplying universal is *noncontingent*. Some members of this group (e.g., Tweedale 1984; Bigelow, Ellis, and Lierse 1992) hold that if F-ness stands in the law-making relation to G-ness, then it is necessarily true that if F-ness is instantiated, then F-ness stands in the law-making relation to G-ness. Other members of the group (e.g., Swoyer 1982) hold that whether the law-making universal is instantiated is a *noncontingent* matter of fact, and hence that laws are necessary truths. Though they are subject to many of the same problems as the more established positions of Armstrong, Dretske, and Tooley, keeping with the spirit of the convictions laid out in Section 1.4 (Chapter 1), I have set aside the positions of these unorthodox universalists. More remarkable differences among the universalists arise with respect to epistemological matters. At one extreme, Brown (1991) believes that knowledge of whether the law-making universal is instantiated is obtained in some a priori manner. At the other extreme, Fales (1990) believes that this knowledge arises directly from perception.

lead to problems.[3] It is in order to avoid these obstacles that I have suggested that we set their discussions of probability aside.

Though it may not be beyond all doubt, there is quite a bit of textual evidence suggesting that Tooley believes that his appeal to universals permits something that is at least very similar to what I have been calling a reduction of lawhood. About a competing account that invokes dispositions, he says:

This answer, however, is unsatisfactory for a number of reasons. In the first place, in offering this sort of answer one is not really making any progress with respect to the problem of explaining nomological language in the broad sense. . . . [O]ne is abandoning the project of providing an account of nomological statements in non-nomological terms (1987, pp. 68–69).

In addition, in a section of his book entitled, "Causal and Nomological Concepts: The Need for Analysis", Tooley explicitly concludes that "Nomological terms cannot . . . be treated as primitive and unanalysable" (p. 28). Further, he is also clear about where he stands relative to the Humeans when he states

. . . that some of the difficulties encountered by other attempts to provide analyses of causal and nomological concepts may reflect over-restrictive ontological assumptions (1987, p. 5; also see pp. 32–33).

As I understand Tooley, his view is that the Humeans appropriately sought a reduction of nomic modality; their big mistake was having burdened themselves with a limited ontology. Though the textual evidence is more limited, plenty still suggests that Armstrong is also committed to something like a reductive analysis of lawhood.

3 *Single-case* probabilities are, roughly, probabilities of a proposition's being true. Supposing that d is a fair die, the following reports one: 'The probability that d shows a four is 1/6'. It might be represented as: 'PR(Fd) = 1/6', where 'Fx' abbreviates 'x shows a four'. *General-case* probabilities are supposedly reported by sentences like: 'The probability of a die showing a four is 1/6'. They are usually represented as something like: 'Pr(F/D) = 1/6', where 'F' names the property of showing a four, and 'D' names the property of being a die. Armstrong and Tooley apparently think that all suitably basic probabilistic laws are statements of a general-case probability. In the text, I say that this may lead to problems, because what is expressed by the sentence 'All radium atoms have a fifty percent chance of remaining stable for 1600 years' is a universally quantified indicative conditional with a single-case probability concept in its consequent. We might represent it as something like: '$(\forall x)(Rx \supset PR(Sx) = 50\%)$', where '$Rx$' abbreviates '$x$ is a radium atom' and 'Sx' abbreviates 'x remains stable for 1600 years'. Why couldn't this be a basic law?

163

In at least two different places, he chides competing accounts for appealing to counterfactuals. His worry is that these accounts ultimately either are circular or leave the counterfactual conditional to "float on nothing" (cf., 1983, p. 31, 62). In addition, there are some brief comments about being nailed to Hume's cross (p. 78) and a lack of metaphysical insight (p. 87) that seem to be directed toward antireductionist views. Furthermore, there are also his own acknowledgments (e.g., p. 85) of the agreement between his position and Tooley's, which I have already argued is reductive. Thus, whatever else Armstrong has in mind, he is interested in providing a reductive analysis. There is far less reason to believe that Dretske is a reductionist. Indeed, there is some reason to believe just the opposite. At one point in his essay, he explicitly takes his position to contrast with "reductionistic" (1977, p. 251) views. Moreover, in contrast to Armstrong and Tooley, when Dretske criticizes a competing account that clearly invokes nomic concepts (see 1977, pp. 261–262), the criticisms are not worries about the ability to find some noncircular analysis of the nomic concepts invoked.

Despite the possible differences in their intentions, and though each injects certain peculiar twists, to be discussed in a moment, our universalists each accept a framework quite similar to this:

(F) That all Fs are Gs is a law if and only if F-ness stands in the to-be-specified nomological relation to G-ness.[4]

Of course, (F) reveals only the *form* of their analyses. In order for this trivial framework to be turned into a genuine analysis, the to-be-specified relation must be specified. Regardless, it is important to see how (F) must be understood if it is to be the first step toward a *reductive* analysis. Its analysans, which might just as well be rendered:

F-ness and G-ness (in that order) instantiate the *to-be-specified* nomological relation,

---

4 For convenience, throughout this appendix, I adopt Tooley's conventions (p. viii) of letting 'F-ness' name the property associated with 'F', and letting 'G-ness' name the property associated with 'G'.

164

must be understood in a certain platonistic fashion. To put the matter in a somewhat simplistic linguistic way, viewed as a framework for reduction, (F) suggests using a *name* that refers to the lawmaking relation. It does not suggest that a *predicate* be used to express that relation. So, the only operative predicate within the analysans is the predicate 'instantiates'. Therefore, even though the law-making relation must turn out to be a thoroughly *nomic* relation, the resulting analysis, strictly speaking, could still be reductive. (Indeed, for Armstrong, the law-making relation turns out to be one of the most central nomic concepts: causation.) Any reductive analysis with form (F) must be quite analogous to Armstrong's (1978) way of answering the One over Many argument. According to Armstrong, for certain predicates '*F*', an object's being *F* is to be analyzed as that object's instantiating *F*-ness. So, for example, assuming that 'accelerates' is one of the appropriate predicates, he would back the following: *x* is accelerating if and only if *x* instantiates the property of acceleration. From a platonistic perspective that sees 'the property of acceleration' as naming a certain universal, this is a noncircular analysis.[5]

Having gained knowledge of the framework they all share to some extent, let me point out a few of the distinguishing features of Armstrong's, Dretske's, and Tooley's schemata.[6] Tooley (cf., 1987, p. 78) is committed to:

5 For some criticisms of Armstrong's employment of the One over Many, which in an indirect way prompted my criticisms of the universalists, see Lewis (1983a) and Devitt (1980).
6 Of course, there are other disagreements between their positions that are not reflected by the form of their analyses, or their reductionist tendencies. Some will become clear as we consider how each attempts to say what his law-making relation is. Also, due to other things they believe, they often disagree on the consequences of their accounts. For example, as part of his theory of universals, Armstrong denies that there are any uninstantiated universals. So he is stuck with the consequence that basic vacuous laws are impossible (1983, pp. 123–124). (Incidentally, this is a relatively serious problem for Armstrong. He attempts to address it by claiming that putative vacuous basic laws are disguised counterfactuals supported by higher-order laws, i.e., laws about laws. For some brief criticisms of Armstrong's attempt, see Carroll 1987, p. 272, and Mellor 1980, pp. 121–124.) For another example, as part of his theory of universals, Tooley denies that there are any universals that include concrete particulars. So, for example, he denies that there is a property of *being in Smith's garden*. As was the case with Armstrong, Tooley's beliefs about universals create problems for his position on laws; he is forced to deny that there can be basic restricted laws (1987, p. 122). There are other disagreements; see especially Armstrong and Tooley's difference of opinion with regard to the basicness of "oaken" laws.

165

(T) It is a law that for all x, if x has property P, then x has property Q if and only if the relation of nomic necessitation holds between the two properties P and Q.[7]

Armstrong (1983, p. 85) adopts a very similar framework:

(A) That Fs are Gs is law if and only if F-ness stands in the nomological relation N to G-ness.[8]

Turning to Dretske, he takes a position on the logical form of sentences with the grammatical form:

It is a law that F's are G (Dretske, 1977, p. 250).

He says that they are to be understood as having the form:

F-ness $\to$ G-ness (p. 253).

In some sense, the '$\to$' is supposed to describe the relationship between the two universals. In an important footnote (p. 253), Dretske goes on to say:

I attach no special significance to the connective "$\to$." I use it here merely as a dummy connective or relation. The kind of connection asserted to exist between the universals in question will depend on the particular law in question, and it will depend on whether the law involves quantitative or merely qualitative expressions. . . . In the case of simple qualitative laws (though I doubt whether there are many genuine laws of this sort) the connective "$\to$" merely expresses a link or connection between the respective qualities and may be read as "yields."

7 In presenting Tooley's position, I have sidestepped some refinements intended to distinguish genuine laws from some other nomologically true propositions (1987, p. 90). My criticisms of his position are independent of the concerns that lead Tooley to introduce the revisions. It is also important to realize that, because he does not believe in negative or disjunctive universals, Tooley thinks that a different law-making relation is required for exclusion laws; laws to the effect that everything with some property P lacks some property Q.
8 A comment is in order about Armstrong's analysandum. He believes that no suitably basic laws are expressed by sentences of the form 'all Fs are Gs'. (See Armstrong, Chapter 4, pp. 39–59.) So, in contrast with (F), he analyzes the locution 'that Fs are Gs is a law' instead of the locution 'that all Fs are Gs is a law'. According to Armstrong, 'Fs are Gs' is not just a stylistic variation of 'all Fs are Gs'; 'Fs are Gs' can be true even if 'all Fs are Gs' is false.

So, Dretske does seem to be committed to a framework that strongly resembles the positions of Armstrong and Tooley; namely, that for all purely qualitative 'F' and 'G',

(D) It is a law that all Fs are G if and only if F-ness → G-ness.

It is important to remember that these three schemata are still not analyses. Merely making up a name or suggesting a symbol is not enough; we must be told what the law-making relation *is*. There is a puzzling aspect of Dretske's key footnote that makes his overall position a little hard to assess. In suggesting that the '→' be read as 'yields' for simple qualitative laws, Dretske may just be offering an arbitrary way to verbalize the '→'. If so, then the '→' is supposed to function much like Tooley's 'the relation of nomic necessitation' or Armstrong's 'N'; Dretske merely would have adopted a framework showing the form of his analysis. Because of this, and because he has little more to say about the '→', I am afraid that there would not be much more to say about Dretske's account; he merely would have offered a schema for an analysis without ever attempting to give the analysis. There is, however, another less common interpretation of Dretske's position. In suggesting that the '→' be read as 'yields', he may intend 'yields' to have something like its ordinary meaning. If so, then he in essence would have specified what his law-making relation is (for certain sorts of laws), and hence would have given an analysis – not merely a schema for an analysis. Simply for convenience, I have adopted the more common interpretation that takes 'yields' as a mere verbalization of the '→'. If this is a mistake, and Dretske is identifying his law-making relation with the relation of yielding, then his position is very similar to Armstrong's. They are so similar that, depending on whether Dretske intends his account to be reductive, all or nearly all my criticisms of Armstrong (to be given below) carry over.

What of Tooley's attempt to fill in his schema? He tries to specify the referent of 'the relation of nomic necessitation' by description, that is, by specifying identifying features. He initially suggests:

The relation of nomic necessitation is the unique relation R such that for any properties F-ness and G-ness, F-ness's standing in relation R

167

to G-ness (i) entails that all *Fs* are *Gs*, (ii) is contingent, and (iii) is not equivalent to its being the case that certain facts about particulars obtain.[9]

There are problems with this suggestion. First, there is a minor confusion in condition (iii). Strictly speaking, there are no facts that are not equivalent to its being the case that certain facts about particulars obtain. Take any relation *R*. The proposition that *F*-ness stands in *R* to *G*-ness is clearly equivalent to the disjunction of this very proposition and any logical truth about some particular. So, *F*-ness's standing in *R* to *G*-ness is equivalent to its being the case that certain facts about particulars obtain. What Tooley must mean by the phrase 'facts about particulars' is 'facts *exclusively* about particulars'.[10] Once we are clear about this confusion there are more serious problems to consider. As I hope is the case, all relations *R* may be such that for all properties *F*-ness and *G*-ness, that *F*-ness stands in *R* to *G*-ness is equivalent to its being the case that certain facts solely about particulars obtain. I hope that nominalism is true. If it is, then all facts are equivalent to facts only about particulars. Giving Tooley the benefit of the doubt, let's grant that there are some facts not equivalent to any facts only about particulars. One good set of candidates includes the facts that humility is a virtue (Schiffer 1987, p. 237; Quine 1960, p. 119), that modesty is a virtue, and so on. Then, consider the relation, *M,* defined as follows:

F-ness stands in *M* to *G*-ness if and only if *F*-ness and *G*-ness are virtues and all *Fs* are *Gs*.

Then, for any properties *F*-ness and *G*-ness, that *F*-ness stands in relation *M* to *G*-ness (i) entails that all *Fs* are *Gs*, (ii) is contingent,

9 I have paraphrased Tooley's specification (1987, p. 80) to keep it in line with my terminology.
10 This interpretation also helps to make sense of two other passages of his (1987) work. On page 76, Tooley considers a relation *R* that holds between two properties *A* and *B* if and only if everything with property *A* has property *B*. He seems to think that his condition (iii) prevents this relation from being the relation of nomic necessitation. On page 91, he considers a different relation *R* that holds between *P* and *Q* if and only if everything with property *Q* *and* another property *S* stands in a certain irreducible relation *W* to another property *T*. Because of the presence of *W*, this relation *R* is thought not to be ruled out by condition (iii). Despite what Tooley suggests, both relations are equivalent to certain facts about particulars. The significant difference must be that the latter is not equivalent to certain facts exclusively about particulars.

168

and (iii) is not equivalent to its being the case that certain facts exclusively about particulars obtain. But now consider the relation K defined as follows:

> F-ness stands in relation K to G-ness if and only if F-ness stands in the relation of nomic necessitation to G-ness and all the coins in my pocket are Portuguese escudos.

We know from Tooley's specification of the nomic necessitation relation that for any F and any G, F-ness's standing in this relation to G-ness satisfies conditions (i)–(iii). But, then, it follows from the definition of K that for any F and any G, F-ness's standing in relation K to G-ness satisfies the same three conditions. Thus, K and M both satisfy all the identifying features other than uniqueness contained in Tooley's specification. Therefore, this relation does not exist; no *unique* relation satisfies the other identifying features. Furthermore, this uniqueness problem is a bit of a red herring. Tooley cannot accept that either K or M is really the relation of nomic necessitation; the resulting analysis would be subject to trivial counterexamples.

Aware of problems of this sort, Tooley (1987, p. 91) revises his attempt to say what the relation of nomic necessitation is. His preferred revision comes to this:

> The relation of nomic necessitation is the unique relation R such that for any properties F-ness and G-ness, F-ness's standing in relation R to G-ness (i) entails that all Fs are Gs, (ii) is contingent, and (iii) *is not analyzable*.

It seems as if Tooley is trying to ensure that the law-making relation be a *purely* theoretical entity, one that is neither expressed by any familiar predicates nor definable solely in terms of these predicates. But, it is for precisely this reason that Tooley's revised specification is disappointing. He has given us no reason to believe that there is one, and no more than one, unanalyzable relation that satisfies the other supposedly identifying features of his law-making entity. Nor has he given us any reason to believe that if there is such a relation, then it is such as to make (T) necessarily true. As Tooley sees it, we should believe both that the relation exists and that it is such as to make (T) necessarily true via a kind of inference to the best explanation: the idea being that if there were such an entity, then (T) would be the best explanation of what it is to be a law. But, as I see it, the explanatory gains promised by Tooley's analysis are nil. Even if there were a relation satisfying the identifying features laid out, and even if this relation were such as to make (T) necessarily true, (T) would offer no more illuminating an explanation of what it is to be a law than a position like mine that maintains that lawhood is irreducible. After all, (T) analyzes lawhood in terms of the law-making relation but then stops there, taking that relation to be unanalyzable; irreducibility enters one uninformative step later.

The problem raised here for Tooley is similar to the problem raised by Bas van Fraassen (1989, pp. 99–103). But there is a difference. Van Fraassen believes that since the relation of nomic necessitation is irreducible, it gives "no logical clue" (1989, p. 102) to what it implies about particulars, and so Tooley is stymied by the *inference problem,* the problem of saying why *F*-ness's nomically necessitating *G*-ness entails that all *Fs* are *Gs.* Though van Fraassen is certainly correct that the entailment could not be purely logical, it nonetheless could still obtain. Take the property of *being a color.* For all I know, it may not be equivalent to certain facts exclusively about particulars. Still, redness's being a color entails that all red things are colored. This is not a *logical* entailment. Instead, it is the ordinary sort of entailment that permits us to move from something's being a vixen to something's being a fox. Why can't this sort of entailment link a relational statement about two universals with a generalization about particulars? Whether there is the required entailment depends completely on whether Tooley's lawmaking relation exists. The real problem for Tooley is that he hasn't given us sufficient reason to think that it does.

Armstrong has recently been very clear about what his lawmaking relation is. In reply to van Fraassen (1989), he says:

It is at this point that, I claim, the Identification problem has been solved. The required relation is the causal relation, . . . now hypothesized to relate types not tokens (1993, p. 422).[11]

With this designation, Armstrong's schema (A) has been turned into an analysis:

11 Also see Armstrong (1983, pp. 95–97; 199?).

That *Fs* are *Gs* is a law if and only if *F*-ness stands in the relation of causation to *G*-ness.

This analysis is subject to two different problems. First, there is the one that plagued Tooley's account: As yet, we haven't been given any reason to believe that the law-making relation exists. The mere promise of a reduction doesn't give us such a reason because Armstrong's account promises no more illumination than a similar nonreductive theory. This nonreductive theory is *so* similar that it could be stated using the very same biconditional that Armstrong does. But, in contrast to Armstrong, the nonreductionist sees the analysans as merely saying that *F*-ness causes *G*-ness, where 'causes' is an unanalyzed predicate, rather than a name for a universal. Though this account is nonreductive, in terms of real elucidation it has just as much to offer as Armstrong's.

There are some arguments that would permit Armstrong an interesting reply to this criticism. These arguments are not available to Tooley because his law-making relation is so much more elusive than Armstrong's, not being expressed by any ordinary predicate. One of these arguments comes from the philosophy of language. It contends that the true semantic theory for English posits a reference for the predicate 'causes' (and most other predicates). Another antinominalist argument is much simpler. It maintains that there are certain undeniable sentences which cannot be paraphrased to avoid apparent reference to causation (e.g., 'Causation is very interesting'). Hence, unlike for Tooley's relation of nomic necessitation, there may be reasons for believing that Armstrong's law-making relation exists, *ones that have nothing to do with the benefits of giving a reductive analysis of lawhood*. To be sure, I am not endorsing these platonist arguments. Indeed, I doubt that they are sound. So, I doubt that Armstrong really is in a position to answer my first criticism. But, since it would be impossible for me to fully address these arguments here, we should turn to my second criticism. It applies even if his law-making relation does exist.

The second problem for Armstrong consists of two counterexamples, and applies equally well to the nonreductive version of his position. Both examples have a similar structure, involving an ordinary situation in which *F*-ness stands in the causal relation to *G*-ness. Suppose that each *x* that is *F* is such that *x*'s being *F* causes *x*'s being *G*. Then, it follows that *F*-ness stands in the causal rela-

171

tion to G-ness. (If there is any doubt about this, notice that for *all* *x*, if *x* is *F*, then *x*'s *F*-ness causes *x*'s *G*-ness.) Yet, we can also suppose that for each *x* that is *F*, the chance that *x* is *G* given that *x* is *F* is only thirty percent. Because there is such a low probabilistic connection linking *F*-ness and *G*-ness, and though it is true that *Fs* are *Gs*, it is not a law that *Fs* are *Gs*, contrary to what Armstrong's analysis says. My second counterexample is similar. Suppose there is a rarely instantiated condition *H* such that for all *x*, if *x* lacked *H* and were *F*, then *x*'s being *F* would prevent *x* from being *G*. The condition *H* is so rare that only one thing, particle *b*, has it. Since everything else lacks *H*, were anything else to be *F*, its being *F* would prevent it from being *G*. Thus, in this situation, it clearly is not a law of nature that *Fs* are *Gs*. (In the previous counterexample, this proposition's lawhood is undercut by the probabilistic relationship between *F*-ness and *G*-ness. In this example, this work is done by the counterfactual relationship between these properties.) To turn this second example into a problem for Armstrong, we should add to our suppositions that, besides being the only *H*, *b* is the only *F*. And, we should also add that *b*'s being *F* causes *b*'s being *G*. Since *b* is the only thing that is *F*, it follows that for *all x*, if *x* is *F*, then *x*'s being *F* causes *x*'s being *G*. Hence, it follows that *F*-ness causes *G*-ness. Thus, Armstrong's analysis again incorrectly says that it is a law that *Fs* are *Gs*. Both counterexamples arise from the fact that *property-level causal sentences*, causal sentences apparently relating two properties, can be *accidentally true*.[12]

Some may be doubtful that in these situations, if every *F* is such that its *F*-ness causes its *G*-ness, then *F*-ness causes *G*-ness. To remove this doubt, consider a slightly different case using some genuine predicates. (Armstrong may have doubts about whether these predicates really express properties, but this is irrelevant to the point I am about to make.) Last year, Green underwent a traumatic and highly unusual medical procedure and lost all his hair. Ever since, and as a result, he has been terribly timid and self-conscious. His baldness, you might say, caused his shyness. Now, as a matter

12 I have discussed these issues at greater length in Carroll (1991, pp. 262–267). My focus there is on nominalization causal sentences (e.g., 'Smoking causes coughing') and generic causal sentences (e.g., 'Sunspots cause electrical disturbances'), but the points are basically the same. One of the main themes of that paper is that so-called property-level causal sentences are not relational. This presents an additional very serious problem for Armstrong. I strongly suspect that causation never relates two universals.

of fact, in this hypothetical situation, up until the present time, Green is the only person who has ever gone bald. So, we would not hesitate to accept about this situation that *baldness caused shyness.* Next week, Peterson, who is psychologically much like Green, will undergo the same medical procedure. He will lose all his hair, and as a result will be bashful. So, not only is it true that baldness *caused* shyness, it is also the case that baldness *will cause* shyness. Supposing that no one else ever goes bald, it is true about this situation that every past, present, and future case of baldness leads directly to an accompanying case of shyness. Thus, it is true about this situation that *baldness causes shyness,* or, in more platonistic terms, that *baldness stands in the causal relation to shyness.* Our judgments about this case would be unaffected by probabilistic knowledge that the chance of any bald person being shy is as low as thirty percent, or counterfactual knowledge that everyone else in this situation besides Green and Peterson would not be shy were they to lose their hair.

Armstrong has three possibly replies to my counterexamples. First, he can stubbornly deny that in the examples, F-ness causes G-ness. But, because of the considerations just raised, such a denial seems completely unwarranted. Second, he can be cagey about the law-making relation invoked in his analysis. That is, he might deny that F-ness stands in his law-making relation to G-ness despite the fact that it would be true to say about these cases that F-ness causes G-ness. On this reply, whether his law-making relation is instantiated is not determined by the truth or falsity of familiar property-level causal sentences. But, if he does make this response, then I lose my grasp on what his law-making relation is. If it is not the relation expressed by the predicate 'causes' in ordinary sentences of the form 'F-ness causes G-ness', then what is it? The third possible reply is the most promising: Armstrong could revise his position, no longer identifying his law-making relation with causation, instead defining it in terms of causation and some other nomic property (e.g., chance or lawhood). The additional nomic concept would be invoked in order to pick out the nonaccidental property-level causal truths from all the others. Of course, I am sure Armstrong would resist such a move. It would diminish the interest of his account. Furthermore, if one makes such a move, one might as well adopt a different reductive analysis – one to be discussed in Section A.3 – that purports to refer to a nomic universal and is ide-

173

ally suited to pick out the laws from the accidents. If its law-making universal were to exist, then it would clearly be perfectly reductive and also perfectly true. Nevertheless, like tempting revisions of Armstrong's analysis appealing to some other nomic property, it would not be a very interesting achievement.

A.2 ABSTRACT PARTICULARS, LAWHOOD, AND REDUCTION

In Chapter 2, I considered Humean analyses of lawhood. These analyses do not appeal to abstract entities – neither universals nor abstract particulars. In Section A.1, I considered universalist positions, accounts of lawhood that propose an appeal to universals. I would now like to complete my survey of reductive positions and ontological items by considering two reductive accounts that invoke abstract particulars. The abstract particulars invoked are possible worlds. This is not surprising. Other abstract particulars like propositions, sets, and numbers are not usually thought to have the appropriate nature to instill the modal character of laws. They are not usually thought to be modality-supplying. Thus, if any appeal to abstract particulars can reductively distinguish laws from accidents, it is an appeal to possible worlds.

a. The physically possible worlds account

The first account is what I call *the physically possible worlds account* (*PPW*, for short). It holds, roughly, that the laws are exactly the propositions true in all physically possible worlds. Though I know of no defenders of the account, it is, in some ways, analogous to David Lewis's analysis of necessity in terms of propositions true at all possible worlds (1973, pp. 84–91).

Before stating PPW, I want to distinguish it from another position equally deserving of its name. The latter is a nonreductive position. Before giving an analysis, it asserts that there is a set of all *possible worlds* and gives that set a name, say, 'W'. Then, the nonreductive analysis of lawhood states:

P is a law if and only if P is true at each member of W that is physically possible.

174

Taking the analysans at face value, this is a nonreductive position because it includes the predicate '. . . is physically possible'. In contrast, PPW asserts that there is a set of all *physically possible worlds* and gives that set a name, say, 'S'. Then, it analyzes lawhood thus:

P is a law if and only if P is true at every member of S.

This is a reductive position. It does not merely assert that there is a set of possible worlds, and then in the analysis rely on the fact that some, but not all, of those worlds are physically possible.

PPW has something in common with the schemata adopted by the universalists. They all use a made-up name to refer to some abstract entity, and a genuine analysis has not been given until the referent of the name is specified. In the previous section, we saw that this presented a serious problem for the universalists. Is it a problem for PPW? Though this problem is not as serious a threat as it is for Tooley, it does put PPW in the same tenuous position as Armstrong. PPW makes it very clear what the law-making abstract entity is supposed to be: It is supposed to be the set of all physically possible worlds. But, there is still the question of whether there really are any possible worlds. The analogous question is what created a devastating problem for Tooley. The only reason he can offer for thinking that nomic necessitation exists is a reason that appeals to the supposed explanatory power of his analysis. As I argued, that is not a good reason. The defender of PPW, however, like Armstrong, has more interesting things to say in support of the existence of his modality suppliers. There are reasons for believing in possible worlds that are independent of the supposed benefits of giving a reductive analysis. I tend to doubt that these are ultimately very good reasons, but I cannot press that point here. Deciding the ontological question of whether there are any possible worlds would take us too far afield.

So let us suppose that possible worlds exist. Another problem for PPW is that, as stated, it has the mistaken consequence that our laws are necessarily laws. Suppose that P is actually a law. So, according to PPW, in the actual world, P is true at every member of S. But, now consider any other possible world. In it, it is also the case that P is true at every member of S; S has not changed. Thus, according to PPW, every one of our laws is a law in every possible world.[13] A tempting revision of PPW that avoids this undesirable consequence is this: P is a law if and only if P is true and P is true at every member of S. The revision, however, does not fare much better. Though some actual laws can fail to be laws in other worlds according to this revised account, no actual nonlaw can be a law in another world. In other words, on the revised account, the laws of each possible world are a subset of the laws of the actual world. That cannot be correct. There are very many propositions that, though they are not in fact laws, could be laws.

There is another problem for PPW. I am assuming that this account does succeed in specifying the referent of the name used in its analysis. But, the way it does so undermines most of the interest of the analysis. A defender of PPW specifies the referent of the name 'S' relying on the concept of physical possibility. Officially, that does not make the analysis nonreductive; the analysis still does not include the predicate 'is physically possible'. Nevertheless, it seems that, in order for this achievement to be nonspecious, there must be some way other than by relying on judgments of physical possibility to determine what the members of S are. We must have some direct or otherwise independent access to the set of physically possible worlds. I see no reason to think that we do. The analogy with Lewis's position on necessity is instructive. If it were the case that our only access to possible worlds were through judgments of possibility, by judging which things are both worlds and possible, then, even though a nonmodal analysis of necessity could be given using a name referring to the set of possible worlds, it is not clear what the point would be. I suspect that Lewis does believe that we have some independent access to possible worlds, access that does not depend on judgments of possibility. That, however, should be little consolation to a defender of PPW.

b. Pargetter's account

In footnote 8 of Chapter 1, I define physical necessity this way:

13 It is interesting to note that the nonreductive position laid out at the beginning of this section does not have this consequence. At each possible world, there is a different set of worlds that are physically possible. So, one of our laws could fail to be a law at another world by not being physically possible in that other world. This advantage of the nonreductive position results from the inclusion of the predicate 'is physically possible'. The ease with which these two accounts are confused gives PPW more plausibility than it deserves.

176

P is physically necessary if and only if P is true in all possible worlds with exactly the same laws as the actual world.

As I say there, the intended notion of actuality is a nonrigid one. So, in a Newtonian world, it is physically necessary that massive bodies exert gravitational forces proportional to the inverse square of their distance, because this generalization is true in all possible worlds with the laws of *that Newtonian world*. In part to avoid the ambiguity in the phrase 'the actual world', and in part to follow a format introduced by Saul Kripke (1963) in his model theory for necessity, many define physical necessity in a superficially different manner. This definition has two parts:

P is physically necessary in w if and only if P is true at all worlds accessible from w.

y is accessible from w if and only if w and y have exactly the same laws.

Of course, 'accessible' is being used as a technical term. Its meaning is exhausted by the second biconditional. No one offering this definition of physical necessity intends for us to rely on any ordinary understanding of accessibility. I am not sure that there is any real advantage to the two-step approach. It avoids the ambiguity associated with the phrase 'the actual world', but it also, I think, incorrectly portrays physical necessity as relational.

Pargetter (1984, p. 337) turns all of this around to offer what he once hoped would lead to a reductive analysis of lawhood. Rather than define physical necessity in terms of accessibility and accessibility in terms of lawhood, he wants to define lawhood in terms of accessibility:

P is a law in w if and only if P is true in all worlds accessible from w.[14]

14 One oddity of Pargetter's account is that it portrays lawhood as a relation to possible worlds. But this is only an oddity. Though he seems to think there is some importance that attaches to working with a relational notion (cf., 1984, p. 337), I see no reason why his analysis could not equally well be given as: P is a law if and only if P is true in all accessible worlds. As far as I can tell, this restatement has all the same attractions and faults.

Of course, the problem with Pargetter's account is that it is not a genuine analysis. It uses a technical notion, the accessibility relation, and we have not been told what it is. It is obviously not the ordinary notion of accessibility. On its ordinary use, like when we say Vancouver is accessible from Seattle, we mean something like it is easy to get to the first place from the second. But, nothing literally gets from one possible world to another. The relevant notion of accessibility is a technical notion that simply has not been specified. Aware of this problem, Pargetter suggests (p. 341) that the situation here is parallel to the situation involving possible world analyses of the subjunctive conditional like those offered by Lewis (1973) and Robert Stalnaker (1968). Such accounts typically appeal to *similarity* as a relation between worlds, but give no complete analysis of that relation. The best they can do is to lay out some constraints on the relation and hope that it will eventually be fully analyzed. Pargetter hopes that the same is true of the accessibility relation. According to Pargetter, we should no more criticize him for failing to define the accessibility relation than we should criticize Lewis or Stalnaker for failing to define the similarity relation.

Despite what Pargetter says, his analogy is not much help. For Lewis, something like the ordinary notion of similarity is the starting point for his analysis of the subjunctive conditional. This notion needs to be refined in certain ways; indeed, in different ways for different contexts of utterance. But here at least we have something with which to start. Stalnaker, in contrast, takes the notion of similarity to be largely empty, and to be of little help with regard to giving a reductive analysis. (See Stalnaker 1984, pp. 128–129). For Stalnaker, the concept of similarity primarily helps generate a model theory for the subjunctive conditional. Thus, Pargetter's analysis, as van Fraassen (1989, pp. 72–73) also very clearly points out, suffers from an identification problem. It uses a made-up predicate, the definition of which has not been given. So, his account fails to include a reductive analysis of lawhood.[15]

---

15 Recently, in a book written with John Bigelow (1990), Pargetter has claimed to define accessibility in *causal* terms. Such an analysis may be interesting but, unless the appeal to causation is something like Armstrong's, it has no pertinence to this appendix on platonistic *reductive* analyses. Causation is a nomic concept, and so the resulting analysis would be nonreductive. Furthermore, my counterexamples to Armstrong's analysis raise some doubts about the possibility of defining lawhood in causal terms.

A.3 ONTOLOGY AND THE PROBLEM OF LAWS

The reductive analyses examined in Chapter 2 are all *nominalistically respectable*. By this, I mean that these analyses include no overt or ineliminable appeal to any abstract entities. As a result, some may think that, in arguing for the irreducibility of lawhood, I have ignored an important sort of position, some *non-Humean* or *platonistic* reductive account. These are accounts that, like the more traditional Humean accounts, attempt to analyze lawhood using only concepts free of nomic commitment but, unlike the Humean analyses, do make obvious and crucial reference to abstracta. Similar concerns might be raised about the nonsupervenience arguments of Chapter 3; perhaps there is some true supervenience thesis that permits facts about modality-supplying abstract entities in the explanatory base.

The conclusions of Section A.1 and A.2 do at least *suggest* that there is no serious omission in either Chapter 2 or Chapter 3. In Section A.1, I consider three universalist positions. I argue that no successful reductive analysis of lawhood is included in these positions, because the authors have not told us what the law-making relation is, have given us no reason to think that it exists, or have offered analyses that are subject to counterexample. My criticisms are fairly general; so much so, that we might expect that any appeal to universals in order to distinguish laws from accidents would be a mistake. In Section A.2, I considered two accounts – PPW and Pargetter's account – appealing to the only other sort of modality-supplying abstract entity: possible worlds.[16] Since they also come up short, we might expect that *any* appeal to abstract entities to dis-

16 The authors discussed in this appendix are representative of the class of nomic platonists, but they do not begin to exhaust that class. Many of the others, however, *seem* less interested in giving a reductive analysis. For example, Vallentyne (1988) recommends an appeal to possible worlds but says his account is informative not because it is reductive, but "because it describes the network of concepts related to the concept of lawhood" (p. 609). It is for this reason, in part, that I have restricted my discussion to Armstrong, Dretske, Pargetter, and Tooley. Incidentally, I suspect that Vallentyne is a reductionist at heart, his goal being to reduce lawhood relying on his technical notion of a *nomic structure*. He may also be subject to criticisms similar to those raised in this appendix, since he never says what it is about a world that determines its nomic structure. He says that a nomic structure is a certain kind of relation or function, but we have not been told, for any given possible world, which relation or function is its nomic structure. Similar considerations apply to McCall's (1969) account of lawhood in

179

tinguish laws from accidents is a mistake. Hence, we have some solid evidence that Chapter 2 overlooks no successful attempts to give a non-Humean reduction. Furthermore, if there are no successful non-Humean analyses, then it is difficult to see how some nonnomic facts about abstract entities could ground the lawful differences in the possible worlds constituting my counterexamples to Humean supervenience.

Unfortunately, matters are not quite that simple. To suggest that they were in two journal articles (Carroll 1987, pp. 275–276; 1990, pp. 218–219) was a minor mistake on my part. There is a universalist position that may well succeed in reducing lawhood. This position has certain relative attractions: A defender of this account is in a better position to argue for the existence of its law-making universal than Tooley is to argue for the existence of nomic necessitation, and yet the new account is not subject to counterexamples in the way that Armstrong's proposal is. Furthermore, as the following statement makes abundantly clear, the new analysis is remarkable simple:

(C) *P* is law if and only if *P* instantiates lawhood.

A defender of (C) is better situated to argue for the existence of its law-making universal than Tooley is to argue for his, because, as was true of Armstrong's position, there are reasons for believing that this law-making universal exists that have nothing to do with the benefits of giving a reductive analysis of lawhood. Perhaps a property expressed by 'is a law' is needed for some sort of semantics for natural language, or maybe there are certain evidently true sentences that cannot be paraphrased to avoid apparent reference to this universal (e.g., 'Lawhood has an important role in the natural sciences'). It should be obvious why (C) is impervious to counterexamples; we might just as well try to counterexample the following analysis: *x* is accelerating if and only if *x* instantiates the property of acceleration. Needless to say, (C) is just as reductive as Armstrong's account that refers to causation, because, like Armstrong's proposal, the analysans is to be understood platonistically;

terms of alternative *possible* futures. The notion of possibility seems to be a technical notion. (It is not physical possibility, since physical possibility is analyzed in terms of it. See p. 429.) But, we are not told what this technical notion is.

the only operative predicate is 'instantiates'. In (C), this predicate supposedly relates P with a certain named universal: the property of being a law.

Officially, I reject (C). I still suspect that the standard antinominalist reasons for believing in lawhood (and other universals) are unsound. So, when the non-Humean defender of (C) insists that the analysans includes the name 'lawhood', still being inclined toward nominalism, I conclude that (C) includes a nonreferring name and hence is false. (As I see it, ordinary uses of the phrase 'P instantiates lawhood' do not include any names, and are just usefully long-winded ways to say 'P is a law'.) If I am wrong, and this latest law-making entity does exist, I am prepared to admit that (C) succeeds as a reductive analysis of lawhood. But, as I hope is clear, this would be a very small admission on my part. In order for (C) to be any sort of genuine achievement, there must be some way to determine whether lawhood is instantiated other than by relying on judgments of whether some proposition is a law. We must have some direct or otherwise independent access to lawhood itself. I see no reason to think that we do. Therefore, my concession that there would be a reductive analysis of what it is to be a law if there were such an entity as lawhood certainly should be of absolutely no consolation to the many reductionists whose positions have been criticized throughout this book. For this reason, and for the reasons given earlier in this appendix, it is hard to see how any position one might take on the existence of any entities of any sort could have any impact at all on our ability to give an *illuminating* explanation of what it is to be a law.

Appendix B:

Defending (SC)

As introduced in Chapter 1, principle (SC), our conceptual bridge from lawhood to the subjunctive conditional, is the strongest (and still reasonably safe) such bridge suggested by the Laplacean picture. Here is what it says:

(SC) If $\Diamond_{\mathscr{P}} P$ and $\Box_{\mathscr{P}}(P \supset Q)$, then $P > Q$.

In Chapter 2, I use this principle to bolster three important types of counterexamples. In Chapter 3, I use (SC) again, this time to provide some extra support for certain key counterfactual premises in my nonsupervenience arguments. Since the counterexamples it fortifies are relatively undisputed, and because the counterfactuals it supports are independently plausible, (SC) is not *essential* to any of my earlier arguments. Nevertheless, additional evidence of its truth could only strengthen my overall position. In this regard, as should be obvious, (SC)'s support of independently plausible counterfactuals is already strong confirmation of its truth, as is the general acceptability of the conclusions reached using those counterfactuals. Still, further support for (SC) is forthcoming from this appendix's replies to some possible challenges.

At least as far as I am aware, no *direct* criticisms of (SC) have appeared in print. There are, however, some that I've formulated, and still others that have been suggested to me in conversation. All of these direct challenges are addressed in Section B.1. There is a well-known *indirect* criticism of (SC) stemming from David Lewis's work on counterfactuals. It is addressed in Section B.2. Before beginning, I advise the reader to become reacquainted with principle (SC*). It is one of the two important consequences of (SC) revealed at the start of Chapter 3. It says that if P is physically possible and Q is a law, then Q would (still) be a law if P were the case. Familiarity with (SC*) is valuable because it so happens that most of the objections to (SC) considered in this appendix apply more simply to (SC*).

B.1 DIRECT CHALLENGES

As some urge, certain restricted laws pose a problem for (SC*). These antagonists ask us to consider, say, the Galilean principle of free-fall. They also correctly point out that it is physically possible that the earth have significantly less mass. Then they contend that according to (SC*), if the earth had significantly less mass, the free-fall principle would still be a law. There lies the apparent problem. Intuitively, if the earth were to have significantly less mass, then the free-fall principle would not be a law. After all, if the earth were to have significantly less mass, then, if Ling-Ling (or some other body) were free-falling, she would not accelerate at 9.81 meters per second per second.

For reasons given in Chapter 2, this example is ineffective. The principle of free-fall is not in fact a law; it is not even true. So (SC*) does not have the implication that it would be a law if the earth had significantly less mass. To generate the counterexample, the challengers of (SC*) are welcome to *suppose* that the free-fall principle is a law, but then they must be careful about exactly what they suppose. I suspect that they will not really suppose that it is a law, and will only suppose that our universe is Newtonian, thinking that this principle would be a law in such a universe. But, this does not generate a counterexample to (SC*) because, as I argued in Chapter 2, the free-fall principle would not be a law if our universe were Newtonian. In order to suppose that this generalization is a law, we need to suppose that the acceleration of free-falling bodies is a much less accidental phenomenon than it would be in a Newtonian world. The objectors are welcome to make this supposition, but then the previously troublesome counterfactuals are now perfectly acceptable. With this supposition, if the earth had significantly less mass, then the Galilean principle would be a law. With this supposition, free-falling bodies (including Ling-Ling) would accelerate at a rate of 9.81 meters per second squared even if the earth had significantly less mass.

A more clever example is proposed by Peter van Inwagen and reported by Jonathan Bennett (1984, p. 84). Suppose it is noon, I am on Earth, and it is a law that no signal travels faster than light. Consider the counterfactual that if I were on Jupiter within half a second, then I would have traveled at a speed greater than the speed of light. If that counterfactual is true, then the following is false:

(1) If I were on Jupiter within half a second, then it is a law that no signal travels faster than light.

If so, then this is apparently a counterexample to (SC*). The antecedent of (1) seems to be physically possible – it is physically possible for me to be on Jupiter at a half second past noon. So, according to (SC*), proposition (1) ought to be true.

Like the first direct challenge, it should be obvious that this second challenge is no threat to (SC*). As Bennett points out, and as van Inwagen was no doubt aware, the key conditional is ambiguous. On one reading, sentence (1) is indeed false, but its antecedent is not physically possible. Hence, it is not a counterexample to (SC*). On that reading, the antecedent says something to the effect that I am millions of miles away from Jupiter at noon and on Jupiter a half second later. On the other reading, the antecedent is physically possible, but the counterfactual is true, just as (SC*) demands. On this reading, the antecedent is something like: I am on Jupiter at a half second after twelve (with no implications about where I am at twelve).

There are certain extreme cases that some philosophers have thought to threaten (SC). While they find it plausible that the laws would be the same given *some* (or perhaps even many) physically possible suppositions, they do not believe the laws would be the same given *any* physically possible suppositions. There are various ways to make this concern more concrete. Here's one. It is physically possible that there be no radium atoms. So, according to (SC*), it should follow that if there were no radium atoms, then it would still be a law that all radium atoms have a fifty percent chance of remaining stable for 1600 years. The objector, however, at least is not confident about the truth of this counterfactual, things being so different. There are even more extreme cases. Isn't it physically possible that no material objects or events exist ever? If so, then (SC*) implies that our laws would still be laws even if there were no such objects or events. Many find this apparent consequence of (SC*) difficult to accept.[1]

There are three remarks to make in reply to this objection. The first is specifically directed toward the first way of making the concern more tangible: It strikes me as very plausible that it would still be a law that all radium atoms have a fifty percent chance of remaining stable for 1600 years if there were no radium atoms. My second remark is directed specifically at the worry about completely empty universes: It is not clear how the objector can both assert the physical possibility of no material objects or events existing, and also doubt that our laws would still be laws if there were no such objects or events. To assert this physical possibility claim is to maintain that a possible world with the same laws as the actual world exists in which there are no material objects or events. So the objector must think it possible that our laws be laws in at least one empty world. But, if so, then the objector has no apparent grounds for denying that our laws would still be laws if our world were empty. (I am inclined to accept both the claim of physical possibility and the disputed counterfactual, though not much turns on this.) My third remark is directed at the general concern. The physically possible suppositions made in the arguments that appeal to (SC) are not at all extreme. In the U_{1*}/U_{2*} argument, which in some ways is the most central argument of my book, the supposition is that a mirror on a well-oiled swivel is in a certain position. In the many other arguments where (SC) is invoked, the suppositions are nearly as restrained. So, this third direct challenge, like the direct challenges involving Galileo's law and traveling to Jupiter, does not undermine my use of (SC).

B.2 AN INDIRECT CHALLENGE

To put the indirect challenge in its proper perspective, suppose that our world is deterministic, and consider the following counterfactual sentence:

(2) If the match were struck, then it would light.

1 This general concern was raised by Lawrence Sklar.

185

How should we evaluate it? In the spirit of (SC), we should suppose that the match is struck, and ask what our world would be like, assuming our laws were still laws. One apparently desperate and demanding way of doing so would be to ask how things would have had to be different in the past for the match to be struck. After *backtracking* several thousand years, we could start working forward to decide what other conditions are present in this counterfactual situation when the match is struck. If the conditions that are present together with the laws entail that the match lights, only then should (2) be accepted as true (cf., Lewis 1986, p. 45; Bennett 1974, p. 391).

The backtracking method *is* a rather hopeless way of evaluating (2). But how is that a problem for (SC)? An apparent problem arises because of Lewis's ingenious suggestion for evaluating this sentence in certain contexts.[2] According to Lewis, we should suppose that the match is struck and suppose that the past stays pretty much the same except for a minor miracle – a violation of the laws of the actual world – that permits the match to be struck. What went on in the distant past is then quite irrelevant to deciding what conditions are present in the counterfactual situation when the match is struck. Thus, we can be sure that other important conditions like the presence of oxygen and the dryness of the match are still present. We can then determine that the match lights. Generalizing his approach, it appears that we should accept:

(3) If the match were struck, then the laws would be different.

Why should we accept (3)? Well, the nearest antecedent worlds for (2) are worlds in which there is a minor miracle. So, since (2) and (3) share the same antecedent, the nearest antecedent worlds for (3) are also worlds in which there is a minor miracle. In those worlds, some law of the actual world would be false, and hence not a law.

Nevertheless, there are plenty of reasons not to abandon (SC) or (SC*). First, and most importantly, it is obvious that the laws do not counterfactually depend on the striking of a match. If the match were struck, the laws would be no different. That is *so* obvious that I have trouble believing that anyone, especially Lewis, would hold that some of our laws would not still be laws if that match were

2 Well, he suggested this method for a slightly different sentence – the Nixon and button example. See Lewis (1986, pp. 43–45).

struck. Second, the reasoning leading to the required conclusion that if the match were struck, the laws would be different requires assumptions that are not part of Lewis's basic theory. Suppose Lewis is correct about the evaluation of (2) in certain contexts, and hence that *in those contexts*, the nearest antecedent worlds for (3) include a minor miracle. It does not follow that those same worlds are the nearest antecedent worlds for (3) *in the present context*. Since it has not been shown that (3) is true in the present context, the conclusion threatening (SC*) does not follow.[3] Finally, it has not been established that Lewis has given the correct method of evaluating sentence (2) in even the contexts that he has in mind. There are other methods to consider. For example, Bennett (1984) suggests, roughly, that for counterfactuals with physically possible antecedents, we should consider the possible world governed by the same laws as the actual world that best matches the actual world with respect to the time that the antecedent is about. If the consequent turns out true in this possible world, then the counterfactual is actually true. (See Pollock 1984 for a different suggestion compatible with (SC).)

Sometimes the indirect challenge begins in a slightly different way. Suppose our world is deterministic and consider the following sentence:

(4) If the match were struck, then the distant past would have been different.

If we suppose in the spirit of (SC) that the match is struck and ask what our world would be like assuming that our laws are still laws, then we are forced to conclude that our world would be different at

3 It is an underappreciated feature of Lewis's theory that it takes the nearness relation that governs counterfactual sentences to be picked out in part by the sentence's context of utterance. Lewis emphasizes this point in his postscript to "Counterfactual Dependence and Time's Arrow" (1986, pp. 52–53). As a matter of fact, he does not use my suggested appeal to context-dependency as an escape from the problem presented by (3). Indeed, in a different paper, he makes some remarks that strongly suggest that he does accept (3) as true for some ordinary contexts. Letting L be the proposition specifying the actual laws, he says, "If I had raised my hand, the law proposition L would not have been true" (1986, p. 292). He plays down this counterintuitive aspect of his position by pointing out that he does not accept the more extreme consequence that his raising his hand would have either been or caused a law-breaking event. Even so, we should not accept this aspect of his position, nor should we accept (3) as true in the present context.

187

every moment of the past. So, those who adopt (SC) are forced to accept (4) as true, and some think that's a mistake. Of course, according to Lewis's theory, if we evaluate (4) in the manner suggested for (2), we conclude that (4) is false. I am no more impressed by this version of the indirect challenge. Though there may very well be contexts in which (4) is false, it seems to me that it would be true in most ordinary contexts and, more important, is true in the present context. Supposing that determinism is true, it is clear that if the match were struck, then the distant past would have been different (cf., Bennett 1984, p. 68; Pollock 1984; pp. 117–118).

For the reasons just given, (SC) does more than hold its own against the indirect reply. But, we should also notice that even if (SC) were to succumb to the Lewisian pressure, the arguments in Chapters 2 and 3 would essentially be undisturbed.[4] In other words, the trouble that Lewis's theory allegedly presents for (SC) is independent of (SC)'s role in the arguments of those two chapters. Let us take my U_{1*}/U_{2*} argument as an example. About U_1, we are asked to consider the following counterfactual: If the mirror were in position d, then L_1 would be a law. As I pointed out in Chapter 3, though it has independent plausibility, this counterfactual proposition also follows from the conjunction of (SC) and the plausible claim that it is physically possible in U_1 that the mirror be in position d. But, now, let us ask whether this key counterfactual turns out true on Lewis's theory. If it does, then, even if the indirect reply succeeds in showing there is something wrong with (SC), it does not show there is a problem with my U_{1*}/U_{2*} argument.

According to Lewis's method, when we suppose that the mirror is in position d, we should also suppose that the past stays pretty much the same, keeping the distant past exactly the same. Assuming that U_1 is deterministic,[5] in order to keep the distant past precisely the same, and yet have the mirror in position d, we also have to suppose that a minor miracle occurs; there must be a violation of the laws of U_1. But, there is no reason to think that L_1 is one of the laws of U_1 that is violated. In fact, there is good reason to think that it isn't. To get that mirror to that spot, some laws of motion or energy conservation may have been violated, but presumably not

4 My appeal to (SC) in Chapter 5 (see footnote 15) would not fare so well.
5 It does not matter to my argument of Chapter 3 whether U_1 and U_2 are deterministic. Assuming that they are only gives the indirect reply more to work with.

L_1, not our law about the spin of X-particles in Y-fields. Given the way that U_1 happens to be laid out, what could that law have to do with the position of the mirror? Thus, according to Lewis's theory, L_1 would be a law if the mirror were in position d; this counterfactual is true. The indirect reply gives with one hand what it takes away with the other. While my focus in this paragraph has been on the first key counterfactual in the U_{1*}/U_{2*} argument, similar considerations apply to all my other applications of (SC) in Chapters 2 and 3. As a quick examination (which I leave to the skeptical reader) would show, each of the counterfactuals that (SC) supports in these chapters also turns out true on Lewis's theory.

References

Anscombe, G. E. M. (1971) *Causality and Determination*. Cambridge: Cambridge University Press.

Armstrong, D. M. (1961) *Perception and the Physical World*. London: Routledge and Kegan Paul.

(1978) *Nominalism and Realism*. Cambridge: Cambridge University Press.

(1980) "Identity through Time" *Time and Cause*. P. van Inwagen (ed.). Dordrecht: D. Reidel Publishing Company.

(1983) *What Is a Law of Nature?* Cambridge: Cambridge University Press.

(1988) "Reply to Van Fraassen" *Australasian Journal of Philosophy* 66, 224–229.

(1993) "The Identification Problem and the Inference Problem" *Philosophy and Phenomenological Research* 53, 421–422.

(199?) "Singular Causation and Laws of Nature" (forthcoming).

Aronson, J. (1971) "On the Grammar of 'Cause' " *Synthese* 22, 414–430.

Ayer, A. J. (1936) *Language, Truth and Logic*. New York: Dover Publications.

(1963) *The Concept of a Person*. New York: St. Martin's Press.

Beauchamp, T. and Rosenberg, A. (1981) *Hume and the Problem of Causation*. New York: Oxford University Press.

Bennett, J. (1974) "Counterfactuals and Possible Worlds" *Canadian Journal of Philosophy* 4, 381–402.

(1984) "Counterfactuals and Temporal Direction" *Philosophical Review* 93, 57–91.

(1988) *Events and Their Names*. Indianapolis: Hackett Publishing Company.

Bigelow, J., Ellis, B. and Lierse, C. (1992) "The World as One of a Kind: Natural Necessity and Laws of Nature" *British Journal for the Philosophy of Science* 43, 371–388.

Bigelow, J. and Pargetter, R. (1990) *Science and Necessity*. Cambridge: Cambridge University Press.

Blackburn, S. (1984) *Spreading the Word*. Oxford: Clarendon Press.

(1986) "Morals and Modals" *Fact, Science and Morality*. G. Macdonald and C. Wright (eds.). Oxford: Basil Blackwell.

(1990) "Hume and Thick Connexions" *Philosophy and Phenomenological Research* 50 (Supplement), 237–250.

190

Blanshard, B. (1962) *Reason and Analysis*. La Salle: Open Court Publishing Company.

Boscovich, R. J. (1966) *A Theory of Natural Philosophy*. Cambridge: The MIT Press.

Braithwaite, R. (1927) "The Idea of Necessary Connection (I)" *Mind* 36, 467–477.

(1928) "The Idea of Necessary Connection (II)" *Mind* 37, 62–72.

(1953) *Scientific Explanation*. Cambridge: Cambridge University Press.

Brand, M. (1980) "Simultaneous Causation" *Time and Cause*. P. van Inwagen (ed.). Dordrecht: D. Reidel Publishing Company.

Broad, C. D. (1935) "Mechanical and Teleological Causation" *Proceedings of the Aristotelian Society* 14 (Supplement), 83–112.

Broughton, J. (1987) "Hume's Ideas about Necessary Connection" *Hume Studies* 13, 217–244.

Brown, J. R. (1991) *The Laboratory of the Mind*. London: Routledge.

Campbell, K. (1976) *Metaphysics*. Encino: Dickenson Publishing Company.

Carroll, J. W. (1987) "Ontology and the Laws of Nature" *Australasian Journal of Philosophy* 65, 261–276.

(1990) "The Humean Tradition" *Philosophical Review* 99, 185–219.

(1991) "Property-Level Causation?" *Philosophical Studies* 63, 245–270.

(1992) Review of *Causation and Universals, Philosophy and Phenomenological Research* 52, 1001–1004.

Cartwright, N. (1983) *How the Laws of Physics Lie*. Oxford: Clarendon Press.

Chisholm, R. (1946) "The Contrary-to-Fact Conditional" *Mind* 55, 289–307.

(1955) "Law Statements and Counterfactual Inference" *Analysis* 15, 97–105.

(1977) *Theory of Knowledge*. Englewood Cliffs: Prentice-Hall.

Cohen, S. (1988) "How to Be a Fallibilist" *Philosophical Perspectives* 2, 91–123.

Collingwood, R. G. (1940) *An Essay on Metaphysics*. Oxford: Clarendon Press.

Costa, M. (1989) "Hume and Causal Realism" *Australasian Journal of Philosophy* 67, 172–190.

DeRose, K. (1992) "Contextualism and Knowledge Attributions" *Philosophy and Phenomenological Research* 52, 913–929.

Devitt, M. (1980) "'Ostrich Nominalism' or 'Mirage Realism'?" *Pacific Philosophical Quarterly* 61, 433–439.

Dretske, F. (1977) "Laws of Nature" *Philosophy of Science* 44, 248–268.

Ducasse, C. J. (1969) *Causation and the Types of Necessity*. New York: Dover Publications.

(1975) "On the Nature and the Observability of the Causal Relation" *Causation and Conditionals*. E. Sosa (ed.). Oxford: Oxford University Press.

Earman, J. (1978) "The Universality of Laws" *Philosophy of Science* 45, 173–181.

(1984) "Laws of Nature: The Empiricist Challenge" *D. M. Armstrong*. R. Bogdan (ed.). Dordrecht: D. Reidel Publishing Company.

(1986) *A Primer on Determinism*. Dordrecht: D. Reidel Publishing Company.

Earman, J. and Friedman, M. (1973) "The Meaning and Status of Newton's Law of Inertia and the Nature of Gravitational Forces" *Philosophy of Science* 40, 329–359.

Ehring, D. (1982) "Causal Asymmetry" *Journal of Philosophy* 79, 761–774.

(1986) "The Transference Theory of Causation" *Synthese* 67, 249–258.

Fair, D. (1979) "Causation and the Flow of Energy" *Erkenntnis* 14, 219–250.

Fales, E. (1990) *Causation and Universals*. London: Routledge.

Fodor, J. (1987) *Psychosemantics*. Cambridge: The MIT Press.

Foster, J. (1979) "In Self-Defence" *Perception and Identity*. G. Macdonald (ed.). Ithaca: Cornell University Press.

(1983) "Induction, Explanation and Natural Necessity" *Proceedings of the Aristotelian Society* 83, 87–101.

(1991) *The Immaterial Self*. London: Routledge.

Frankel, L. (1986) "Mutual Causation, Simultaneity and Event Description" *Philosophical Studies* 49, 361–372.

Gasking, D. (1955) "Causation and Recipes" *Mind* 64, 479–487.

Geach, P. (1965) "Assertion" *Philosophical Review* 74, 449–465.

Goldman, Alan (1988) *Empirical Knowledge*. Berkeley: University of California Press.

Goldman, Alvin (1986) *Epistemology and Cognition*. Cambridge: Harvard University Press.

Goodman, N. (1947) "The Problem of Counterfactual Conditionals" *Journal of Philosophy* 44, 113–128.

(1958) "The Test of Simplicity" *Science* 128, 1064–1069.

(1983) *Fact, Fiction, and Forecast*. Cambridge: Harvard University Press.

Hahn, R. (1967) *Laplace as a Newtonian Scientist*. Los Angeles: William Andrews Clark Memorial Library.

(1986) "Laplace and the Mechanistic Universe" *God and Nature*. D. Lindberg and R. Numbers (eds.). Berkeley: University of California Press.

Hanson, N. R. (1969) *Perception and Discovery*. San Francisco: Freeman, Cooper and Company.

Harman, G. (1986) *Change in View*. Cambridge: The MIT Press.

Hempel, C. (1966) *The Philosophy of Natural Science*. Englewood Cliffs: Prentice-Hall.

(1971) "Problems and Changes in the Empiricist Criterion of Meaning" *Readings in the Philosophy of Language*. J. Rosenberg and C. Travis (eds.). Englewood Cliffs: Prentice-Hall.

Hempel, C. and Oppenheim, P. (1948) "Studies in the Logic of Explanation" *Philosophy of Science* 15, 135–175.

Hesse, M. (1967) "Simplicity" *The Encyclopedia of Philosophy*. P. Edwards (ed.). New York: Macmillan Publishing Company.

Hume, D. (1955) *An Inquiry Concerning Human Understanding*. Indianapolis: Bobbs-Merrill Educational Publishing.

Humphreys, P. (1989) *The Chances of Explanation*. Princeton: Princeton University Press.

Jackson, F. (1977) "A Causal Theory of Counterfactuals" *Australasian Journal of Philosophy* 55, 3–21.

(1987) *Conditionals*. Oxford: Basil Blackwell.

Johnson, W. E. (1964) *Logic, Part III*. New York: Dover Publications.

Kim, J. (1973) "Causation, Nomic Subsumption, and the Concept of Event" *Journal of Philosophy* 70, 217–236.

(1974) "Noncausal Connections" *Nous* 8, 41–52.

(1984) "Concepts of Supervenience" *Philosophy and Phenomenological Research* 45, 153–176.

Kitcher, P. (1989) "Explanatory Unification and the Causal Structure of the World" *Scientific Explanation*. P. Kitcher and W. Salmon (eds.). Minneapolis: University of Minnesota Press.

Kneale, W. (1949) *Probability and Induction*. Oxford: Clarendon Press.

(1950) "Natural Laws and Contrary-to-fact Conditionals" *Analysis* 10, 121–125.

(1961) "Universality and Necessity" *British Journal for the Philosophy of Science* 12, 89–102.

Kripke, S. (1963) "Semantical Considerations on Modal Logic" *Acta Philosophica Fennica* 16, 83–94.

(1972) *Naming and Necessity*. Cambridge: Harvard University Press.

Langford, C. H. (1941) Review, *Journal of Symbolic Logic* 6, 67–68.

Laplace (1951) *A Philosophical Essay on Probabilities*. New York: Dover Publications.

Lewis, C. I. (1946) *An Analysis of Knowledge and Valuation*. La Salle: Open Court.

Lewis, D. (1973) *Counterfactuals*. Cambridge: Harvard University Press.

(1983a) "New Work for a Theory of Universals" *Australasian Journal of Philosophy* 61, 343–377.

(1983b) *Philosophical Papers, Volume I*. New York: Oxford University Press.

(1986) *Philosophical Papers, Volume II*. New York: Oxford University Press.

Lyon, A. (1977) "The Immutable Laws of Nature" *Proceedings of the Aristotelian Society* 77, 107–126.

McCall, S. (1969) "Time and the Physical Modalities" *Monist* 53, 426–446.

McGinn, C. (1981) "Modal Reality" *Reduction, Time and Reality*. R. Healey (ed.). Cambridge: Cambridge University Press.

Mackie, J. L. (1974a) "Counterfactuals and Causal Laws" *Philosophical Problems of Causation*. T. Beauchamp (ed.). Encino: Dickenson Publishing Company.

(1974b) *The Cement of the Universe*. Oxford: Clarendon Press.

(1977) *Ethics*. London: Penguin Books.

Mellor, D. H. (1971) *The Matter of Chance*. Cambridge: Cambridge University Press.

(1980) "Necessities and Universals in Natural Laws" *Science, Belief and Behavior*. D. Mellor (ed.). Cambridge: Cambridge University Press.

193

(1987) "The Singularly Affecting Facts of Causation" *Metaphysics and Morality*. P. Pettit, R. Sylvan and J. Norman (eds.). Oxford: Basil Blackwell.

Mill, J. S. (1947) *A System of Logic*. London: Longmans, Green and Company.

Molnar, G. (1974) "Kneale's Argument Revisited" *Philosophical Problems of Causation*. T. Beauchamp (ed.). Encino: Dickenson Publishing Company.

Moore, G. E. (1958) *Philosophical Studies*. London: Routledge and Kegan Paul.

Musgrave, A. (1981) "Wittgensteinian Instrumentalism" *Theoria* 47, 65–105.

Nagel, E. (1961) *The Structure of Science*. London: Harcourt, Brace and World.

Numbers, R. (1977) *Creation by Natural Law*. Seattle: University of Washington Press.

Otte, R. (1981) "A Critique of Suppes' Theory of Probabilistic Causality" *Synthese* 48, 167–189.

Pap, A. (1962) *An Introduction to the Philosophy of Science*. New York: The Free Press of Glencoe.

Pargetter, R. (1984) "Laws and Modal Realism" *Philosophical Studies* 46, 335–347.

Peacocke, C. (1980) "Causal Modalities and Realism" *Reference, Truth and Reality*. M. Platts (ed.). London: Routledge and Kegan Paul.

Plantinga, A. (1974) *The Nature of Necessity*. Oxford: Clarendon Press.

Pollock, J. (1984) *The Foundations of Philosophical Semantics*. Princeton: Princeton University Press.

(1990) *Nomic Probability and the Foundations of Induction*. New York: Oxford University Press.

Popper, K. (1959) *The Logic of Scientific Discovery*. New York: Basic Books.

Putnam, H. (1978) "There Is at Least One A Priori Truth" *Erkenntnis* 13, 153–170.

Quine, W. V. O. (1960) *Word and Object*. Cambridge: The MIT Press.

(1980) *From a Logical Point of View*. Cambridge: Harvard University Press.

Ramsey, F. (1978) *Foundations*. London: Routledge and Kegan Paul.

Reichenbach, H. (1947) *Elements of Symbolic Logic*. New York: The Macmillan Company.

Reid, T. (1970) *An Inquiry into the Human Mind*. Chicago: University of Chicago Press.

Rescher, N. (1969) "Lawfulness as Mind-Dependent" *Essays in Honor of Carl G. Hempel*. N. Rescher et al. (eds.). Dordrecht: D. Reidel Publishing Company.

Robinson, H. (1982) *Matter and Sense*. Cambridge: Cambridge University Press.

Salmon, W. (1980) "Probabilistic Causality" *Pacific Philosophical Quarterly* 61, 50–74.

Schiffer, S. (1987) *The Remnants of Meaning*. Cambridge: The MIT Press.

194

(1990a) "Meaning and Value" *Journal of Philosophy* 87, 602–614.

(1990b) "Physicalism" *Philosophical Perspectives* 4, 153–185.

Scriven, M. (1961) "The Key Property of Physical Laws – Inaccuracy" *Current Issues in the Philosophy of Science*. H. Feigl and G. Maxwell (eds.). New York: Holt, Rinehart and Winston.

(1971) "The Logic of Cause" *Theory and Decision* 2, 49–66.

Shalkowski, S. (1992) "Supervenience and Causal Necessity" *Synthese* 90, 55–87.

Shoemaker, S. (1980) "Causality and Properties" *Time and Cause*. P. van Inwagen (ed.). Dordrecht: D. Reidel Publishing Company.

(1984) *Identity, Cause, and Mind*. Cambridge: Cambridge University Press.

Skyrms, B. (1980) *Causal Necessity*. New Haven: Yale University Press.

Smart, J. J. C. (1985) "Laws of Nature and Cosmic Coincidences" *Philosophical Quarterly* 35, 272–280.

Stalnaker, R. (1968) "A Theory of Conditionals" *Studies in Logical Theory*. N. Rescher (ed.). Oxford: Basil Blackwell.

(1984) *Inquiry*. Cambridge: The MIT Press.

Strawson, G. (1989) *The Secret Connexion*. Oxford: Clarendon Press.

Suppes, P. (1970) *A Probabilistic Theory of Causality*. Amsterdam: North-Holland Publishing Company.

Swain, M. (1978) "A Counterfactual Analysis of Event Causation" *Philosophical Studies* 34, 1–19.

Swartz, N. (1985) *The Concept of Physical Law*. Cambridge: Cambridge University Press.

Swokowski, E. W. (1975) *Calculus with Analytic Geometry*. Boston: Prindle, Weber and Schmidt.

Swoyer, C. (1982) "The Nature of Natural Laws" *Australasian Journal of Philosophy* 60, 203–223.

Taylor, R. (1963) "Causation" *The Monist* 47, 287–313.

Tooley, M. (1977) "The Nature of Laws" *Canadian Journal of Philosophy* 7, 667–698.

(1984) "Laws and Causal Relations" *Midwest Studies in Philosophy* 9, 93–112.

(1987) *Causation*. Oxford: Clarendon Press.

(1990) "Causation: Reductionism Versus Realism" *Philosophy and Phenomenological Research* 50 (Supplement), 215–236.

Toulmin, S. E. (1953) *The Philosophy of Science*. London: Hutchinson University Library.

Tweedale, M. (1984) "Armstrong on Determinable and Substantival Universals" in *D. M. Armstrong*. R. Bogdan (ed.). Dordrecht: D. Reidel Publishing Company.

Unger, P. (1966) *Experience, Scepticism, and Knowledge*. Oxford D. Phil. Thesis.

(1986) "The Cone Model of Knowledge" *Philosophical Topics* 14, 125–178.

Vallentyne, P. (1988) "Explicating Lawhood" *Philosophy of Science* 55, 598–613.

van Fraassen, B. (1980) *The Scientific Image*. Oxford: Clarendon Press.
(1989) *Laws and Symmetry*. Oxford: Clarendon Press.
Vogel, J. (1990) "Cartesian Skepticism and Inference to the Best Explanation" *Journal of Philosophy* 87, 658–666.
von Wright, G. H. (1971) *Explanation and Understanding*. Ithaca: Cornell University Press.
(1974) *Causality and Determination*. New York: Columbia University Press.
(1975) "On the Logic and the Epistemology of the Causal Relation" *Causation and Conditionals*. E. Sosa (ed.). Oxford: Oxford University Press.
Wilson, F. (1986) *Laws and Other Worlds*. Dordrecht: D. Reidel Publishing Company.
Winkler, K. (1991) "The New Hume" *Philosophical Review* 100, 541–579.
Woodward, J. (1990) "Supervenience and Singular Causal Statements" *Explanation and Its Limits*. D. Knowles (ed.). Cambridge: Cambridge University Press.
(1992) "Realism about Laws" *Erkenntnis* 36, 181–218.

Index

deductive-nomological model of explanation, 4n
DeRose, K., 37n
Descartes, 28, 55, 56, 85, 99, 148
Devitt, M., 165n
direct realism, 105–6
directionality
of causation, 141–7
of time, 141–4
dispositions, 6, 14, 78n–9n
Dretske, F.
induction, 96–9
universalist theory, 6n, 161–2, 162–7
Ducasse, C. J., 119n

Earman, J., 30n, 45n–6n, 48, 102n, 108
Ehring, D., 120n, 148
Ellis, B., 162n
empirical concepts, 30–1
empiricism (see also empiricist framework) 12–15, 57, 86, 87
empiricist framework (see also empiricism) 75, 86, 87, 92
empty universes, 64n, 180–1
entrenchment, 42n
epiphenomena, 127–34, 147
epistemology, 3–4, 28–9, 40, 40–3, 45, 46, 49, 54–5, 55, 98, 112
error theories, 90–2, 102
essential properties, definition of, 10n
ethics, 4, 28, 57, 81–5
explanation, 4n, 6, 53, 74, 118

Fair, D., 120n
Fales, E., 24n, 25n, 107n
Fodor, J., 13
Foster, J., 91n, 96–9, 119n, 138n
Frankel, L., 144
Friedman, M., 46n
functionalism, 89

Galileo's law of free-falling bodies, 2, 27, 36–9, 47, 183
Gasking, D., 120n
Geach, P., 94
Goldman, Alan, 108
Goldman, Alvin, 42, 110
Goodman, N., 4, 12, 20n, 30n, 40–3, 51n, 164n
grue, 40–1

Hahn, R., 17n, 18

Hanson, N. R., 23
Harman, G., 42, 110
Hempel, C., 4n, 14, 30n, 47n, 86
Hesse, M., 51n
Hume, 4, 23, 28n–9n, 86, 125n, 167
Humean analyses, 28–56
Goodman's account, 40–3
naive regularity analyses, 29–40
systems approach, 45–55
Humean supervenience, 57–85
about causation, 74
about chance, 68–74
about counterfactuals, 78n–9n
about explanation, 74
about dispositions, 78n–9n
first weak thesis, 76–80
about lawhood, 58, 60–8, 73, 77, 183, 184
second weak thesis, 76–80
Humeanism, the argument for, 102–18
(see also Hume's argument)
Hume's argument, 4–5
Humphreys, P., 124n, 130n

IBE (see inference to the best explanation)
idealism, 28–9, 55
identification problem, 170–8
identity over time (see persistence)
independence of causation, 119–20, 130–4, 139, 146–7, 150–65
indicative conditionals, 31n
induction, 40–3, 96–9, 100
inference problem, 170
inference to the best explanation, 96–9, 108–9
instrumentalists, 23
intentionality, 13, 15

Jackson, F., 31n, 64n
Johnson, W. E., 32n

Kepler's first law of planetary motion, 1, 2, 27, 39n, 47n
Kim, J., 57, 75n–6n, 122–3, 125n
Kitcher, P., 102n
Kneale, W., 87n
knowledge, 3–4, 5, 28, 29, 37–8, 40, 87, 102–16, 157, 162n
Kripke, S., 24, 159, 177

Langford, C. H., 4n
Laplace, 17n

198